SECURITIES

- **What They Are**
- **Their Markets**
- **Regulations**
- **Analysis**
- **Financial Planning**

by Raymond H. Jacobs

Volume 1   **AN INTRODUCTION TO THE SECURITIES BUSINESS**

SECOND EDITION

PUBLISHED BY KALB, VOORHIS & CO.

OTHER KALB, VOORHIS PUBLICATIONS:

- The Financial Planning Workbook
- The Financial Planning Study Series
- The Pocket Summary of Mutual Funds
- Current Data (Mutual Funds)
- KV Convertible Fact-Finder
- The Convertible Bond Chart Book
- The Convertible Preferred Chart Book

ACKNOWLEDGEMENT

The author wishes to express his gratitude to the staff of Kalb, Voorhis & Company, including its Research Department and Financial Planning Division, for great assistance in the preparation of this text. Especial thanks are due Edward G. Reisdorf and Miss Bebe Zadek for their valuable contributions of time and ideas.

FOREWORD

This edition of Securities expands considerably the coverage of the first edition published in 1964. Including changes in Federal securities laws enacted by the Congress in 1964, it also treats several subjects in greater depth. A new chapter has been added to describe the various types of customer accounts with broker/dealers, their inception and maintenance, and their internal handling. This chapter also covers the related subject of supervision and regulation of the registered representatives who form the important link between the public and the securities markets.

As in the previous edition, Volume 1 defines the various types of securities and presents an overall view of their markets. It covers the basic reasons for investments in the different kinds of securities, how they are evaluated, how they are bought and sold, and how their markets are regulated.

Volume 2 deals in broad terms with the subject of financial planning and gives detailed coverage of all aspects of open-end investment companies, popularly known as mutual funds.

Intended to help individuals in understanding securities and their markets so that they may better plan their own investment programs, the text will provide important information for those who are preparing for the regulatory examinations required of persons entering the securities business.

August 15, 1967   Raymond H. Jacobs

Table of Contents

CONTENTS

CONTENTS

CONTENTS

CONTENTS

CONTENTS

CONTENTS

CONTENTS

INDEX
For detailed index, please
see back of Volume 2.

Chapter 1

Speculation and Investment

INTRODUCTION

"Secure" came from the Latin, meaning "without care." Similarly, "security" gives the meaning of safety. By extension, the term came to mean something given, pledged or deposited to make secure the fulfillment of an obligation. Later, "security" applied to the *evidence* of debt, such as a bond, or the evidence of ownership, such as a stock. As used in this text, "securities" refers to bonds, both governmental and corporate, and to corporate stocks. However, these form only a part of the broad spectrum of investment and speculation involved in our economy. For an understanding of the relative importance of securities in the economy as a whole and in personal financial planning, it is necessary to know something about the alternatives in the use and flow of money.

The term *investment* is commonly used to mean the purchase of securities or of tangible properties that (1) provide either income and eventual return of capital or (2) which offer a reasonable expectation of good income and capital growth over a period of time.

Speculation, on the other hand, refers to dealings in properties, securities, or commodities whose safety, possible income, and growth are unknown. Further, any security or property that provides no income and that is purchased solely for possible safety (such as precious gems) or for possible appreciation (such as unimproved land) must be termed as a speculation rather than as an investment.

FORMS OF SPECULATION

Securities are the most popularly discussed and often the most publicized speculations. Certainly, if the purchaser of a corporate security is intent on making a profit by "buying low, selling high," he is speculating.

In this sense, a speculation could be the purchase of shares of a *new issue* of stock in a young electronics corporation which is attempting to manufacture and market a new product. The business is unproven; nothing really can be known about the income or growth of a new company. But the speculator calculates that there will be a wide public interest which will create a demand for the stock and thus increase its price. Then he will sell at a profit. Naturally, he might be wrong too: the company may spend the money realized from the stock sale without any tangible result; public interest may diminish rapidly; the trading price of the stock may fall below the speculator's purchase price.

However, purchase of a new issue of stock of the multi-billion dollar duPont Corporation is not speculative in the same sense. Because of duPont's prodigious assets and reliability, the purchaser's money is far safer from loss. Nevertheless, such investment-type securities are also objects of speculation — if they are bought and sold in anticipation of an increase in market price, rather than for income or long-term increase in value.

If a purchaser acquired duPont stock at $160 a share with the intention of holding his shares for several years (assuming that they continued to do well), he would be *investing*. But if he made the same purchase expecting (and hoping) that the stock would jump to $200 a share in a few months and he then intended to sell at that price for a profit, he would be *speculating*.

Another speculative purchase is that of a *special situation*, which occurs because some particular development might cause, or already has caused, the value of the security to increase. Such a situation has no relation to business conditions or the general trend of the securities market. Special situations include securities of companies undergoing internal changes: reorganizations, mergers, consolidations, receiverships, or liquidations. Sometimes certain special advantages may suddenly make a corporation into an attractive speculation. Because of the expected price advance, special situations are a speculation, not an investment.

Speculation is not *gambling*. Gambling is defined as the risk of money on a *chance* outcome, the result of which cannot be foretold, controlled, or guided by the gambler. The speculators in the duPont and electronics examples were taking the calculated risk that the price of the stock would increase . . . such an increase would not occur as the result of pure chance, but rather on management skills or general market action.

There is a special type of speculation in securities which is known as a *short sale*. This is discussed on page 1–66. Also, some *securities options* are used speculatively as described on page 1–67.

In addition to speculation in securities, there can be speculation in *cash, real estate, personalty,* and *commodities.*

Cash is a speculation when it is not used to produce income. If kept in a safe deposit box or under the mattress it is "safe" only in the sense that it cannot lose in dollar amount. But it *may* lose in two ways: it does not produce the income of a business investment or the interest of a bank deposit, and its dollar value at any future date cannot be predicted.

Cash varies as to its real value. The man who put $10,000 into the mattress in 1928 and took it out to spend in 1933 enjoyed a very real increase in the value (puchasing power) of his money. It bought $13,250 worth of goods at 1928 prices. However, an additional $10,000 set aside in 1939 and spent in 1966 would have bought only $4303 worth of goods at 1966 prices. Inflation had shrunk the dollar to 43% of its 1939 value. The unfortunate facts show that in the longer 37 year-period ending in 1966 the dollar gained in real value in only seven years and lost in 30 years.

Real Estate may be considered as a speculation or as an investment. Unimproved real estate, not rented out, is speculative by nature. It produces no income and its value at a later date may be more or less than its original cost. Improved real estate as an investment is discussed later in this chapter, but it should be noted that it may also be purchased speculatively in the same way as investment type securities. Successful real estate speculation requires either considerable knowledge and experience, considerable luck, or a combination of the two. Although fortunes have been made in real estate, the would-be purchaser who seeks short-term growth of capital should be fully aware of its speculative nature and the risks of loss involved.

Personalty consists of personal property (other than securities) in the form of objects of art, paintings, stamp collections, antiques, and the like. Again, since money put into such items can produce no income and the value of the items at some future date cannot be predicted, this is a speculation. To be successful requires a great deal of knowledge of the particular field involved and usually substantial sums of money.

Buying **commodities** or the buying and selling of commodity futures is always a speculation (except in the normal course of business by people or concerns who deal in commodities). Like personalty, commodities can provide no income and their future value cannot be foretold.

TYPES OF INVESTMENT

There are two general types of investment:

1. Investment in other people's debts.
   a. Government E and H bonds
   b. Savings accounts in banks

 c. Life insurance cash values
 d. Savings and loan share accounts
 e. Mortgages
 f. Treasury bonds
 g. Municipal bonds
 h. Corporate bonds

2. Investment in ownership (equity).
 a. Real estate
 b. Proprietorship
 c. Partnership
 d. Small Business Investment Companies
 e. Corporate stocks
 f. Investment companies

The table at the end of this chapter summarizes the basic characteristics of the above investments.

Other People's Debts

With the possible exception of savings and loan accounts, all investments in other people's debts have two factors in common: a guaranteed * return of principal and a specified rate of return. All types listed in item 1 will return to the investor the principal amount involved either on demand (a, b, c, d) or at maturity (e, f, g, h). Not all of them, however, have the same dollar value at all times. E and H Bonds, savings accounts, cash values in life insurance policies or annuities, and the share value of savings and loan accounts have a known "market" value at any time. Mortgages, Treasury bonds, municipal bonds, and corporate bonds fluctuate in market value. These fluctuations are generally around the interest on "prime" paper † at any particular time. Municipal and corporate bonds may also fluctuate in market value to reflect public confidence in the financial strength of the issue.

 a. **E & H Bonds** are very widely held. Many people consider them the safest type of investment. These bonds increase in liquidation value at their maturity, but they never fluctuate in value. They are ordinarily not transferable and they cannot be used as collateral for a loan. They are as safe as any investment can be in terms of actual dollars and are excellent for investment of emergency funds. Like cash, however, their value in terms of what those dollars will buy is an unknown.

 b. **Savings Accounts** in banks are very secure indeed, particularly those insured by the Federal Deposit Insurance Corporation. Money

---

 * "Guaranteed" is used in this discussion in its generally accepted sense. For the special meaning used in connection with certain securities, see page 1–17.

 † "Prime" paper refers to securities considered by bankers as top quality collateral.

deposited in a savings account is actually being loaned to the bank. In return for its use, the bank pays a specified rate of interest, which may change from time to time. The bank also guarantees to pay back money in savings accounts practically on demand. Incidentally, money borrowed from a bank is actually the money of other depositors, not the money of the bank itself. This is why banks are so conservative about making loans. From the standpoint of dollar safety and some return, a savings account is an excellent investment. However, it offers no growth potential and interest paid has been frequently lower than the loss of purchasing power incurred through inflation. Like the E and H bonds, a savings account is an excellent place for emergency funds.

c. **Cash values** are the cash surrender values or cash reserves which are found in all life insurance policies except pure term insurance. They derive from a portion of the insured's premiums. Although no income is received directly from them, they earn interest at about $2\frac{1}{2}$ to $3\frac{1}{2}$ per cent which is added to the cash reserves. The actual cash surrender value at any time for any particular policy is spelled out in the policy itself. For many people, the cash surrender value of their life insurance policies represents their only true emergency fund. One great advantage of cash values is that the holder does not have to surrender his policy to get cash. He can always borrow in amounts up to the surrender value without additional collateral although he must pay interest on the loan. Life insurance companies have an excellent safety record. As with money in the bank, this type of investment offers no growth opportunities and the earnings may not equal the loss of buying power during inflationary periods.

d. **Savings and Loan** (sometimes referred to as building and loan) share accounts are not truly debt-type accounts like savings accounts in banks. They are actually "share accounts" rather than "dollar accounts," but they do not classify as equity type investments because the share value is fixed and the share account owners do not share in the profits of the institution. Savings and loan companies refer to earnings on their accounts as "dividends," not as interest, because they are not loans by the depositor to the institution (as in a bank). Instead, the "deposits" buy a type of shares in the savings and loan company. Under normal circumstances, money "deposited" will be returned on demand. There are two other important differences between a savings and loan company and a bank. First, all of a savings and loan company's loaned-out capital is invested in one industry — real estate. Banks are limited by law as to the amounts that can be loaned in any one category of investment. Thus their loans must be diversified and are not dependent upon a single segment of the economy for safety. Second, the type of insurance on savings and loan accounts is *not* the same as the type on savings accounts in banks. The insuring agency is a different one and the terms of the insurance are quite different. It is well-known that savings and loan companies pay higher rates of return than banks. The difference is a good example of the general investment rule that "the higher the return, the greater the risk."

e. A **mortgage** is a document which shows that real property (land or buildings) has been pledged as security for a loan. Investors have long favored mortgages for investments because usually a fairly high rate of interest is returned with respect to the risk involved. They are reasonably safe when the amount of the mortgage is not too great relative to the market value of the underlying real estate. In addition, unless the mortgage holder is faced with a situation reminiscent of the Florida boom-bust debacle of 1925, he will always find that land has a certain intrinsic value.

The mortgage holder is faced with several major disadvantages. His capital is tied up for a long period of time. Because there is no ready market for individual mortgages, a forced sale to realize capital might require a marked discount on its face value to attract a buyer. Mortgages are not good for emergency funds and they do not offer growth possibilities.

Considerable capital was required for investment in mortgages until the advent of real estate syndicates and real estate investment trusts. The syndicate allows small investors to invest units of $500, $1,000, $2,000 or more. Income is often tax-free in the early years of such ventures because of generous Federal income tax depreciation rulings, and because the profit on property sold by the syndicate is taxed according to low long-term capital gain rates. Syndicates and trusts are more fully discussed in the Financial Planning section of Volume 2.

Bonds, which represent a debt of the issuer to the holder, are defined in the next chapter. There are three general types: Treasury, Municipal, and corporate.

f. **Treasury bonds, notes,** and **Bills,** like E and H bonds, offer absolute dollar safety when held to maturity. Interest rates on each issue are fixed and payments are guaranteed by the full faith and credit of the United States. Treasury paper is considered prime collateral for loans and represents immediate cash when it is needed. Unlike E and H bonds, Treasury bonds fluctuate in market value. Their value in the market place varies with supply and demand which, in turn, varies with the stated rate of interest, the length of time to maturity, and the rates of interest generally available in other forms of investments. Typically, Treasury bonds of $1,000 face value amount will vary from $870 to as high as $1,040 or more between different issues on one day. Generally speaking, the longer the time to maturity, the higher the yield to maturity that is demanded by investors. The possible disadvantages of this type of investment are the lack of growth possibilities and the unknown value of the investment at any future time in terms of buying power.

g. **Municipal bonds** are those issued by any government authority (state, county, city) other than the Federal government. These bonds are usually considered relatively safe as to interest and principal. Their strength lies in the ability of the issuer to tax. Like Treasury bonds, municipal bonds vary in market value with the prevailing interest rates and the length of time to maturity. Occasionally, municipal bonds will drop drastically in market value when there is reason to believe the bonds may be defaulted or refunded, but this is rare. These bonds are particularly attractive to wealthy people whose income tax bracket is high because interest on most municipal bonds is exempt from Federal income tax. The net return after taxes from a three per cent municipal bond is equivalent to a six per cent return from other securities for tax payers in the 50 per cent tax bracket. The higher the bracket the more favorable the return from municipals to the taxpayer.

h. **Corporate Bonds** are evidence of debt of a corporation to the bondholders. As with municipal and Treasury bonds, the interest is fixed and the loan is to be repaid at a stated date. Corporate bonds also vary with respect to the price on the bond market and the prevailing interest rates and length of time to maturity. While some corporate bonds are considered as safe — or safer — than some municipal issues, others are considered as risky as the most speculative common stock issues.

Ownership or Equity Investments

a. **Real estate,** when considered as an investment, is sometimes referred to as income propery. Such property may be land alone, rented out for such purposes as farming or parking lots. More generally, investment real estate refers to "improved" property, property that includes buildings. These vary from a single house, apartment house, or office building to shopping centers and manufacturing plants. From an investor's point of view, real estate offers income on a fairly predictable basis, favorable tax treatment and the possibility of growth of capital. Offsetting these advantages, considerable amounts of money are usually needed, and the property must be properly supervised and maintained. More time and knowledge are required than in the ownership of debt-type investments.

b. **Proprietorship** — a business of one's own — is part of the American dream. Comparatively few, however, have the capital, experience and overall know-how required to go into business as sole proprietors. The opportunities are great indeed, but the lists of business failures released periodically by the government attest to the great risks involved. Because both income and capital are directly affected by the actions of the proprietor himself — and are dependent in large degree upon his health — no one should tie up all of his capital in his own business. At least some of it should be so invested that its safety and income are independent of the success or failure of the business venture. The one feature of this type of investment that differs from all others (except that of a working partner in a partnership) is that the *services* as well as the capital of the investor usually are involved. *Personal corporations* are sometimes formed by sole proprietors to lessen their liability, for tax reasons, or other purposes. In such companies all of the common stock is owned by the proprietor.

c. A **Partnership** differs from a sole proprietorship mainly in that more than one principal is involved. There is perhaps more risk in a partnership than in a sole proprietorship because every partner is personally liable for the actions of all of the other partners — and even his personal property is at stake. But unlike a proprietorship, an investor can contribute capital and no services. He is then a limited (or "silent") partner whose liability for firm actions is usually limited to the amount of capital he has contributed. To this extent, a limited partner's capital investment is similar to an investment in the common stock of a corporation.

A *joint venture* is a temporary partnership of persons or corporations formed for the purpose of carrying out a particular venture, such as the building of a supermarket or the underwriting of a securities issue. Once the objective has been accomplished, the organization is dissolved.

d. **Small Business Investment Companies (SBIC's)** were authorized by Congress in 1958 to lend money to or invest in the stock of small growth companies whose current assets and net profits are limited, and who would thus find it difficult to obtain conventional financing. An SBIC obtains funds by borrowing from the government at low rates; in addition, it receives certain tax advantages. Anyone with capital — a bank, a group of businessmen, a professional investment counselor — can organize an SBIC. Shares in some SBIC's are traded publicly; that is, they can be bought through a stockbroker. Others are privately held.

e. **Corporate stock** basically represents shares of a corporation, which is an organization formed under laws of any of the states to carry on a business enterprise. The entire corporate interest is divided into shares of *stock* owned by individual stockholders who are each, therefore, part owners of the corporation. Different types of stock may be issued by a corporation with varying rights and privileges; these are described in the next chapter. By buying stock, an investor may become a part owner of a multi-billion dollar corporation or of a neighborhood enterprise. Perhaps there is no other form of property ownership that offers as many variations in safety of principal, growth possibilities, income return, and liquidity (ability to sell on short notice) as common stock. There are approximately 30,000 issues of common stock being actively traded in the United States. To select a quality stock from such a list — indeed to select one from the roughly 1600 issues listed on the New York Stock Exchange — is no task for an amateur. Few professional investment advisers would care to select just one stock for a client's entire investment. Thus, while common stock ownership is easy to obtain, it is difficult indeed to obtain on a knowledgeable basis.

f. **Investment companies** offer one solution to the problem of selection of individual securities issues. Of the two types, the open-end investment company, popularly known as a "mutual fund" is the more widely known. These companies invest and reinvest their shareholders' money in a broad portfolio of securities under professional management. Their shares are continuously offered to the public at the actual value per share based on the current market value of their portfolio holdings. Most such companies have a sales charge and all charge a management fee. They are referred to as "open-end" because they stand ready to redeem their shares from the shareholders at any time at the actual net asset value at that particular time. As with individual securities or other forms of property, if the shareholder chooses to redeem at a time when the value is less than his cost, he will incur a loss. The "closed-end" investment company differs from the mutual fund in that it issues a fixed number of shares during an initial offering. Thereafter, anyone wishing to purchase shares must do so from a shareholder in the same way as any other common stock. Also, the company does not redeem its shares. Characteristically, closed-end investment company shares sell at discounts or at premiums which may represent wide variations from the actual asset value of the shares based on the current market value of its portfolio securities. Investment companies are discussed in depth in Volume 2.

A convenient reference table showing the features of the principal types of investments appears on the next page.

REVIEW QUESTIONS

1. What are the differences between investment and speculation?
2. A new issue of corporate stock may be either speculative or non-speculative. Why?
3. What is a "special situation"?
4. In what respect is there a significant investment difference between personal property and real property?
5. What are the significant differences between investment in debt and investment in equity?
6. What is "prime paper" and why is it important?
7. What is meant by the cash surrender value of life insurance and the loan value?
8. How does the interest paid by a bank differ from the "dividends" paid by a savings and loan company?
9. Why are mortgages considered desirable investments? What are their disadvantages?
10. What are the advantages of Treasury bonds?
11. What are the similarities and differences among corporate, municipal, and Federal bonds?
12. What is "improved property"? What are its advantages and disadvantages for investment purposes?
13. What are the differences between owning a business as a sole proprietor and other investments?
14. Why are personal corporations formed?
15. How does a sole proprietorship differ from a partnership?
16. How is the investment of a "silent" partner similar to investment in corporate stock?
17. What is a joint venture?
18. What is the purpose of small business investment companies?
19. What is corporate stock?
20. What relationship does a stockholder have with a corporation?

FEATURES OF PRINCIPAL TYPES OF INVESTMENTS

Investment	Safety of Principal [1]	Income	Possible Growth of Capital	Liquidity	Ease of Accumulation [6]	Management or Services Required
E Bonds	Absolute	Fixed	No	Immediate	Very High	No
H Bonds	Absolute	Fixed	No	Immediate [3]	Low	No
Savings Accounts (banks)	Very High	May vary	No	Immediate [4]	Maximum	No
Cash Values	Very High	None [2]	No	Immediate [4]	Very High	No
Savings & Loan	High	May vary	No	Immediate [4]	Maximum	No
Mortgages	High to Medium	Fixed	No	Low	Low	Some
Treasury Bonds	Absolute [5]	Fixed	Some	Extremely High	Low	No
Municipal Bonds	Very High to High	Fixed	Some	Very High to Low	Low	No
Corporate Bonds	Very High to Low	Fixed	Some	Very High to Low	Low	No
Real Estate	High to Low	Variable	Yes	Low	Low	Yes
Owner or Partner	High to Low	Variable	Yes	Low	Low	Yes
Stocks	High to Low	Variable	Yes	High to Low	Very High	No
Investment Companies:						
Open-end	High to Low	Variable	Yes	Immediate	Very High	No
Closed-end	High to Low	Variable	Yes	High to Low	Very High	No

[1] Refers to dollars, not purchasing power.
[2] Fixed interest accumulates as part of cash value.
[3] Maximum 30-day delay for H-bonds.
[4] Under normal circumstances.
[5] When held to maturity; otherwise, very high.
[6] Through small periodic investments.

Chapter 2

The
Nature
of
Securities

CORPORATE SECURITIES

The Corporation

A corporation is an organization chartered by a State government to carry on an enterprise. It is a legal entity with an existence that is legally distinct from the men who own and control it. Because it is legally considered as a "person," it can sue or be sued, buy and sell property in its own name, and even enter into contracts with its own stockholders. In most cases its life is perpetual.

Ownership in a stock corporation is shared by stockholders, whose varying holdings are represented in proportion to their holdings of shares of stock. The stockholders elect a board of directors to administer the corporation.

The words of John Marshall, first chief justice of the United States Supreme Court, are as valid now as in an 1819 decision where he stated: "A corporation is an artificial being, invisible, intangible, and existing only in contemplation of law . . .".

In addition to its status as a "person," a corporation has certain other advantages. Because it never dies, the corporation can obtain continuous credit for expansion and other purposes through long-term bonds, and its owners can transfer stock without fear of disrupting the internal corporate life. Thus the corporation can expand or change to fill shifting business needs.

But there are disadvantages also. The larger the corporation, the more complicated and costly its administration becomes. Taxes are heavy and are assessed from many sources. There are more governmental regulations and controls than in the other forms of business enterprise. These disadvantages explain why many businesses are operated as proprietorships or as partnerships. However, most large business enterprises and thousands of small companies are incorporated on the basis that the advantages outweigh the disadvantages.

Formation

To form a corporation is quite simple. A group of individuals, known as incorporators, apply to the authorities of a state for a charter to carry on a business for profit (or non-profit, as in the case of philanthropic, religious, or educational institutions) or for public or governmental functions (municipal corporations).

A corporation's *charter* is also referred to as Articles of Incorporation or Certificate of Incorporation. This document details the name of the corporation, its purpose and the nature of its business, the authorized number of shares of capital stock that may be issued with a description of the various classes of such stock, the amount of indebtedness the corporation may incur, a statement of the duties of the officers of the corporation, and the names and addresses of the original directors. The charter usually authorizes the making, altering or repealing of *by-laws* which reflect permanent policies of the corporation.

Some states, like Delaware, have fairly easy requirements for incorporation. Other states, like New York, have rigid requirements. Thus, because of the complications and expense involved in some states, it is not unusual for a company to incorporate in a different state from that in which it intends to establish its main offices. In such a case a corporation maintains a "statutory" office in the state in which it is incorporated.

Different types of laws apply to a corporation that seeks to qualify to do business within a state and to one that seeks to sell its securities within a state. For example, a manufacturing company might be incorporated in Maryland, have its main offices and plant in Indiana, and wish to sell shares of its stock in Florida. It would have to comply with the requirements for incorporation in Maryland, of which it would be considered a "domestic" corporation. In Indiana, the company would have to meet the legal requirements that qualify it to "do business" within the state. In Florida, the company would have to comply with the "Blue Sky" regulatory laws of that state with respect to the marketing of shares of a "foreign" corporation.

Corporate Stock Ownership

Corporate stock is defined as an interest in the corporate property, all of which is owned by the individual stockholders of the corporation. Each share of stock is a percentage, however small, of the joint ownership held by all the stockholders of the corporation. Municipalities, and non-profit corporations generally, do not issue stock; they are excluded from the following discussion.

Stock is characteristic of a corporation organized for profit. Every such corporation must have shares of stock issued and outstanding as evidence of ownership by certain individuals. A business corporation may issue other types of securities, but does not necessarily do so; it must issue stock.

Ownership of a corporation through stock holdings differs from ownership through a partnership or sole proprietorship in one important respect: limited liability. Personal liability of each owner is ordinarily limited to the amount paid for the shares of stock—he cannot lose more than the amount of his investment. In a sole proprietorship or partnership, liability for business debts extends to all of the owners' assets, including personal property. While a corporation is a person at law and is liable for its own acts of commission or omission, the stockholders are not ordinarily liable for its debts. Thus, if the corporation is sued successfully, the individual shareholders are not personally responsible. Aside from tax considerations, limited liability is one of the greatest advantages of the corporate form of ownership.

A secondary, though very important, advantage to stock ownership is the ability to buy in extremely small units. The average price of all stocks listed on the New York Stock Exchange is about $40 per share. One could not become a sole proprietor or buy even a small percentage of a partnership for such a small amount.

Stockholders' Rights

As part owner of a corporation, each stockholder has certain rights and privileges. Generally these are detailed in the by-laws or in the charter itself. Usual rights include:

Stock Certificate. Each stockholder is entitled to one or more stock certificates which constitute physical evidence of ownership. A certificate shows: (1) the name of the issuing corporation; (2) the number of shares represented by the certificate; (3) the name(s) of the registered owner(s); (4) the names of the transfer agent and the registrar; and (5) the signatures of the corporation's officers authorized to sign the certificate. The *transfer agent* keeps a record of the name of each registered shareholder, his address, and the number of shares owned. It is the transfer agent's responsibility to see that properly-endorsed certificates presented to his office for transfer are cancelled and that new certificates are issued to the new owner. The *registrar* is usually a bank or trust company that has the responsibility to prevent the issuance of more stock of a company than the amount authorized by the corporation's charter.

Right of Transfer. The stockholder usually has the right, which is stated on the certificate, to transfer the ownership of his shares to someone else without the consent of the corporation. In some cases, particularly when original management has acquired shares by reason of providing original capital or services, the right of transfer may be withheld. Such stock is known as *restricted stock.*

Dividends. Stockholders are entitled to receive dividends when declared by the directors. Except in the case of cumulative preferred stock (page 1–16), a stockholder has no claim to dividends until they have been declared by the directors. On common stock, the amount declared by the directors is within their discretion and may represent a large percentage of earnings or a small one. In some cases, they may exceed earnings (being paid from surplus). However, no dividend may be paid on common stock in any year unless the required dividend has been declared and paid on preferred stock, including any arrears on cumulative preferred.

Liquidation Rights. The stockholder almost always has the right to share in the proceeds of liquidation of the corporation. Here, the preferred usually takes precedence over the common stock, but only after all bonds and other liabilities of the corporation have been paid. Common stock has the last claim upon liquidation.

Voting Rights. Each holder of voting stock of a corporation has the right to attend the annual meeting to vote in person for the directors and on any measure that has to do with changes in fundamental policy of the company. The stockholder has the right, also, to attend in person any special meeting in which such measures are to be voted on. Most stockholders do not find it convenient to attend such meetings. Instead they vote by *proxy*. A proxy is merely a power of attorney granted by the stockholder to someone else to vote his stock in one of two ways—either as directed by the stockholder, or at the discretion of the person holding his power of attorney. Usually, the management of a corporation selects the directors to be voted on in advance and makes certain recommendations to the shareholders, asking them to vote in accordance with management's recommendations. Most of the time, the shareholders as a group will vote as management requests. Sometimes, however, one or more shareholders get sufficiently dissatisfied with present management to seek to replace it. "A "proxy fight" then occurs in which management and the other group compete for the shareholder's proxies. Management has a distinct advantage. While the corporation pays the costs of the mailings on the part of management, the group that is fighting for control has to pay its own expenses, unless it wins control, in which case the corporation may pay them. Short of such proxy fight, the shareholder's right to vote is largely academic since management will almost always automatically receive the required majority endorsing itself and its policies. Solicitation of proxies for most companies is regulated by the Securities and Exchange Commission, which requires that a *proxy statement* containing certain definite information be furnished shareholders whose proxies are solicited. This statement is required whether solicitation is by the corporation's management or by others.

There are two general types of voting used by corporations, *cumulative* and *non-cumulative*. In non-cumulative voting, typically each share is allowed one vote for each director. Thus, any person or group of persons who owns more than 50 per cent of the outstanding shares can be sure of electing an entire board of directors satisfactory to it. Under the cumulative method, each share usually has a number of votes equal to the number of directors to be elected. The total number can be cast in any combination the shareholder wishes: all for one director, half for one and half for another, etc. Thus, a large minority stockholder or perhaps a group of dissident stockholders who own *over* 10 percent of the voting stock, can vote as a group and are sure to elect one man of a nine-man board. Such assurance they cannot have under the non-cumulative (or statutory) method. The cumulative method is now required by law in some state.

Right of Inspection. Each stockholder normally has the right to inspect the stockholder list, the minutes of stockholder meetings, and the corporate records and books. The stockholder list may not always yield meaningful information, however, because of the practice of registering many stock certificates in *street name*—the name of a broker, brokerage firm, or a nominee. Registration in street name allows convenient handling and sale and delivery of stock left with a broker.

Pre-emptive Rights. In many corporations, shareholders have what are known as pre-emptive rights. In the issue of any new stock, the present shareholders have the right to buy the new shares (in direct proportion to the number of shares already owned) before the new issue is offered to the general public. It is customary for a company issuing additional stock to price it somewhat below the market. If the present shareholders did not have this right, the new shareholders would benefit at the expense of the old shareholders. Not all states require that the shares of a corporation carry pre-emptive rights.

CLASSES OF CORPORATE SECURITIES

The capital structure of a corporation consists of all of its outstanding bonds preferred stock and common stock. A stock certificate represents ownership in a corporation. A bond certificate represents debt. Within themselves, there are distinctions among the several types of stocks and bonds. In the following text, the various classes of corporate securities are discussed as to their characteristics with only general comments as to their investment qualities. For a detailed discussion on the evaluation of stocks and bonds, see the later chapters on Securities Analysis.

Stocks

All corporate stock is called *capital stock*, which includes all common and preferred issues of a corporation. Whether or not a corporation issues other types of stock, it always issues one class of stock, usually called *common stock*, which represents the basic ownership of the corporation.

Sometimes a corporation will issue more than one class of common stock, though this practice is not as prevalent now as it used to be. When more than one class (class A, class B, etc.) of common stock is outstanding, the classes may vary as to voting power (some have none), participation in dividends, and rights on liquidation of the company. No broad statement can be made that would apply equally to all issues of common stock. Each issue must be examined to determine the rights and privileges of the holder.

Preferred stock was created originally to yield a specified return that compared favorably with that of bonds, without creating the funded debt incident to a bond issue. At the same time, preferred stock has a safety factor; it is preferred over common stock in regard to dividends and usually as to assets on liquidation. Preferred stock usually possesses the same rights and privileges as common stock, except that in many cases it does not have voting power. In some cases, it has voting rights if dividends are in default. Frequently, corporations will have more than one issue of preferred stock outstanding. If one of these takes precedence over the others (that is, its dividend must be paid before a dividend may be paid on the others), it is referred to as a *prior preferred*. Sometimes, preferred stock has more safeguards added to make it more attractive to investors. These include such provisions as a sinking fund to retire the stock, a required dividend reserve, or a protection against dilution of equity by later issues.

In its simplest (non-cumulative) form, preferred stock is one that requires the payment of a specified dividend before any dividend can be paid on common stock. Except for *participating preferred*, the dividend on preferred stock is at a fixed rate. It may be *passed* (i.e. not paid), but the rate does not increase, regardless of how great earnings are.

Participating preferred stock (not a very common type of issue by companies in good financial health) has a very unusual feature. Once its holders have been paid the required preferred dividend, they also share to a stated extent with the common stock holders any earnings that are to be paid out as an ordinary dividend.

Cumulative preferred stock carries the additional advantage that any arrears in dividends must be paid by the corporation before *any* dividend can be paid on common stock. Thus, the owners have a claim to the dividends whether they are earned or not. All other preferred stock is *non-cumulative*, which simply means that the preferred dividends must be paid in any one year before a dividend can be paid on the common stock in that year.

Convertible preferred stock can be converted into a stated number of shares of common stock under specified conditions. The conversion terms are all fully disclosed at the time of the first issuance.

The convertibility feature is normally not of immediate advantage to the owner because the preferred stock is usually issued with the "break-even" conversion rate above the market. For example, the common stock of a corporation is selling at $15. The corporation then issues convertible preferred at $100 per share which can be converted into five shares of common stock. Thus, if the common stock rises to $20, the holder of each convertible preferred share would receive common shares of exactly the market value of his investment should he convert. The price of the preferred may have little or no relationship to the selling price of the common stock below $20. However, when the market value of the common makes conversion advantageous, the price of the convertible preferred will react to changes in the market in much the same way as the common stock itself. For example, should the price of the common rise to $25, each convertible preferred share would rise correspondingly to about $125 (five shares times 5=$25 + the original $100). It should be noted that this example is an oversimplification. Actually, the market price of the convertible preferred would usually be somewhat more than $125.

Preferred stock that is not convertible usually is less volatile than common stock because of its fixed dividend rate.

Callable preferred stock is preferred stock that can be called for redemption by the issuer under specified conditions at a specified price, known as the *redemption price*. Sometimes the entire issue is callable after a certain date. Sometimes part of the issue is callable after a certain date at a stated price with the remainder callable at a later date at either the same or at a different stated price. Each issue must be studied separately to determine all of the conditions surrounding it; the same company may have two or more issues of callable preferred stock outstanding, with different conditions for each.

A *guaranteed stock* is one on which a stated dividend return is guaranteed by someone other than the issuer. It is similar to a guaranteed bond. These securities are usually found in the railroad industry where some large companies use the tracks of smaller companies on a leased right-of-way basis. To ensure the economic health of the smaller road, the larger company may "guarantee" the preferred stock dividends or bond interest of the smaller company.

Authorized stock represents the number of shares that may be issued by the company. This authorization is contained in the company's original charter; it may be changed (upwards or downwards) at a later date by common consent of the shareholders. Frequently, more stock is authorized for issue than is actually issued. The unissued stock is held for issue at a later date, if desired.

Outstanding stock has been issued to persons other than the corporation itself and is still held by persons other than the corporation. Holders of outstanding stock at any time are not necessarily the same persons to whom the stock was originally issued, of course. The outstanding stock is always equal to the total number of shares issued less the treasury stock.*

Treasury stock is stock that was once issued to persons other than the corporation itself and then bought back by the corporation, either on the open market or directly from the holders. For example, a family-held corporation may have issued stock to the general public to obtain needed funds for expansion. At a later date, with more money available, the family (majority) stockholders may wish to reduce the broad ownership of the company by having the corporation buy its own stock on the open market, paying the market price for it. Treasury stock also differs from other common stock in that no dividends are paid on it and it cannot be voted. Also, it may be used in any way the company sees fit—to acquire other properties, for bonus payments to employees, or for sale at any price desired. When so used, the stock is reissued and then becomes the same as the rest of the outstanding stock.

A *right, stock right,* or *subscription right* is a privilege extended to a present shareholder to buy additional shares of stock at a price below that of the market. They are issued by a company when it wants to raise money without increasing its debt. Because the rights usually permit the holder to buy shares at less than the current market value of the stock, the rights ordinarily have a market value of their own and are actively traded. They usually expire within a short period of time.

A *warrant* is a privilege to buy shares of stock at a specified price under specified conditions. Warrants differ from rights in the manner of their issue and in the fact that they usually have a comparatively long time limit. Some warrants are "perpetual." Some securities are issued with detachable warrants to make the issue more attractive to investors. The warrants may be detached either for conversion or for sale. There is usually an active market for most warrants.

Voting trust certificates, some of which are listed on the New York Stock Exchange and other exchanges, are "certificates of beneficial interest." Sometimes, during a reorganization, control of a corporation is transferred to a group of trustees by the stockholders, who turn over their stock to the trustees. The stock is transferred on the books of the corporation, so that the trustees then have the right to vote the stock. In turn, the trustees issue to the former shareholders voting trust certificates which entitle the holders to receive the dividends paid on the stock. When the trust terminates, each shareholder receives the number of shares of the original stock to which he is entitled through his beneficial interest. Since voting trust certificates are actively traded, ultimate ownership of the underlying stock at termination of the trust is transferred to the latest holders of the voting trust certificates.

---

* There is an exception in the case of open-end investment companies. See page 2–77.

Bonds

A *bond* is evidence of a loan made to the issuer of the bond. Basically, it is an IOU or promissory note, usually in $1,000 units, though $100 and $500 denominations are not uncommon. The issuer may be a national government or municipality as well as a corporation.

The bond issuer promises to pay to the holder a specified rate of interest for a specified length of time and then to repay the face amount of the bond to its holder on the maturity date. There are certain exceptions in that some bonds are perpetual and some have a contingent interest provision. Depending upon interest rates in general, the interest rate of the bond itself, and the public attitude as to the financial health of the issuer, a bond may sell on the open market at a price above its face amount (at a premium) or it may sell at a price below its face amount (at a discount).

Bonds, like any loan, are either secured or unsecured. A secured bond is a note that is backed by real property, equipment, or other actual assets of the issuer that can be seized by the bondholder should the issuer fail to meet the terms of the bond. Interest on a bond is usually paid twice a year, but it may be paid annually or at other intervals. Interest and principal payments on corporate bonds are usually made by a corporate trustee under an *indenture of trust* or *deed of trust* which gives all the details of the bond issue.

Bonds mature, i.e., become due for payment of principal, at various periods of time from the date of issue. *Short-term* bonds mature within five years; *medium-term* bonds have a life of from five to twenty years; and *long-term* bonds have maturity dates of more than twenty years from the date of issue. Short-term bonds are common issues of industrial corporations but are rare among railroads or public utilities.

A *mortgage bond* is an evidence of indebtedness that is secured by a mortgage or lien on some underlying real property. When the term "bond" alone is used, it usually refers to a mortgage bond. The value of the property against which the bond is issued may or may not be equal in value to the amount of the bond issue. A first mortgage bond has a first claim to the underlying assets. Thus it is generally considered better than any other bond issued by a particular corporation.

There are types of senior mortgage bonds other than first mortgage bonds. In railroads, first lien bonds on a particular operating division of a road are known as divisional bonds. *Prior lien bonds* sometimes are placed ahead of first mortgage bonds in reorganization, but this can only be done with the consent of the holders of the first mortgage bonds. Joint bonds are those issued and guaranteed by two or more companies which own and operate a particular property.

Second mortgages, common in the real estate industry, are given different names in the world of finance. Junior mortgage bonds take precedence both as to interest and as to principal after senior issues. In addition to the general mortgage bond described below, these may be termed as consolidated mortgage bonds or refunding (mortgage) bonds (see below).

A general mortgage bond is one that is backed by a blanket mortgage, not necessarily a first mortgage, on all of the fixed assets of a corporation. The general mortgage bond differs from the simple mortgage bond in that the latter is secured by certain specified fixed assets rather than by all of them.

An open-end mortgage bond is like an open-end mortgage on a house. It is one that permits additional borrowings, but it requires inclusions of additional property under the mortgage as the borrowings are increased.

A closed-end mortgage bond specifies that the original issue has priority on claims and prohibits additional borrowings under the bond.

A *collateral trust bond* is one that is backed (secured) by other securities that are held by a trustee. The collateral is often the stocks or bonds of companies controlled by the issuing company but may be other securities.

When the interest alone or both interest and principal repayment of a bond are guaranteed by someone other than the issuer, the security is known as a guaranteed bond. Payment is made by the guarantor only in the event of default by the issuer. An assumed bond is one on which the interest payments and ultimate payment of principal is directly undertaken by a corporation other than the issuer; this occurs most commonly in cases of acquisitions and mergers.

A *debenture* or *debenture bond* differs from a secured bond in that it is not backed by physical assets; it is backed only by the general credit of the issuer. Because of this factor they are often issued as convertibles to make them more attractive to potential buyers. In fact, most convertible bonds are debenture bonds. A holder of a subordinated debenture agrees to waive his claims to interest or principal payments until after certain other obligations of the issuer have been paid.

The interest on an *income bond* is normally paid only out of available income. Such a bond may be cumulative or non-cumulative. In some cases, unpaid interest may accumulate as a claim against the corporation when the bond becomes due. An income bond resulting from financial reorganization of a corporation is termed an adjustment bond. One type of income bond that is usually an adjustment bond is the split-coupon bond which entitles the holder to a fixed rate of interest plus additional interest when corporate earnings exceed a specified amount. Such bonds may also be termed participating bonds.

The interest on a *revenue bond* is paid from operating revenue. It is a type of income bond frequently associated with railroads and municipalities.

A *refunding bond* is issued to permit reorganization of the capital structure of a corporation or municipality. It is frequently used to retire an existing bond issue.

A *sinking fund bond* requires the setting aside of funds for the redemption of the bond during its lifetime. Such redemptions may be by call or by purchase on the open market.

A *coupon bond* is one with coupons attached; each coupon represents the interest payment due on a specified date. The coupons are presented for payment of the interest. Coupon bonds are normally *bearer bonds;* that is, the name of the owner is not recorded. Whoever holds the bonds can sell them, redeem them when due, or surrender the coupons for interest payments.

A *registered bond* has the owner's name recorded on the books of the issuer or its agent. When such a bond is sold by its owner to another person, a transfer of ownership must be made in the same manner as the transfer of ownership of stock certificates.

Some bonds are registered as to principal but not as to interest and carry attached coupons which may be presented for payment by anyone, either to the company itself or to a bank for collection. Because of this, these bonds are also referred to as bearer bonds, like coupon bonds. However, payment of principal will be made only to the registered owner.

Fully registered bonds have no coupons attached.

Like some types of preferred stock, bonds can be *convertible*. A *convertible bond* can be converted to a specified number of shares of preferred or common stock under specified conditions at a stated price. When the price level of the stock into which the bonds can be converted rises to a level where conversion would be advantageous, the bonds will also rise and react to market changes in much the same manner as the stock itself. However, the bond will tend to seek its own value (based on current interest rates) when the stock is falling in price.

A *callable bond* can be called in for redemption at the corporation's volition. When bonds are called, the corporation usually sets the call price (*redemption price*) a few points above the face value. Called bonds pay no more interest. Unless redeemed, the bondholder's capital will be stagnant. A *non-callable bond* is subject to redemption only at its expiration.

When bonds issued on the same date of the same issue have varying dates of maturity, they are called *serial bonds*. These should not be confused with *series bonds* which, although they are secured by the same mortgage or pledge of assets, are issued on different dates. Designated as Series A, Series B., etc., the terms of each series may differ, but a later series may not have an earlier maturity date than a prior series. Series bonds are sometimes called *limited open-end mortgage bonds*.

When a business is insolvent, a court may appoint a receiver to operate, reorganize or liquidate the business. Usually, such companies are short on cash. The receiver may get permission from the court to sell *receivers' certificates* to raise any necessary money. Such certificates are liens on the property and usually have first claim on any earnings or assets.

On rolling stock, railroads frequently issue *equipment trust certificates* which actually constitute title to the movable equipment. Ownership of the equipment is vested in a trustee who may lease it back to the railroad. Payments by the railroad cover interest, expenses, and amortization of the principal amount. These generally run about 15 years to maturity, with certificates maturing in series. The rate at which the series mature is faster than the rate of depreciation of the equipment, so that the safety of the certificates increases as they approach maturity. After all payments have been made, the equipment again becomes the property of the railroad. Should the railroad fail to make the required payments, the trustee may seize the equipment for the benefit of the certificate holders.

GOVERNMENT PAPER

Corporations issue bonds to obtain money for construction of facilities, expansion, working capital, or other matters related to the running of their businesses. Likewise, the Federal and local governments must raise money for similar purposes. Corporations borrow money on their ability to make profits; governments borrow money on their right to tax.

U. S. Government bonds are really debentures, backed by the general credit of the United States.

Treasury bonds, issued in $1,000 units, are traded like any other bonds. They have maturities of five years or longer. The market value of each outstanding issue can be determined by consulting the daily financial columns. In general, the value of any particular issue will vary as the prime interest rate varies from time to time. Treasury bonds are good collateral for loans.

Treasury notes differ from Treasury bonds principally in that they are for shorter terms (one to five years) and are not legally restricted as to interest rates.

Certificates of Indebtedness are issued by the Treasury with maturities of up to one year.

Treasury Bills are short-term paper with no stated interest rate; they are sold at a discount through competitive bidding with maturities of 90 days or less.

Savings bonds, (E and H bonds) differ sharply from all other bonds in that they cannot be used (by law) as collateral and do not fluctuate in value.

Municipal Bonds

Municipal (a broad term to include those of state, county, city and town) bonds may be bonds or they may be debentures. Their value on the market varies with the prime interest rate and also with public confidence in the ability of the issuer to meet interest and principal payments. The interest on most municipal bonds is exempt from Federal income tax, which makes them attractive to investors in the higher income tax brackets.

State Obligations. Bonds issued by the states, though broadly included in the term "municipals," actually fall into a separate category. Generally speaking, because the entire state is concerned, state bonds have a greater degree of inherent security than those of the sub-divisions of the state. On the other hand, except for New York, they have the disadvantage that the state can be sued for failure to meet its commitments only with the consent of the state itself. Municipalities can be sued without such consent as they are sued in the state courts. For the most part, towns, counties and other sub-divisions of a state depend on real property taxes for meeting their obligations. A state generally does not tax real property. Instead, it depends upon income taxes, gasoline taxes, taxes on corporations, sales taxes, tobacco and liquor taxes, and fees of various kinds.

Types of Obligations. Basically, there are two types of municipal obligations. One is the *general obligation;* the other is the *limited obligation,* of which the revenue bond is an example. A general obligation means that all of the taxing power of the municipality (or state) is pledged for its payment. A limited obligation means that something less than the full taxing power is pledged for its payment; usually the taxes from a specific source (such as gasoline taxes) are pledged. If, in addition to the specific pledging of one source of taxes, the deficiency (if any) is to be made up from general revenue, the obligation is a general one rather than a limited one. Some authorities classify this special type as a third type of obligation, but essentially any obligation that has claim on all of the resources of a municipality is effectively a general obligation.

Limited and Unlimited Tax Bonds. Just as there are two types of obligations, so there are two types of tax situations that affect the quality of a bond issue. A state may through its constitution or through its statutes place a limit on the taxing power of a municipality. For example, it might be illegal for a city to exceed a tax rate of $30 per $1,000 of assessed valuation. Bonds of that city would be termed *limited tax bonds.* In other cases, there is no constitutional or statutory limitation on the taxes a municipality may assess. In these cases, their bonds are known as *unlimited tax bonds.* The fact that the taxing power is unlimited is not necessarily indicative of a higher quality security. States and municipalities have, on occasion, made the tax rates and assessed valuations so high that business is driven out of the area, and a net reduction in collectible taxes has resulted.

Floating Debt. Floating debt is the non-funded obligations of a state or municipality. Unpaid bills is one example, particularly when they are overdue, rather than current. Because a local government receives most of its tax revenue once or twice a year, rather than in an even flow throughout the year, there are short periods when it is "in funds" and other, longer periods when it is very short on cash. To meet its current bills, payroll, and so on, the government may issue *tax anticipation notes*—IOU's to be paid from current tax receipts. They are a part of the floating debt, but are usually not considered in the overall debt burden as they will usually be paid off during the current year. *Bond anticipation notes* are also a part of the floating debt. Because these may be outstanding (i.e., unredeemed) for several years, bond anticipation notes are usually added to the municipality's funded debt in determining overall net debt.

Overlapping Debt. The same property may be subject to taxation by two different taxing authorities. For example, residential property in a town may be taxed by the town itself for service of the town's debt. At the same time, it may be taxed by the county for bonds of the county school system. This situation is known as *overlapping debt*. In one county in Maryland, for example, the same property is taxed (at different rates) for general operating expenses of the county government, for the operating budget of the school system, for retirement of school bonds, for sanitary services and for the road system. In addition, taxes are collected on the property by the county for remittance to the state.

FOREIGN SECURITIES

Foreign securities follow the same general classifications as domestic securities, but terminology varies to some extent. Many investors have been interested in foreign securities over the years because of the comparatively high yields often available. However, there are special risks involved in foreign investments that are absent from investments in domestic issues. Foreign government securities have not as a whole been as safe nor as dependable as U.S. government issues, particularly in areas affected by wars or Soviet encroachment. Stockholders have lost when foreign governments have expropriated holdings of their companies. And variations in currency values and convertibility have often been detrimental to the U.S. investor.

Without doubt, there are definite opportunities in foreign investments, but more than usual care and knowledge is needed to evaluate them. For the average individual, the foreign securities market is full of pitfalls.

Interest Equalization Tax

Money which leaves the United States for foreign investment sources is lost to our economy, at least temporarily. Because it does not directly

return any corresponding amount in the form of trade or reciprocal investment, it is a debit against the U.S. balance of payments. During the past
few years, the balance of payments has shown annual deficits since, invariably, more capital has left the United States than has entered it. This has resulted in a severe drain on our gold supply.

Among the measures proposed by the administration to reduce this
deficit and to conserve gold was the *"interest equalization tax"* suggested as
an excise tax by the Treasury Department in July 1963. It called for a tax
to be imposed on U. S. taxpayers who purchased new and outstanding foreign
securities. Enacted as Public Law 88–563 on September 2, 1964, the Interest
Equalization Tax Act imposed a tax of 15 per cent on foreign equities purchased from foreigners payable by the purchaser. Debt obligations of foreign
issuers with maturities of three years or more were given a tax imposition
on the purchaser of 2¾% to 15% on a sliding scale, the tax increasing with
the length of time to maturity. The purpose of the tax was stated "in order
to equalize costs of longer-term financing in the United States and in markets
abroad, and for other purposes." Since the tax effectively adds to the cost
of a security, the yield on such foreign investments is correspondingly
reduced. All purchases made on or after July 19, 1963 became taxable under
the Act. As enacted the law imposed the tax through December 31, 1965, but
expiration was extended in October 1965 to July 31, 1967. Further extension
is probable so long as the balance of payments remains unfavorable.

Since the Act was intended to help solve the balance of payments
problem, the tax was not imposed on purchases of foreign securities from
American owners. Also, there are several exclusions and exemptions under
the Act including exclusion for investments in "less developed countries"
as defined in the Act.

American Depository Receipts

To facilitate trading in foreign securities, certain American banks and
trust companies issue American Depository Receipts (ADR's). These
receipts are issued against the deposit of shares of the foreign company
in an overseas branch of the American bank. When these shares are
sold, there is an exchange of the ADR's, not of the shares themselves. The
investor pays for his ADR's in U. S. dollars and receives his dividends in
U. S. dollars. His costs may be a little higher because of the charges by the
depository bank. In most cases, ADR owners do not have customary
stockholders' rights of attending meetings and voting.

A COMPARISON

	Stocks	*Bonds*
Basis for Issuance	As a share in the corporation.	As a debt of the corporation.
Return	No fixed rate. Must be declared by directors.	Fixed. Payment precedes stock.
Voting Rights	Stockholders elect directors.	No voice in management.
Mandatory Issuance	Yes.	No.
Degree of risk	Varies as to corporation and type of stock.	Some, but not as much as stock.
Maturity Date	None.	Yes, as stated.
Claims Preference	After bonds and other creditors.	Precedes stockholders.

REVIEW QUESTIONS

1. In what important respects does a corporation differ from a partnership?
2. What form of security *must* be issued by a corporation organized for profit?
3. What are a stockholder's rights?
4. What is the limited liability of a stockholder? Of a limited partner?
5. When is a stockholder entitled to receive dividends?
6. To what extent does a common stockholder share in the proceeds of liquidation of a corporation?
7. Define "proxy." What is a proxy fight?
8. Explain the difference between cumulative and non-cumulative voting.
9. What are pre-emptive rights?
10. Under what circumstance is the capital stock the same as the common stock of a corporation?
11. How does preferred stock differ from common stock?
12. What type of preferred stock may react to changes in the market at certain times in the same manner as common stock of the same corporation?
13. What is a "callable" security? Are all such issues alike?
14. Who issues the guarantee of a "guaranteed" security?
15. Discuss the relationship of authorized, issued, outstanding and treasury stock.
16. How does treasury stock differ from common stock?
17. In what respects are rights and warrants the same? Different?
18. What are voting trust certificates?

19. Must a bond be secured?
20. What determines the market price of a bond?
21. Distinguish between a mortgage bond and a general mortgage bond.
22. What kind of a bond is issued under terms that permit additional borrowings if additional property is pledged as collateral?
23. What are the differences among the following: revenue bond, income bond, adjustment bond, split-coupon bond?
24. What special feature does a sinking fund bond have?
25. What desirable feature is afforded by a registered bond that is lacking in a coupon bond?
26. What are serial bonds? Series bonds?
27. How does a debenture bond differ from a mortgage bond?
28. What is a receiver's certificate? What claim does it have on a company's earnings and assets?
29. What is an equipment trust certificate? What special feature does it have with respect to safety?
30. Corporations borrow money on their ability to make profits. On what do governments borrow?
31. What principal differences are there among the different U.S. Treasury obligations?
32. What types of bonds cannot by law be used as collateral?
33. Define a municipal bond. What specific advantage does it have?
34. What two general types of obligations are issued by states? Municipalities?
35. What is floating debt? Overlapping debt?
36. What is the difference in security offered by a state as compared with a municipality?
37. Explain the difference between limited and unlimited tax bonds.
38. Distinguish between tax anticipation notes and bond anticipation notes. Which is included in floating debt? Which in overall net debt?
39. What are the special risks involved in foreign securities?
40. What is the purpose of ADR's?

Chapter 3

The
O-T-C
Market

THE MARKETPLACE FOR SECURITIES

Types of Markets

Securities are bought and sold in two general types of markets: the stock exchanges, which deal in securities of companies which have applied and qualified for trading on them, and the over-the-counter market, which handles all other securities transactions. Buying and selling of securities listed for trading on the exchanges is frequently effected off the exchanges. When this is done, it is termed as dealing in "the third market."

The over-the-counter market is a national *negotiated* market, without a central market place, composed of a network of thousands of brokers and dealers in the United States who make securities transactions for themselves and their customers. Professional buyers and sellers seek each other out by telephone and telegraph and negotiate prices on the most favorable basis that can be achieved. Often these negotiations are accomplished in a matter of seconds or minutes.

The stock exchanges are *auction* markets where buyer and seller meet. While each exchange is located in a single city, the market is made nation-wide through the offices of member firms in all major cities. A customer's order placed in New Orleans, for example, may be relayed by telephone or teletype to New York, the order be executed on the floor of the exchange, and the confirmation be given orally to the customer within a matter of minutes.

The over-the-counter market is the larger, accounting for at least 75% of the gross value of all securities sold in the United States. Through this market, over 25,000 issues are traded. Only about 3,000 securities are listed on the New York Stock Exchange, American Stock Exchange, and the regional exchanges. More than three million investors own OTC securities exclusively; another three million people hold mutual fund shares and a large percentage of 13 million other individuals have some type of over-the-counter issue in their portfolios. The percentage of people owning OTC securities exclusively has increased sharply over the years according to the 1965 Census of Shareowners compiled by the NYSE—by more than 23 per cent since 1962.

Some authorities have called the trading of securities the only "capital-istic" business remaining in the United States. Manufacturing, agriculture, and trade are subject to a multitude of Federal, state, and local laws and regulations which ultimately are of inestimable importance in determining the worth of the business or product. On the other hand, the securities of corporations are freely traded according to their worth and their projected future value, and hence are subject to the laws of supply and demand in the marketplace.

Functions of the Over-the-Counter Market

Over-the-counter transactions fall into three categories:

a. All publicly held securities not listed on the stock exchanges. These are the stocks of most corporations and most banks and insurance companies; most corporate bonds as well as U.S. Government secu-rities, municipal bonds, and railroad equipment trust certificates; many foreign corporate securities; and all open-end investment companies (mutual funds).

b. *Primary distributions*, or *new issues* of securities which are being sold to the public for the first time.

c. *Secondary distributions* of issues which may already be traded on an exchange but, because of the size of the offering, are divided into smaller parcels and traded apart from the regular exchange trans-actions. These avoid the price drop and instability which might result from the sudden sale of a large block of securities on the exchange floor. Technically, this differs from general "third market" activity which is a more routine over-the-counter marketing of listed securities.

UNDERWRITING AND THE INVESTMENT BANKER

The Investment Banker

For marketing new issues, companies usually seek the services of an *investment banker*, the expert who can offer efficient marketing through proper advertising and selling practices.

He is one of the three types of bankers who serve corporations. The other two are the commercial banker and the institutional banker.

The investment banker deals with long-term capital for equity financing (that is, for common and preferred stocks) and borrowings (bonds). The capital he seeks may go to a new corporation, which is seeking operating capital (a new issue) or to an already established corporation which may need capital for expansion or other activities (usually a secondary issue).

The investment banker provides valuable aid as an adviser and as an underwriter.

As an adviser. Because he thoroughly understands the methods and effects of different types of financing and has a close working knowledge of the investment market, the investment banker can advise a corporation in such matters as:

a. Whether additional capital should be sought through equity financing (the issuance of stock to the public) or whether the capital should be borrowed. If it is to be borrowed, the investment banker can help the corporation to determine whether the borrowing should be private (as a loan from a lending institution or the private placement of a bond issue) or should be through a public bond issue.

b. If a security is to be issued, the type that is best suited to the corporation's needs in terms of its own capital structure and its appeal to the public.

c. The condition of the investment market. Could an issue be marketed effectively at the time?

d. The terms or conditions of the security to be issued, including rates on a preferred stock or bond, to make the issue reasonably competitive with other securities on the market.

e. The best method of marketing the issue.

As an underwriter. The second important function of the investment banker is that of *underwriter*. This is a term borrowed from the insurance industry in which, for a fee, an underwriter assumes a risk. In the type of security underwriting described in the next paragraph, the investment banker assumes the risk and guarantees the issuing corporation a fixed sum of money.

In the simplest form of underwriting, an investment banker buys the entire issue from the company at a set price and then offers shares or bonds to the public. To compensate for promotion expense and the risk that the issue may not readily be sold, the underwriter offers the securities to the public at a price higher than the price he paid to the issuer. This difference in price, *underwriting spread*, *mark-up*, or *underwriting discounts and commissions*, makes up the underwriter's gross profit. Under present laws and regulations, the underwriter must continue to offer the securities at the price first set by him until the entire issue has been sold. There can be no "free" market for regular trading until then. These regulations are designed to prevent an underwriter from "holding back" a substantial block of shares of a desirable issue to take advantage of a possible rise in price due to the scarcity of the securities.

Underwriting Syndicate

Frequently, an investment banker is not willing to take an entire issue by himself. He may not be able to finance it alone, or there may be other reasons for his wanting to take only a part of an issue. When this occurs, or to obtain wider distribution, the investment banker may enlist the services of other investment bankers to form an *underwriting syndicate, purchase group,* or *underwriting group.* Each member of the syndicate underwrites a specific amount of the issue. The syndicate organizer is sometimes referred to as the *principal underwriter,* the *syndicate manager,* or the *managing underwriter.* To assist in selling the issue to the public, the services of other dealers are sought to become a part of the *selling group.* Each such dealer agrees to sell a specified amount of the issue. If he fails to do so he may be penalized, but his commitment does not extend to the actual purchase of his unsold allotment as it does with the syndicate members. An *Underwriting Agreement* is entered into by the managing underwriter with the issuing corporation. In addition, *Agreements among Underwriters* (or *Purchasers*) are signed by the managing underwriter and the other syndicate members; these specify the commitment of each underwriter and the price to the underwriter, which is usually higher than the price to the manager. Because of his lesser risk, the dealer in a selling group pays somewhat more than a member of the underwriting group. Regardless of the price to any of the sellers, the price to the purchasers (the public) is the same whether the purchases are made from an underwriter or from a dealer.

In the instances given, the *issuer* (the company whose securities are being sold) is guaranteed a fixed amount for the entire issue. It often happens that no investment banker or group will guarantee to underwrite an issue. To reduce their risk, they may undertake to underwrite an issue on a *best efforts* basis. This means that they will try to dispose of all of the issue, but will not guarantee to do so. In such cases, the issuer may agree to reimburse the underwriter for certain advertising and promotional expense incurred in the selling of the issue. Such reimbursement is over and above the mark-up on the securities.

It is not uncommon for a best efforts underwriting to fall far short of its objective. Only a small percentage of a stock issue may actually be sold. When this happens, the company issuing the stock receives insufficient money into its treasury to accomplish the purpose for which the stock was issued. Because this is unsatisfactory both from the point of view of the company and of its shareholders, the *best efforts, all or nothing* underwriting has become increasingly popular. Here, the shares are not actually issued until the entire issue has been subscribed to. Should anything less than the full issue find buyers, the offer is withdrawn. Investment bankers are usually very careful about undertaking this type of underwriting because all of their selling expenses are a net loss should the entire issue not be sold.

In cases where a corporation is increasing an issue of securities through the issuance of rights to its present shareholders, a type of underwriting known as *standby underwriting* is sometimes employed. If the holders of the rights do not buy the entire issue, the standby underwriter is obligated to take the remainder. Because of the time factor involved, during which the market may change radically, the risk to the underwriter in this type of underwriting is considerably more than in other types.

Some new issues, particularly of municipal bonds, are so sure of a market that they are offered to underwriters on a *competitive bid* basis. The underwriter or underwriting syndicate which offers the issuer the most favorable terms of net interest cost on the money received usually is the successful bidder. The price to the issuer is established by the bidding. In the *negotiated* type, the price is determined by negotiation. The manner of price determination is the major difference between these two types of underwritings.

When an entire issue is bought by a single purchaser, such as an insurance company, the transaction is generally referred to as a *private placement*. This may be done directly by the issuer or the services of an investment banker may be used.

Occasionally, an issue may be sold by the issuing corporation itself without employing an underwriter. This is most often done by small corporations or when the offering is one of stock rights only.

Prospectus

Under the Securities Act of 1933 (Chapter 5) any offer to the public of a new issue can only be made by a *prospectus*, a descriptive booklet containing information about the company and the issue, which must meet the "full disclosure" provisions of that Act. The Securities and Exchange Commission reviews all prospectuses before they are issued to make sure they conform to the requirements of the Act, but in no sense does the SEC pass on the merits of the issue either as a speculation or as an investment.

Information in a prospectus includes the purpose for which the solicited funds are to be used, the underwriter's and dealers concessions, the net amount of proceeds to the issuer, the business of the corporation, biographical information on the officers and directors including the extent of their experience in the business, financial statements and any other material the SEC considers necessary to give a potential investor a basis for making a considered investment decision.

A prospectus must always be used during the period of the underwriting. In addition, there is a minimum period of time during which the prospectus must be used, even if the actual underwriting has ended. For a new issuer (a corporation that has not previously sold securities to the public pursuant to an earlier effective registration statement), this minimum time period is 90 days, unless the SEC specifies a shorter period. For others the period during which a prospectus must be delivered prior to a sale is 40 days. In the special case of open-end investment companies, a prospectus is always required because the underwriting is continuous; *new* shares are being offered for sale.

Many best efforts underwritings are called *Reg A's*. These are underwritings in which the total dollar amount is $300,000 or less and which have been registered under a "Regulation A exemption." Because of the limited nature of the offering, the SEC has modified its prospectus requirements to some extent. These issues are offered by an *offering circular*, instead of by a regular prospectus.

Sometimes a company's stock is owned by one individual or a small group of individuals. Such stock has been bought on a *private offering*. It has never been offered to the general public. At a later date, that individual or group of individuals (or perhaps an estate) decides to sell its shares to the public. A primary distribution is again involved because the stock, which had been previously bought and held, was not originally sold on a public offering basis. Therefore a prospectus must now be used, just as in the case of a completely new issue.

In addition to SEC requirements, the provisions of the individual state securities laws must be complied with in these states in which an offering is to be made.

Stabilization

For the duration of an underwriting of a new issue, the public offering price is maintained by the distributing firms at a fixed price. Should an active market be formed in the issue at a price below this offering price, it would be difficult for the underwriters to market the issue at the higher price. To prevent such a market from forming, the principal underwriter usually stipulates that he may buy on the open market for his own account. When he does so, he is buying at less than the public offering price and selling at the offering price. Such activity is known as *stabilization*. If it is to be done, the '33 Act requires that the prospectus carry a notice, in capital letters of at least 10-point type, that reads:

IN CONNECTION WITH THIS OFFERING, THE UNDERWRITERS MAY OVER-ALLOT OR EFFECT TRANSACTIONS WHICH STABILIZE OR MAINTAIN THE MARKET PRICE . . . AT A LEVEL ABOVE THAT WHICH MIGHT OTHERWISE PREVAIL IN THE OPEN MARKET. SUCH STABILIZING, IF COMMENCED, MAY BE DISCONTINUED AT ANY TIME.

Indication of Interest

While waiting for effective registration of a new issue, the principal underwriter is vitally interested in the potential market for the issue. He needs to know approximately how many shares should be allotted to each of the *other* underwriters *and the dealers* in the selling group. Each of these, in turn, wants to know his potential market before making any kind of commitment to the principal underwriter. A preliminary *red herring* prospectus is therefore issued to be shown by dealers to prospective customers. Thus the underwriter looks to dealers and the dealers to their customers for *indications of interest* in the new underwriting.

Note that the red herring is only permitted to get an indication of interest. As a prospectus, it is incomplete in that it lacks certain information such as the price. It must not be used in any direct or indirect manner to sell securities. In this connection, any recommendation or favorable opinion with respect to the securities is construed as selling. Also, any stressing of the favorable features as against the unfavorable aspects is considered a violation of the law.

After the effective registration date, a bona fide offer to sell is made by the *final (effective)* prospectus. Any further use of the red herring requires that it be preceded or accompanied by the effective prospectus.

Due Diligence Meeting

A due diligence meeting will be called close to the end of the cooling period (the period between the date of filing and the date the registration statement becomes effective) to enable the underwriters, officers of the issuing corporation, and their respective legal and accounting staffs to discuss the registration statements and prospectus, to review the current status of the corporation, and to insure that proper supervision of the offering continues up to its completion.

Secondary Distribution

Sometimes an estate or an institutional owner of a large block of shares (of a stock previously offered to the public) wishes to sell them. Placing such a large order through a stock exchange might drive the price down so that the results of the sale would be unsatisfactory. To prevent such an adverse effect on the current market price, large blocks are frequently handled in the over-the-counter market through a *secondary distribution*. Brokers all over the country offer the shares at a *net (i.e. without commission)* price fairly related to the current market, but often slightly below it in order to make the offer attractive to their customers. When so handled, the large block is in effect broken up into many small blocks and the market is unaffected.

Other procedures for disposing of large blocks of stock and special procedures for buying large blocks without unduly affecting the market are described in Chapter 4. In adidtion, as with a new issue, a private placement may take the place of a secondary distribution.

"When, as, and if..."

When a company wishes to sell additional shares of stock, thus increasing the number of shares outstanding, it will either issue rights to its existing shareholders (when they have pre-emptive rights) or will offer its new shares directly to the public. While waiting for the securities to be issued, the rights or shares may be traded on a *when, as, and if basis*. If, for any reason, the securities are not issued, all trades are automatically cancelled. In other words, there is no actual money commitment unless the rights or shares are actually issued. This type of trading is normally handled over the counter.

TRANSACTIONS

Brokers and Dealers

Once an entire issue has been sold to the general public, purchases and sales of these securities could theoretically be made directly between owners and would-be owners. However, if there were no organized ready market, each buyer would have to look for a seller and each seller would have to look for a buyer. This would, of course, be completely impractical. The need for a ready market in which securities of all types could be bought and sold resulted in the *broker*.

Regardless of the type of market, *auction or negotiated*, a *broker*, as defined in the Securities Exchange Act of 1934, is one who buys and sells securities for the account of another person. However, this definition does not apply to a bank which buys or sells for the accounts of others. A broker may be an individual, a corporation, or any other legal entity except a bank.

Because a broker buys and sells for the accounts of others, he acts as an *agent* for the buyer or seller, or both. He is a go-between and does not enter into the transaction. For his services, he charges his customers a commission on both purchases and sales. When he confirms an order either to buy or sell, he must detail the number of shares, the cost per share, the total cost for the shares, and his commission on the transaction. He must also show the transfer taxes that are paid by a seller. The confirmation also shows his customer that he has acted as a broker or agent and not for his own account, and must show (or offer to provide) the other party to the transaction and the time of execution.

There is no difference in the *registration* of a broker and a dealer. Actually, brokers and dealers alike are registered as "broker/dealers." However, there is a sharp distinction *in function* between a broker and a dealer. A *dealer* is one who buys or sells securities for his own account as a regular business. Should he sell securities to a customer or buy securities from him, the dealer acts as a *principal* and not as an agent. He provides his customers with confirmations, just as a broker does, but he must indicate that he has acted as a principal and for his own account. He gives the identical information to his customer that the broker gives, but there is no commission shown. A dealer as principal buys or sells "net."

Most broker/dealers act sometimes as brokers and sometimes as dealers. However, some act only as brokers and others act only as dealers.

Further, there are specializations among brokers and among dealers. Some firms, known as *bond houses*, act as dealers only in the marketing of municipal bonds. Others deal only in local issues. Some restrict their activities to the sale of shares of mutual funds. Others trade only for their own accounts.

How Transactions Are Made

If all broker/dealers were to operate strictly as brokers, accepting orders from customers to buy or sell unlisted securities, a market could exist. It would be a somewhat scattered and confused market because Broker A who had an order to sell 100 shares of BCD stock would have no way of knowing that Broker X had an order to buy 100 shares of the same stock. It is doubtful whether such a market could be made profitable for the brokers themselves, who would have to spend excessive time finding buyers and sellers.

Fortunately, large numbers of broker/dealers act as dealers by creating and maintaining markets in selected securities. How does a dealer "create" a market for a security? Simply by publishing an offer to buy at a certain price (a *bid*) and to sell the same security at another (higher) price (an *offer*). He publishes this bid and offer in the "pink sheets" issued daily to more than 1800 subscribing firms by the National Quotation Bureau, Inc.

The dealer's published bid and offer states that he is willing to buy one trading unit (usually 100 shares of stock or five $1000 bonds) at the lower of the two prices and that he is willing and able to sell one trading unit at the higher of the two prices. The difference between the two prices is known as the *spread* which represents the dealer's profit on a two-way transaction. If the dealer is *inventorying* a stock, he may make more profit through an increase in value of the stock, but he may also lose through a decrease in its value. When a dealer is carrying an inventory, he is said to have a *position* in that security. When he buys more of the security, he adds to his inventory;

when he sells, he sells from the inventory. He is like any other merchant except that his goods are bonds and stocks.

Quotations in the daily pink sheets (green sheets in Chicago; white sheets in San Francisco) come in from dealers all over the country and cover thousands of stocks. When a broker/dealer receives an order from a customer to buy or sell a stock, he consults the sheets to determine who "has a market." He may find that several firms are quoting. For his customer's best interest, the broker may query (shop around) some of these dealers to get the best (highest) bid and best (lowest) offer to sell.

Let us imagine that his order is to buy 100 shares at the best price possible. After checking with several dealers, the broker finds that the lowest price offered is 42. He might say to the dealer, "I can buy 100 shares at $41\frac{1}{2}$." If the dealer is anxious to make the sale, he might reply, "Will sell at $41\frac{3}{4}$." Since the broker was instructed by his customer to buy at the best price, the broker will accept that offer, and the sale has been made.

To further improve the mechanics of the OTC market, the National Association of Securities Dealers, Inc. (NASD) is currently studying the possible use of automated equipment in the dissemination of quotations information. Automation properly applied in the informational area of the OTC market could assist in quickly and efficiently identifying market makers, help insure firmness of quotations, provide up-to-date price information and other attending statistical figures such as volume and timed changes in quotes.

It is important to realize that the expression "His word is as good as his bond" is vital in this business. In many transactions every hour, a customer gives an order to a broker on the telephone, the broker completes the transaction with a dealer on the telephone and all parties understand that a valid contract has been entered into by all parties just as though formal documents had been drawn up. Without the ability to rely on the spoken word, there could be no effective market operation. Probably in no other business is so much reliance placed on the integrity of others in the business. It is essential that that integrity be maintained.

Whether a dealer is selling directly to or buying directly from a customer or a broker is acting as an agent for a customer, each has a definite obligation to the customer. He must act in the customer's best interest. If a dealer, he must make sure that any transaction with a customer is at a price reasonably related to the market. In other words, if a dealer knows that a stock can be bought at a price of 41 (net) from another dealer, he would be guilty of unethical practice were he to charge his customer a price of 42. If a broker, he must get the best buying or selling price he can for his customer and his commission must not be excessive.

Commissions on stock exchanges are standardized, the exchanges being auction markets in which such standardization is practicable. Because of the different nature of the negotiated over-the-counter market, no standard commissions are set. Many over-the-counter firms normally use standard stock exchange commission rates on over-the-counter transactions, but such rates are not always feasible, particularly with infrequently traded issues or with very low-priced issues.

Newspaper Quotations

Widespread public acceptance of a particular security as an investment medium depends to a large extent on the marketability of the security; that is, the ease with which it may be bought or sold. In turn, marketability depends largely on the public's knowledge of the current market value of the security. The pink sheets are not widely enough distributed to give the public the information it should have. A query must be made to a broker/dealer, and not all of them are subscribers.

To assist investors in determining the market value of certain OTC securities, the National Association of Securities Dealers supplies more than 300 newspapers with daily quotations on almost 4,000 different issues.

The NASD provides inter-dealer or wholesale quotations on some 1,300 nationally traded and active securities published in major metropolitan newspapers. The Association also supplies newspapers in 120 different geographical areas with quotations on less widely traded local issues. Because the over-the-counter market is spread across the country with thousands of transactions taking place almost simultaneously at many different locations, it is impossible to record and publish the actual prices at which transactions are made; hence, these inter-dealer quotations do not represent actual transactions that may have occurred in a particular security.

As a guide for investors, these inter-dealer quotations are gathered by the NASD from the firms who maintain continuous markets in the securities quoted. The quotations reflect what that dealer is willing to pay to acquire the security (the *bid*) and the price at which that dealer is willing to sell the security to another dealer (the *asked* price).

The masthead carried above this list of inter-dealer quotations designates the approximate time of the day that the quotations were obtained from these market makers and emphasizes that price changes occur continuously. With these quotations reflecting only a single point in time, actual transactions could naturally take place at higher or lower prices during the day.

In addition, the public can normally expect to pay a markup, markdown or commission on actual transactions. However, the NASD scrutinizes OTC markups through a policy which states that member firms must buy or sell securities at fair and reasonable prices or be subject to disciplinary action.

In their listings, over-the-counter stocks are separated into categories: Industrial and Utility Stocks; Bank Stocks; Insurance Stocks; Corporation Bonds; Public Authority Bonds.

Over-the-Counter Markets

Thursday, April 27, 1967

These quotations, supplied by the National Association of Securities Dealers, are bids and offers quoted by over-the-counter dealers to each other as of approximately 3 p.m. (Eastern time). The quotations do not include retail markup, markdown or commission, and do not represent actual transactions.

Additional quotations are included in a weekly over-the-counter list published each Monday on this page.

Stock & Div.	Bid	Asked	Prev. Bid	Stock & Div	Bid	Asked	Prev. Bid	Stock & Div.	Bid	Asked	Prev. Bid
InvCoun .12	2¼	3	2½	OreMet .0575	17⅝	18	17⅞	TamarEl	5⅛	5½	5⅝
Ionics	29½	30½	28	OrePrt .20f	15½	16	15½	Tampax 2.40a	143	145	143
IowaBeef	47½	48½	47¼	OtterTail 1.28	23	23⅜	23	Tappan 1.40	22	22¾	22
IaEP4.80pf 2.40	42½	44	42½	OzarkAir	14¾	15	14⅞	TaylorPub .64	24¾	25¼	24¾
IowaSoUt 1.28	28⅝	29	28¾	**P**				TaylrWine .84	35	35⅜	35¼
IrwinRD .32b	25¾	26¾	25	Pabst .50f	52¾	53½	53	TechAnim	3¾	4⅛	3¾
J				PacFarE 2.40	38	39	38⅛	TecumPd 2.40a	73	76	71
Jack-in-Box	25	25¾	25¼	PacGamR .80	11⅜	11⅞	11⅜	TejonRnch .40	23½	24½	23½
Jacquin S3%g	9⅞	10⅝	9⅜	PacS&L .30	12¾	13¼	13	Telex	12¼	12⅝	12¼
JamWat 1.08	27	28	27	PacVegO	10⅛	10½	10	TennNG .18f	13¼	13⅞	13¼
Jamesbury	20¼	21	21	PackMach 1	27	28½	26	TexAmOil S5%g	6¼	6½	5⅝
Jantzen .80b	14¾	15¼	14¾	PackInst	9	9½	8½	TexCap .28b	7	7¼	7
				PalmBCn .40b	29¼	29⅝	29¼	Texize .10	11	11½	11¼
								TexotaO	7¾	8¼	7⅝

(left margin partial column) e-- Bid 6½ !9 .2½ 21 14¾ 29 17⅞ 21 11⅝ 10⅝ 7⅞ 1⅝ 15¼ 19¾ 10 16⅜ 20 19¾ 21½ 10¾ 19¼ 16¾ 12 13⅜ 6 18¼ 4⅜ 36½ 9 11¾/

(right margin partial column) Stock & · Fidlty-F · FidltyN · 5thThrd · 1stMRc · FrstBnc · 1stBkSt · 1stCtHo · 1stCam · 1stMer/ · 1stNAtl. · 1stNBir · 1stNBos · 1stNChi · 1stNCin · 1stNDa · 1stNFt\ · 1stNJer · 1stNMd · 1stNMp · 1stNOr · 1stNPa · 1stNSD · 1stNSJ · 1stNTu · 1stNCE · 1stNStl · 1stOkl · 1stSec(· 1stUni · 1stVaC

Opposite each listing of a security in the Industrial and Utility Stocks, Bank Stocks, and Insurance Stocks sections are three columns of figures: "Bid," representing the offer to buy; "Asked," the offer to sell; "Prev. Bid," the bid of the previous day. For the buyer and seller, transactions during the day will be somewhere in the range of the asked and bid prices. The difference between the two is the *spread*.

An 'x' preceding the bid price stands for 'ex-dividend.' A dividend has been declared which will be paid to the seller of the stock, not the purchaser. The 'pf' after a listing means 'preferred.' Other letter symbols are explained at the end of the listings. When checking for the meaning of letters or other symbols, be sure to consult the table associated with the particular column or columns being used. The same letter symbol may have different meanings in different listings within the same paper; in different papers, completely different symbols are not uncommon.

The bid and asked prices on these stocks are given by dealers who are maintaining markets in the securities. No dealer, however, can set the spread on the type of investment company called a mutual fund. The law states that he must sell shares at only the asked, or offering, price.

Unlike other over-the-counter stocks, the mutual fund bid price is the actual net asset value per share, usually the price at which the fund will redeem its own outstanding shares. The asked, or offering price, is the price a purchaser will pay for new shares issued by the fund. The difference between the bid and asked prices is the sales charge. Daily changes result from re-evaluations (often twice-daily) of the prices of the securities in the fund's portfolio.

Mutual Funds

Thursday, April 27, 1967
Price ranges for investment companies, as supplied
by the National Association of Securities Dealers:

	Bid	Asked	Prev. Bid		Bid	Asked	Prev. Bid
Aberdeen	3.12	3.41	3.09	Istel	21.28	21.94	21.11
Advisers	8.68	9.53	8.69	Ivest	16.07	17.56	15.79
Affiliated	8.93	9.66	8.88	Johnstn (v)	21.13	21.13	21.00
Am Bus	3.80	4.11	3.79	**Keystone Custodian Funds:**			
AmDivInv	11.80	12.89	11.72	Inv B-1	22.96	23.96	22.97
Am Grwth	7.01	7.62	7.01	MdG B-2	23.36	25.48	23.35
Am Inv (v)	37.73	37.73	37.46	Disct B-4	10.21	11.15	10.21
Am Mut	10.62	11.61	10.58	Inco K-1	9.40	10.26	9.38
Am Pac	7.07	7.07	7.09	Grth K-2	7.20	7.86	7.10
Assoc FdTr	1.57	1.71	1.56	Hi-Gr S-1	22.90	24.98	22.81
Assoc Inv	7.59	7.74	7.54	Inco S-2	10.80	11.79	10.75
Axe-Houghton:				Gr S-3	10.32	11.27	10.23
Fund A	(z)	(z)	7.61	Lo Pr S-4	7.17	7.83	7.06
Fund B	(z)	(z)	10.49	Keyst Intl	13.82	14.95	13.75
Stock	(z)	(z)	6.73	Knickrbck	7.53	8.25	7.48
Axe Sc	(z)	(z)	21.02	Knickr Gr	12.14	13.30	12.09
Blue Ridge	(z)	(z)	13.90	Lazard	16.12	16.37	16.12
Bondstock	6.80	7.43	6.80	Lex Inc Tr	9.90	10.82	9.91
Boston	9.38	10.25	9.35	Lf Ins Inv	6.86	7.50	6.86
Broad St	15.75	16.03	15.63	Lf Ins Stk	4.88	5.33	4.89
Bullock	15.52	17.01	15.44	**Loomis Sayles Funds:**			
Can Gen	9.85	10.77	9.86	Canadian	30.39	30.39	30.38
Canadian	18.97	20.52	18.91	Cap Dev	12.44	12.44	12.29
Capital Inc	8.66	9.49	8.62	Mutual	16.13	16.13	16.09

On this particular day, Aberdeen Fund could have been bought for $3.41 per share, which included a sales charge of 29¢. The net asset value or redemption price was $3.12. Some funds are sold without a direct sales charge; their bid and asked prices, as for Am(erican) Investors, is the same. Funds also sell ex-dividend; the 'x' before the bid price of a mutual fund is its net asset value less the amount of dividends it has declared. A fund may also sell ex-distribution ('d'); the bid and asked prices then show the drop in value caused by a declared distribution of capital gains (i.e., profits from sale of securities) that has not yet been paid to the fundholders. A (z) indicates that the price was not available at the time quotations were supplied to the newspapers.

Elsewhere in *The Wall Street Journal* (and other papers) is another over-the-counter group: Government, Agency and Miscellaneous Securities. This includes Treasury bonds, notes, and bills, as well as the bonds of some Federal and state agencies.

Government, Agency and Miscellaneous Securities

Over-the-Counter Quotations: Source on request.
Decimals in bid-and-asked prices represent 32nds (101.1 means 101 1-32). a-Plus 1-64. b-Yield to call date. c-Certificates of indebtedness.

Thursday, April 27, 1967

Treasury Bonds—

	Bid	Asked	Prev. Bid	Yld
2½s, 1962-67 June	99.29	99.31	99.29	2.73
5¼s, 1967 Aug.(c)	100.13a	100.15a	100.13	3.54
3⅝s, 1967 Nov.	99.28	100.0	99.28	3.63
3⅞s, 1968 May	99.25	99.29	99.25	3.97
3⅞s, 1968 Aug.	99.13	99.17	99.13	4.13
3⅞s, 1968 Nov.	99.15	99.19	99.15	4.15
2½s, 1963-68 Dec.	97.22	97.26	97.21	3.90
4s, 1969 Feb.	99.14	99.18	99.14	4.26
2½s, 1964-69 June	96.26	96.30	96.25	4.02
4s, 1969 Oct.	99.2	99.6	99.2	4.36
2½s, 1964-69 Dec.	96.2	96.6	96.2	
2½s, 1965-70 Mar.				

Bonds, whether government or corporate, are quoted differently from stocks. Bond prices are always given as if they were issued in denominations of $100, although most traded bonds have a face value of $1,000. A bid or asked price of 99 means 99 per cent of the face value, or $990 for a $1,000 bond.

Take the third treasury bond in the sample.

The first column indicates that the bond was issued to pay interest at the rate of $3\frac{5}{8}$ per cent of the par (face) value. The second and third columns show that the bond *matures*, or is due for redemption, in November 1967. In the next column, the '.28' is not .28 per cent; treasury bonds are always quoted in fractional parts of 32, not 100. So the .28 is $\frac{28}{32}$ or .875 per cent. The bid price is therefore $998.75. When maturity is close to the date of the listing, the bid price may be quoted extra finely—an 'a' means that another $\frac{1}{64}$ or .0156 per cent must be added. The asked and previous bid prices are then quoted in separate columns. The last column shows the percentage yield to maturity.

Corporation bonds and public authority bonds (turnpikes, etc.) traded over-the-counter are also quoted in the *Journal* but in a more condensed fashion. They are quoted on a strictly percentage basis of the face value. Their rate of yield is not given. Foreign Securities, including ADR's, and Foreign Bonds are listed separately.

A stock or bond traded over-the-counter only is an *unlisted* security, even though it is regularly quoted. A *listed* security is one that is listed and traded on a regular stock exchange (chapter 4).

Deliveries

Deliveries for over-the-counter securities are specified under certain rules of the NASD.* Page references following are to the NASD Manual.

Cash delivery means that delivery of securities sold is required at the office of the purchaser on the day of the transaction. Although no time of day is stated, such delivery must be made during the hours established by rule or practice in the community. The seller can require that the buyer pay for the securities at delivery. (Page 3512.)

Regular way requires delivery on but not before the fifth business day following the date of the transaction. Earlier delivery may, however, be accepted at the option of the buyer. The buyer's rights are not prejudiced by rejection of early delivery. Regular way delivery for U. S. Government bonds means delivery is due on the first business day following the day of the contract. (Page 3512).

---

* For a full discussion of these and other specific requirements, see Uniform Practice Code, NASD Manual.

Seller's option requires the exchange of written contracts. The duration of the option varies. In the cases of stocks and convertible bonds, the options may call for delivery in not less than six business days nor more than 60 calendar days. For U. S. Government bonds, the delivery may be in not less than two business days nor more than 60 calendar days. Other bonds may be delivered in not less than eight nor more than 60 calendar days. The seller in each case may deliver earlier by giving written notice, on or after the day when delivery would have been due if the contract had been made the "regular way," of intention to make delivery on the next business day following the day of the notice. (Page 3512.)

There is also a *buyer's option* contract. Delivery must be made on the date on which the option expires. If the seller tenders delivery before that time, acceptance is at the option of the buyer with no prejudice to his rights should he refuse to accept delivery. (Page 3513.)

Delayed delivery seller's option and buyer's option contracts maturing on Saturday, a half-holiday or a holiday carry over to the next full business day.

One general requirement is that all securities transactions be for *good delivery*. When a sale is made, the old certificate(s) showing the name of the seller must be cancelled by the *transfer agent* and a new certificate issued in the name of the buyer. The *registrar* then checks the new against the old to make sure that the same number of shares are still outstanding to insure that the new shares issued are equal to the old shares cancelled. This is a comparatively simple matter if the old certificates are delivered in a manner that satisfies certain requirements. When these requirements are met, there is a "good delivery." The buyer has the right to expect such good delivery. Failure to make or to insist upon good delivery can be costly in terms of time, money, and customer good will.

(a) When a contract is for 100 shares or multiples, certificates must be for 100 shares each. If less than 100-share certificates, they must be capable of being combined into 100-share units.

(b) If a contract is for less than 100 shares, any combination of certificates that will make the exact odd-lot is acceptable.

(c) An assignment must be executed on the back of the certificate itself or the certificate must be accompanied by a separate assignment, called a *stock power*, for each certificate. The assignment, in each case, must be signed exactly in the same manner in which the shares are registered, as shown on the face of the certificate.

(d) The assignment must be witnessed and the witness must still be living at the time of delivery.

(e) The signature must be guaranteed by someone satisfactory to the transfer agent. This is usually a national bank or a member of a stock exchange.

(f) When registration is in the name of two or more owners as joint tenants or as tenants in common, all must sign the assignment. (Pages 3521-3528.)

Buying in. Should a seller fail to deliver certificates on time, the buyer (on notification to the seller) has the right to *buy in* the securities for the account and risk of the seller. A combination notice of failure to deliver and intent to buy in is sent to the seller. If delivery is not effected by the time stated in the notice, the securities are bought in the open market for the account and risk of the seller; confirmation of the buy in must be made to the seller on the execution date with a copy to the Secretary of the National Uniform Practice Committee of the NASD. (Pages 3573-77.)

Marking to the Market. When a short sale (Chapter 4) is made, the buyer has the right to expect delivery of the certificates. Assume that Broker A sells (short) to Broker B 1000 of XXX common. Broker B expects regular way delivery. Broker A must deliver or have Broker B buy in to close the contract. Broker A doesn't want to have this happen. He, therefore, borrows 1000 shares of XXX from Broker C for delivery to Broker B and makes a deposit for the credit of C to the value of the shares as of that date. If the market price of the shares rises while the shares are on loan, Broker C is *partially unsecured*. He then has the right to demand that Broker A make an additional deposit equal to the change in market value of the 1000 shares. If the shares have risen $2 per share, he could demand an additional $2,000 deposit. This is marking to the market. (Pages 3572-3.)

On the other hand, should the value of the shares drop, Broker A has the right to demand a refund in the amount of the reduced value. This is also marking to the market.

The examples above refer to short sales. The same rights of marking to the market exist for "when, as, and if issued" and "when, as, and if distributed" sales.

Stock Clearing. In the over-the-counter market, when Broker A sells 100 shares of a stock for a customer to Broker B for his customer, Broker A must deliver the stock certificate directly to Broker B and receive the money from Broker B. Now, regardless of how many sales Broker B has made, he must be able to pay for all of the purchases of the same day before he receives the stock certificates. This means that regardless of how much money he may expect to receive from other brokers, he must always be ready to meet deliveries to him with cash. Should all deliveries of a particular day be made to him before he has received cash for his deliveries to other brokers, he may have to pay out substantial amounts of money even though the amounts he will receive later will be greater than what he has paid out. Temporarily, at least, his credit is severely extended. And note that he cannot receive collateral against which to get a loan until after he has paid for the securities.

Aside from the credit difficulties involved, this system requires individual delivery of securities from a broker to every broker who has purchased from him. Yet in any particular security, a broker may be required to deliver 2,000 shares on one day to one group of brokers and receive from others 2,100 shares. His net change in holdings is actually only one 100-share certificate. He may have had to write several checks and receive several others, yet the net change in his dollar accounts may have been only a small amount. At an average price of $10 per share, for example, he would have paid out a total of $21,000 and received a total of $20,000 (disregarding commissions and taxes). Thus, his net change in money position was only $1,000.

Further, consider the following situation:

On a particular day Broker A sells 100 shares of XYZ stock to Broker B. Broker B sells 100 shares of the same stock to Broker C.

The result of this very simple illustration is that on the settlement date A must deliver 100 shares of XYZ to B who, in turn, must deliver 100 shares to C. However, it is obvious that the same net result could be achieved simply by having A deliver 100 shares of XYZ directly to C. Broker B merely "pairs off" his purchase and sale transaction within his own office. Note that by this technique A will deliver 100 shares of XYZ to C even though they were not the original contracting parties. No real problems are caused by the fact that A's sale to B might have been at a different price than B's sale to C since a *settlement price* can be used for the delivery of such balances.

Therefore, in order to reduce the minimum the number of deliveries and of the total shares resulting from one day's transactions, and to reduce the amount of funds needed, it is desirable that securities be cleared and settled through a centralized facility.

In August 1963 the National Over-the-Counter Clearing Corporation started operations. It now clears over 1400 issues in the New York City area.

MARKET TERMS

Some terms familiarly used with transactions in the over-the-counter market are:

Bid and Offer

> *Bid Wanted* (or BW)—a security is being offered for sale and prospective buyers are requested to submit a bid for it.

> *Offering Wanted* (or OW)—a security is being sought for purchase and prospective sellers are requested to submit an offering.

> *Firm Bid*—a valid offer to buy a specified amount of a security at a definite price, whether for a brief moment only or for a specified period of time.

Firm Offer—a valid offer to sell a specified amount of a security at a definite price, whether for a brief moment only or for a specified period of time.

Market Prices and Orders

Actual Market—the prices at which a given security may be bought or sold.

Subject Market—the prices at which it is believed a given security may be bought or sold, subject to confirmation.

Workout Market—a subject market. The prices at which it is believed a given security may be bought or sold within a reasonable length of time. Also termed an *indicated* market.

Market Order—an order to buy or sell at the best obtainable price prevailing in the market when the order is entered.

Open order—an order entered at a specific price and is good until cancelled (G.T.C.).

Trading and Settlement

Dividend On—the buyer is entitled to the dividend declared on a security.

Ex-Dividend—the buyer is not entitled to the dividend declared on a security. The dividend will be paid to the seller.

Traded "Flat"—when referred to a bond, no accrued interest is included in the price. When not so traded, accrued interest must be added to the price quoted.

Cash Trade—a transaction requiring delivery of the securities on the day of sale.

Record Date—the day on which a list is compiled of the registered owners of shares who will receive dividends from a corporation.

Ex-Dividend Date—the day on and after which the buyer of a common stock is not entitled to a previously declared dividend. This is usually the third full business day before the record date. Except for mutual funds, the ex-dividend date is determined by the NASD's Uniform Practice Committee. For mutual funds, the ex date is that designated by the fund or its principal underwriter; it is customarily the same as the record date.

Trade Date—the day on which a transaction is made between two parties.

Settlement Date—the date on which securities sold must be delivered and payment must be made for securities bought. The settlement date is normally the fourth business day after the trade date.

Good Delivery—a security delivered in such form that record ownership may readily be transferred.

REVIEW QUESTIONS

1. What is the significant difference between the operation of the over-the-counter market and that of a stock exchange?
2. What type securities are traded "over-the-counter"?
3. Describe a primary distribution. What must be used in such a distribution?
4. When is a secondary distribution used in security sales?
5. What are considered to be the two important roles of the investment banker?
6. In what ways can an investment banker advise a corporation?
7. What is the basic function of the investment banker as an underwriter?
8. Why are underwriting groups or syndicates formed?
9. How is a member of a selling group obligated?
10. What are the different types of underwritings?
11. What is a "best efforts" underwriting?
12. What are the essentials of a "prospectus"?
13. When is an underwriting called a "Reg A"?
14. When is a distribution classed as a "private offering" and when is it a "primary distribution"?
15. What is stabilization? Under what circumstances is it legal?
16. What is meant by "indication of interest"?
17. What is a red herring prospectus?
18. Under what circumstances are stocks sold on a "when, as and if" basis.
19. When are prospectuses not essential for securities sales?
20. Describe the role of the "broker" in the securities market.
21. What must a broker tell a customer when a transaction is confirmed?
22. What are the differences between a "broker" and a "dealer"?
23. How is a market for securities "created"?
24. Define: bid; asked; spread.
25. Why does a dealer sometimes maintain an inventory of securities?
26. In whose interest does a broker act?
27. Explain how commissions are determined in the O-T-C market.
28. What information is given in a newspaper listing of over-the-counter stocks?
29. What do the mutual fund listed prices reflect?
30. At what price must a dealer sell shares of a mutual fund?
31. What type security usually is published with its yield?
32. Who specifies the delivery rules for o-t-c deliveries?
33. When must a "for cash" delivery be made?
34. What is "regular way" delivery? For U.S. Government bonds?
35. What is meant by "seller's option"? "Buyer's option"?
36. Explain "good delivery."
37. When does the purchaser of securities have the right to "buy in"?

38. Discuss "marking to the market."
39. What is the principle of stock clearing?
40. Distinguish between the following:
    a. Bid wanted and offering wanted
    b. Firm bid and firm offer
    c. Actual market, subject market
    d. Workout and indicated market
    e. Market order and open order
    f. Record, ex-dividend and trade dates
    g. Settlement date and delivery date

Chapter 4

The
Stock
Exchanges

BACKGROUND AND HISTORY

A stock exchange is "an auction market where buyer and seller meet."

Besides the New York Stock Exchange and the American Stock Exchange in New York City, there are twelve regional exchanges which are registered with the Securities and Exchange Commission are national securities exchanges. The most important are the Midwest Stock Exchange, with offices in several midwestern cities; the Pacific Coast Exchange, which includes Los Angeles and San Francisco; and the Philadelphia-Baltimore Stock Exchange, which also includes Washington, D.C.

In the year 1966, a total of 3,187,900,000 shares representing a value of more than $123 billion were traded on the exchanges. The New York Exchange accounted for 80.1 per cent of the dollar value and 69.2 per cent of all shares traded. The American Exchange accounted for 11.5 per cent of the dollar value and 22.9 per cent of the share volume. The regional exchanges together had only 8.4 per cent of the dollar volume and 7.9 per cent of the share volume.

This chapter deals with the New York Stock Exchange. Principles of operation of the other exchanges are similar, though not identical.

The introduction to the New York Stock Exchange *Fact Book, 1966* states:

The New York Stock Exchange is the largest organized securities market in the United States.

It is both national and international in character and operations. The Exchange itself does not buy, sell, own or set the prices of stocks traded thereon. The prices are determined by the decisions of millions of investors, who are able, through the Exchange Community's network of Member Firm offices and through the Exchange's market place, to carry out their investment needs quickly, economically and conveniently.

The Exchange is an unincorporated association. It is governed by a 33-man Board—29 members and allied members who are elected by the membership; and a president and 3 governors representing the public viewpoint, who are elected by the Board.

To these men—from all sections of the country—fall the responsibility for guiding the Exchange's programs and policies.

The programs and policies of the NYSE are based on the most important objects of the Exchange, contained in Section 2 of its Constitution: ". . . to maintain high standards of commercial honor and integrity among its members and allied members; and to promote and inculcate just and equitable principles of trade and business."

The complex, organized exchanges of today bear little resemblance to their simple beginnings of the New York Stock Exchange in the year 1792.

At that time, only a government issue to help pay for the Revolutionary War and a few bank and insurance stocks were being actively traded. A group of brokers formed a loosely knit organization to establish a regular market for these securities and in their agreement agreed "to give preference" to those within the group with respect to commissions charged and other matters related to buying and selling for their own accounts or for the accounts of others. In the beginning, these few broker/dealers met outdoors on Wall Street, but moved indoors the following year.

Even at this early stage, the "stock exchange" was an auction market, but its method of operation was quite different from that used today. There was no formal organization and no formal method of procedure until 1817 when the first formal constitution of the "New York Stock and Exchange Board" was adopted. Every member was required to be present at every session "unless when sick or out of the city." At that time, there were still very few securities in which the general public had an interest. The "auction" was conducted by the president who called out the name of each security in succession. A short period of time was allowed after the calling of each security for the assembled members to make their bids and offers. It wasn't until 1871 that this "call" market gave place to the continuous market which now exists.

CURRENT OPERATING PROCEDURES

As the number of securities offered to the public increased, it became impossible for the "call" market to continue. There just wasn't time enough in the day to call all of the securities in turn. Through a gradual evolution, there developed the present trading procedures on the New York Stock Exchange. There now are nineteen *trading posts* on the floor of the Exchange at which about 1,600 listed stock issues are traded. Certain stocks are traded at each of these posts, where a continuous auction market is maintained. In addition, there is the "Bond Crowd," where about 1,200 bond issues are dealt in. Some 800 to 900 active members may be represented on the trading floor at any one time. To assist these members, there are about 950 member firm employees. In addition, there are about 600 employees of the Exchange itself. During the average trading day in 1966, over 7,500,000 shares were traded. During the first four months of 1967, this number had risen to 9,800,000.

Unlike the usual auction market, this is a two-way auction in which some brokers are seeking to buy at the lowest possible price for their customers and other brokers are trying to sell at the highest possible price for their customers. If all orders from customers were "market" orders—to be executed at the most advantageous price—no great problem would exist in establishing a direct auction market at each post. However, many holders of securities wish to sell only at a specified price (a limit order) and prospective buyers will not pay more than a specified amount per share on a definite (limit) order.

The Specialist

Obviously, a broker cannot remain indefinitely at a trading post to execute limit orders. He must service many customers' orders in the course of the day. This problem is solved by the *specialist* (one of the five types of floor members). At each post, there are specialists who "make a market" for one or more stocks. These specialists are charged with the responsibility for maintaining an orderly market. They accept orders to buy and sell from brokers at prices that are not effective at the particular moment; they will accept orders to buy at prices lower than the current market and to sell at prices higher than the current market. Each such order is entered in the specialist's "book" to be executed whenever the change in the market makes the prices effective. Because the specialist's book reveals the entire picture of the market for a particular security that could permit "insider" manipulation, the specialist cannot at any time show his book to anyone except Floor Governors, Floor Officials, and authorized Exchange Staff.

When executing orders for other brokers as an agent, the specialist acts as a broker. When so acting, he is paid part of the commission the customers' brokers receive. But the specialist also acts as a dealer. He frequently will buy at a slightly higher price than the market or sell at a slightly lower price in order to narrow the "spread" between the bid and asked prices. Stock exchange regulations with respect to what a specialist may or may not do are extremely strict. Not only is he charged with maintaining an orderly market, but he must subordinate his own interests to those of the general public. He cannot, for example, buy or sell for his own account at a given price until he has executed all public orders at that price.

The specialist has other activities also, but they are all geared to "maintaining a continuous and orderly market."

Other Floor Members

The registered *Floor trader* buys and sells for his own account, not for the accounts of others. Using fluctuations of as little as an eighth or a quarter point for profit, the Floor trader may buy and sell the same security many times in a single day under strict rules of procedure that give the benefit of the best prices to the public. A Floor trader generally operates on a day-to-day basis, cleaning out his positions before the market closes, or sometimes, on longer cycles. He is not interested in the quality of a stock—only in its price movements. A successful trader must be unemotional, knowledgeable, and in close touch with the market at all times. He is considered as a dealer, not as a broker. A *commission broker* may also act as the Floor trader for his firm, but when he does so he must observe the very strict regulations imposed on all Floor traders. The trader's activities help to maintain a continuous and orderly market by providing liquidity.

The *independent Floor broker* (sometimes referred to as a *two-dollar broker*) is one who acts for commission brokers on the Floor. A commission broker may have orders to execute for two or more different securities at the same time. Obviously, he cannot be at more than one post at a time. Therefore, he employs the services of one or more independent Floor brokers to handle those transactions he is personally unable to handle. The independent Floor broker's fee is paid by the commission house that uses his service; it is not an additional cost to the commission broker's customer.

About one-third of the buy and sell orders from the general public are for *odd-lots*, or for orders of less than the *round-lot unit of trading* of 100 (sometimes 10) on the Floor of the Exchange. These orders are consummated by the *odd-lot dealer*, who thus obviates the burden of executing many small orders on the Floor of the Exchange itself.

A Typical Transaction

To see how the transactions are actually handled on the floor of the Exchange, let us assume that an order to buy 100 shares of General Electric has been given by a customer to the registered representative of a member firm in Kansas City. The order is a "market" order (i.e., an order to buy at the lowest possible price at the time the order reaches the floor of the Exchange). The order is telephoned by direct wire or is teletyped to the New York office of the member firm, which in turn telephones the order to its clerk on the floor of the Exchange.

The floor clerk causes his broker's call number to appear on three large annunciator boards situated so that one is always in view. These boards are constantly watched by each broker so that he will know when he is wanted at the telephone. Seeing his number on the board, the broker hurries to his telephone station and receives the order to buy 100 shares of GE "at the market." Acting as a *commission broker*, he immediately goes to the *trading post* where the specialist in GE is stationed and asks "How's GE?" The specialist might reply, "85 to a quarter." By this he means that he has an order to sell at least 100 shares at 85¼ and an order to buy at least 100 shares at 85. (Or he may be ready to buy or sell for his own account at those prices.)

Having a market order, the broker *could* say "Take 100 at 85¼" and thus execute his order. However, he is charged with buying at as low a price as possible. Knowing that there may be other brokers at the post who have orders to sell, but who may not wish to sell at 85, he will bid 85⅛ for 100 shares in a loud enough tone of voice so that the other brokers will hear him. If there are no takers, he will then buy the 100 shares at 85¼ through the specialist. However, if there is another broker in the group who has a market order to sell, that broker will probably then call out "Sold 100 at 85⅛." (The specialist does not become involved in this transaction.) The transaction is then noted by both brokers who return to their telephones to confirm it to their offices. At the same time, the notation of the transaction is recorded by Exchange personnel at the post who send it to the ticker department for transmission over the ticker network. It is printed simultaneously on 3,300 tickers in 628 cities in this country and Canada. These transactions appear in a type of shorthand. A one-, two-, or three-letter symbol indicates the stock sold. Just below the symbol and to the right appear the number of shares sold and the price at which executed. If there is no number ahead of the price, the sale was of 100 shares. From 200 shares to 900 shares, the number 2, 3, 4, etc. appears ahead of the letter "s." Thus, 6s86 on the tape would mean that 600 shares had been sold at a price of $86 per share. Above 900, the actual number of shares appears. A sale of 4,000 shares at $56½ would appear on the tape as "4000s56½."

It frequently happens that two or more brokers have orders to execute at the same price at the same time. There are strict rules of precedence as to which order is executed first. These rules, like all others, are designed to give preference to the general public—not to members of the exchange—on a first-come first-served basis. It is not unusual for an investor who has entered an order to buy or sell a stock at a certain price to see transactions at that price on the ticker tape or reported in the newspaper while his own order has not been executed. All this means is that there was *stock ahead* . . .

other orders at the same price came to the specialist first and had precedence or priority.

LARGE BLOCK PROCEDURES

Most of the 66,000 buy and sell orders executed on a typical day on the New York Stock Exchange are in 100-share or multi-hundred share lots. Among these thousands of orders, however, are some hundreds of orders to buy and sell thousands of shares. Any offer to buy or sell that is excessive with respect to the market situation in that stock will inevitably cause a sharp change in the market price of that stock of the particular security involved. In other words, the law of supply and demand is at work. When a buyer or seller instructs his broker to "take your time," large orders may be executed without any appreciable effect on market price . . . the broker will buy or sell in comparatively small lots over a period of days at prices satisfactory to his client. However, when an individual or an institution wants to effect a purchase or sale of a large block of stock *quickly*, special methods may be utilized to prevent a disadvantageous price reaction.

The Stock Exchange auction market functions without interruption during the course of a block procedure. Indeed, the special block methods, as employed by the Members Firms, supplement and strengthen the resources of the auction market and the Stock Exchange community. They serve as an added means of channeling securities to and from the investing public. Such procedures take into account particular problems that may face institutional investors and are available for the relatively infrequent order that calls for special measures.

The information that follows with respect to these special methods has been taken directly from a pamphlet published by the New York Stock Exchange entitled "Marketing Methods for Your Block of Stock."

Consider the case of the investment manager who must *quickly* buy or sell a block which clearly exceeds the immediate supply or demand in the current auction market.

For this, the Stock Exchange has developed special block procedures which supplement the regular-way market, and yet make use of all the resources of the Exchange community. *These special block procedures include the following—as they usually occur in ascending order of size:*

ON THE *BUY* SIDE

    Specialist Block Sale
    Exchange Acquisition
    Special Bid

ON THE *SELL* SIDE

    Specialist Block Purchase
    Exchange Distribution
    Special Offering
    Secondary Distribution

These seven special block methods are available to you through your Member Firm in teamwork with Members working on the Stock Exchange floor.

Your Member Firm makes all the necessary arrangements. While prior Exchange approval is required each time a special block procedure is used, authorization usually is given within a matter of minutes, unless Exchange officials determine that the order indeed can be accommodated in the auction market—and would cost the customer less there.

Assume, then, that the auction market has been explored. But the institution's need for speed calls for unusual measures. The investment manager and his Member Firm then may determine that a special block method is in order.

Specialist Block Purchase or Sale

These are seldom-used procedures: The following description is included as of interest as to what has been and can be done.

Your broker will probably start at the hub of the auction market itself —with the specialist. As a dealer, the specialist's function is to buy and sell for his own account stock in which he specializes, thus helping to maintain fair and orderly markets. However, his participation as a member of the investment manager's floor team need not end with the vital functions he performs in the regular-way auction market.

Indeed, the first of the Stock Exchange's special block procedures available to the investment manager and his Member Firm is called the Specialist Block Purchase or Sale.

Example: A pension fund manager gave his Member Firm broker an order to sell 5,000 shares of an issue then priced at 58. In the auction market, the stock was trading in orderly 100-share lots. But there did not appear to be depth enough in the auction market to absorb the block, short, of selling the stock down perhaps 5 or 6 points. Speed was required, and obviously, the situation called for special measures. A Specialist Block Purchase was explored and decided upon. Step by step, here's what happened:

Following discussions between the client and the Member Firm, the floor broker disclosed the details of the order to the specialist—told him *privately* how much stock was involved and stressed the need for speed. By thus confiding in the specialist, the floor broker enlisted a strong ally. The specialist, after weighing the current market picture (57⅞ bid—58⅛ offered) and assessing his own dealer position, decided he could make a net bid of 57 for the entire block. The broker reported the specialist's bid to his firm. The customer was satisfied that he could do no better, and instructed his Member Firm to accept the specialist's block bid.

At this point, the proposed Specialist Block Purchase was reviewed on the spot by a Floor Governor of the Stock Exchange. He quickly agreed that the block could not flow into the auction market, within the existing framework of volume, and in an orderly sequence of prices. On the other hand, the block transaction would not affect the price structure in the auction market adversely. Stock Exchange approval thus was forthcoming in a matter of minutes.

The trade was made privately. There was *no* print on the ticker . . . *no* announcement of any kind, before or after . . . *no* entry in the specialist's book. The Specialist Block Purchase developed as a logical outcome of assessing the auction market *first*.

The specialist Block Purchase method is convenient and fast. It serves to bring renewed strength to the auction market—for by making a block purchase, the specialist acquires shares for his own inventory. Invariably, this supply comes back into the regular-way market as he sells in response to subsequent public demand.

The same procedure on the buy side—the Specialist Block Sale—enables the investment manager through his Member Firm to *acquire* a block quickly from the specialist. In either case, this technique depends, of course, upon the specialist's position in the stock, his ability at the moment to buy or sell, and the condition of the market.

Exchange Distribution or Acquisition

Assume now that the investment manager and his Member Firm have a good-sized block to sell or buy—ranging perhaps from 10,000 to as many as 80,000 shares. They have explored and assessed the auction market and find that, at the moment, it cannot absorb the block. To the institution, time is important.

They may turn to the Exchange Distribution or Acquisition—perhaps the most flexible and adaptable of the special block procedures. These techniques involve a carefully charted search for offsetting orders to take up the block amount, with the block seller or buyer paying all brokerage costs.

Through the private communications system of your Member Firm—without public announcement—offsetting buy or sell orders are accumulated.

These orders are crossed with the block order on the floor, within the current auction market "bid-and-asked" range.

Only after a "cross" has been executed does the Stock Exchange ticker disclose that a distribution or acquisition has been accomplished, as illustrated by this ticker message reporting an Exchange Distribution of a sizable block of an equipment manufacturing stock.

....DIST.XYZ

10.900.s.435½...

Example: The portfolio manager of an insurance company consults his Member Firm on how to sell a block of 10,900 shares of a stock—market value upwards of $4,700,000. Currently, the stock is selling at close to 437 in the Stock Exchange auction market. It is a high-priced issue, enjoying widespread investor interest. But, once again, the investment manager's specifications call for speed beyond the immediate capacity of the regular-way market. The Member Firm recommends an Exchange Distribution.

This offering was conducted by the originating Member Firm alone, relying on its own partners, branch managers and representatives to generate offsetting buy orders among their customers. The Firm, however, could have enlisted one or more additional Member Firms. *No* prior public announcement of a forthcoming Exchange Distribution is made.

As in the case of all special block procedures, Stock Exchange approval was required. Governors of the Stock Exchange reviewed the current auction market situation and, since it was clear that the block required special marketing effort, approval was forthcoming within a few minutes—as is usually the case.

In an Exchange Distribution, the Member Firm employs its private communications system to generate buy orders. Buyers are attracted to the offering, of course, because the seller pays all brokerage costs. These offsetting buy orders are crossed on the Exchange floor with the block sale order. In this case, from the time the Firm advised its customers privately that the stock was available, it took but four hours and nine minutes to complete the transaction.

An Exchange Distribution is accomplished at a price within the prevailing bid and offer in the auction market. When the block was sold, for example, the Exchange market was 434 bid—436 offered. The price to the buyers participating in the Exchange Distribution was 435½ net.

When the investment manager, through his Member Firm, wants to acquire a block of stock, the same procedure is available. It is called an Exchange Acquisition.

Special Offering or Bid

Like the specialist block transactions, the Special Offering or Bid is not common. It is described primarily because it is an available procedure.

Good-sized blocks—made up of as many as 65,500 shares, with market values as high as $2,439,000—have been distributed or acquired effectively by the simple procedure of announcing an attractive, fixed *net* price over the Exchange's nation-wide ticker system—and then relying on the widespread resources of the entire Stock Exchange community to bring in buy or sell orders quickly and in volume. This method is called a Special Offering or Bid. Its success lies in letting interested investors in more than 700 cities know that a Special Offering or Bid is open to them. The amount of stock involved must be at least 1,000 shares with a market value of $25,000 or more. *The procedure can best be illustrated by the following step-by-step case history:*

A mutual fund decided to sell quickly a block of 28,000 shares of a public utility at about 55. There was not a sufficient floor market at the time to readily absorb the entire block. The Member Firm recommended a Special Offering to the investment manager in the belief that widespread investor buying interest could be encouraged.

A fixed price was determined by the customer in consultation with his Member Firm. They also fixed the incentive commission to be paid to brokers producing buy orders. The offering price was 54⅜ (the auction market quotation was 54⅜ to 54¾) and the seller offered an incentive commission of $1.00 a share to induce brokerage interest throughout the Exchange community. The regular commission would be about 45 per cent of this figure.

As in other procedures, Stock Exchange approval was requested. Once the need for a special marketing effort was established, authorization was quickly granted.

A ticker message, appearing simultaneously across the country, summed up the terms of the Special Offering:

```
.. SPECIAL.OFFERING.BY.WALL.BROAD.&.WILLIAMS



                       XYZ    COMMISSION    STAt
         28.000         54⅜           $1..
```

Buy orders, generated by this widespread publicity and by the special efforts of Member Firm partners and representatives, were received, recorded and fulfilled by the originating Member Firm.

Not only that, but sufficient buy orders to take up the 28,000-share block were received within 32 minutes after the offering was published on the ticker.

In sum, the Special Offering method is an efficient procedure whereby the investment manager and his Member Firm may command the aid of the entire Exchange community in achieving a large block distribution. Buyers, in turn, are attracted by the net price offering. The incentive commission invites special brokerage efforts on the part of Member Firms.

To acquire a large block, the reverse procedure, known as a Special Bid, is also available. Sellers, in this case, find the net price offering attractive, and the special commission invites Member Firm brokerage efforts.

Secondary Distribution

Occasionally, the investment manager faces the problem of selling a block of stock which is exceedingly large in relation to the current market—so large, in fact, that it obviously will require distribution efforts similar to those employed when a new issue is offered to the public.

It is in just such situations that the Secondary Distribution can come into play. Again, the investment manager may turn with confidence to his Member Firm.

The Secondary Distribution method enables the Member Firm and its associates in the securities business to act either as agents (as in the case cited below) or as principals.

A Secondary Distribution follows these simple steps:

The institutional investment manager agrees on a net price per share for his block, somewhat *under* the current auction market level.

The selling group, which has been formed to handle the distribution, offers the stock to buyers at a net price reflecting the current auction market level. Buyers are attracted by the net price—that is, they pay no commission.

Example: A block of 152,100 shares of an oil issue—involving nearly $6,500,000 worth of stock—was sold via a Secondary Distribution. The last sale in the stock was 42½. The institutional investment manager agreed to accept $41.05 a share. The Member Firm group offered the stock to the public at the Stock Exchange closing price of 42½, net, no commission. The institutional seller's cost: $1.45 per share.

As in the case of all special block procedures, Stock Exchange authorization by the Member Firm usually can be obtained quickly.

Newspaper Quotations

Quotations for securities traded on national exchanges are those for actual transactions and are considerably more informative than those for over-the-counter securities. As shown in the following reproduction from the *Wall Street Journal*, much information is given about each security traded during the preceding day on the New York Stock Exchange. Listings for other exchanges are similar.

30 THE WALL STREET JOURNAL,
Thursday, May 4, 1967

Volume, 11,550,000 Shares

Volume since Jan. 1:	1967	1966	1965
Total sales	834,450,952	751,784,584	482,801,150

MOST ACTIVE STOCKS

	Open	High	Low	Close	Chg.	Volume
Avco Corp	44⅛	48¼	44	48	+4⅜	247,000
Brunswk	14⅜	14½	14¼	14¼	....	166,700
McDonnD	38⅝	43⅝	38½	43⅜	+4⅞	159,500
Int Miner	36⅝	36¾	35¾	36	– ⅜	156,500
Lionel Corp	6⅛	6¼	5⅞	6	......	142,600
Sperry Rnd	31	31¾	30¾	31½	+ ¼	117,300
Chrysler	43⅞	45¼	43⅞	45⅛	+1¼	116,500
Studebaker	59⅜	62⅜	58	62⅛	+3⅜	110,400
Std Oil NJ	63	63⅞	63	63¾	+ ¾	101,200
Oxford Pap	29¼	30½	29⅛	30⅜	+1¼	98,000

Average closing price of most active stocks: $38.05.

A—B

–1967–				Sales in					Net
High	Low	Stocks	Div.	100s	Open	High	Low	Close	Chg.
15½	13	Abacus	1.07t	1	15½	15½	15½	15½	+ ⅜
50	41⅜	Abbott Lab	1	78	50½	50½	49⅞	49⅞	– ⅜
24½	16⅞	ABC Con	.80	126	24	24⅛	23⅝	23¾	– ½
34⅞	28	Abex Cp	1.60	17	32⅜	32⅜	32	32⅜	– ¼
51⅞	38⅛	ACF Ind	2.20	64	51¾	52	51⅜	52	+ ⅛
46¾	38¼	Acme Mkt	2b	9	40	40¼	40	40¼	+ ¼
28⅜	27	AdamE	2.11g	13	27⅞	27⅞	27⅝	27⅝	– ¼
34⅞	14½	AdMillis	.40b	99	35¼	35⅜	34⅝	34⅝	.....
59¼	46⅞	Address	1.40	733	56⅝	60⅛	55¾	60⅛	+3⅜
38	25	Admiral	.50	213	27⅛	27½	26⅝	27	– ¼
47	35	Aeroquip	1b	18	46	46	45½	45½	– ¼
42¼	31⅝	Air Prod	.20b	44	37⅝	38⅜	37⅝	38	– ⅛
124	103⅝	Air Pd	pf4.75	2	119½	119½	119½	119½	– ¾
86	63¼	Air Reduc	3	16	85⅝	85⅞	85¼	85¼	.....
43	42½	AirReduct	wi	3	42⅝	43	42⅝	43	+ ½
5¼	3½	AJ Industries		477	4⅝	4⅞	4½	4¾	+ ⅛
33⅞	30⅞	Ala Gas	1.80	7	33⅞	34	33⅞	34	+ ⅜
25⅜	16¾	Alberto C	.20	x112	21½	22⅜	21⅜	22¼	+ ⅜
33¾	27¼	AlcanAlum	1	131	31⅛	31⅛	30¾	30¾	– ⅜
13⅜	7⅞	Alleg Cp	.10g	31	10⅞	11¼	[illegible]		

The first two columns give the "high" and the "low," the highest and lowest prices at which the stock was bought and sold during the year to date, but do not include changes in the latest day's trading. (In the early part of the year, the range of the preceding year is included to give meaning to this information.) The third column gives the name of the security. If a regular dividend is paid, the annual rate follows. The small letter after the rate is keyed to an explanation at the end of the listings. The letter 'b' after the dividend rate, for example, indicates that the corporation also paid a dividend in stock. The fourth column gives the sales in 100's; thus the figure 37 indicates that 37 round lots, 3700 shares, were traded during the day. The fifth through the eighth columns quote the amount of the opening transaction, the highest transaction recorded during the day, the lowest recorded, and the closing or last transaction. The ninth and last column carries the "net change," or difference in closing price compared with the close of the previous day. All quotations reflect the fact that stocks are traded to eighths of a dollar—⅛ represents 12½¢, ¼ represents 25¢, and so on.

Elsewhere in the financial section are usually listed the closing bid and asked prices of stocks which were not traded. And, to round out the day's picture, are the very significant list of the most actively traded stocks and the total volume of shares traded. These are usually placed in a prominent position on the page.

Corporation bonds are quoted separately and in a different fashion.

Corporation Bonds

Volume, $17,080,000

A—B

—1967— High	Low	Bonds	Sales in $1,000	High	Low	Close	Net Chg.
136½	105	Air Red cv3⅞s87	38	135⅞	135	135⅞	.....
135	110	Allegh L cv4s81	22	134¾	134	134	−1
65¼	61½	Alleg West 4s98	2	61	60⅞	61	− ½
101½	97⅝	Allied Ch 5.20s91	6	97¾	97¾	97¾	.....
86¼	83½	Allied Ch 3½s78	5	85¾	85¾	85¾	.....
120	92½	Allied St cv4½s81	30	119¾	119	119¾	+ ½
130¾	114¼	Alcoa cv5¼s91	102	128	127	127	− ½
94	88½	Alcoa 4¼s82	5	89½	89½	89½	− ⅛
129⅛	113⅞	Am AFilt cv4⅞s87	19	126	124⅞	125¼	+ ¼
159¼	125	AmAirlin cv5½s91	110	160	159	160	+ ¾
156	119	Am Airlin cv4s90	25	155⅛	153⅝	153⅝	− 1⅜
106	86	Am Dist cv4⅜s86	31	94	93	93⅜	−1
81	75	Am FP 5s2030	55	78¾	78	78¾	+ ⅝
78⅝	73½	Am FP 4.80s87	9	77⅝	77½	77½	− ½
84	72½	AmMFdy cv4¼s81	39	84⅞	84	84	...
95	89	Am Smelt 4⅝s88	6	91¾	91⅛	91⅛	− ⅛
97	90	Am Sug 5.30s93	2	92¾	92¾	92¾	− ⅛
93⅛	87½	Am T&T 4⅜s85	77	88½	87½	87¾	...
86¼	81¼	Am T&T 3⅞s90	1	82	82	82	+ ½
91⅛	87½	Am T&T 3⅜s73	28	88½	88	88⅜	+ ⅝
81	76	Am T&T 3¼s84	7	77½	76	77½	+ ¾
74	69⅛	Am T&T 2⅞s87	7	70	69¼	69¼	−1¾

The first two columns give the high and low for the year as a percentage of par value. A quotation of 114¾, for example, represents 114.75% of $1,000 or a price of $1,147.50. The third column gives the corporation name followed by the type of bond, the yield, and maturity date. The fourth column gives the total sales. The fifth, sixth, and seventh columns give the high, low, and close for the day. The last column shows the closing sale difference from the previous day's close with each ⅛ representing $1.25.

Exchange Bond Auction

The auction market for bonds on the New York Stock Exchange differs in two important respects from the stock auction market. First, the majority of listed bonds are relatively inactive issues and are traded as "cabinet" bonds. About 5 per cent of the approximately 1,200 listed bonds are traded in the bond crowd as "free" bonds. Second, no specialists take part in the auction itself. When a broker has a transaction to make in any of the free bonds, he steps into the "ring" (a space about eight feet in diameter bounded by a brass octagonal ring in the floor) and makes his bid or offer. He may successively raise his bid or lower his offer until some broker accepts it.

Bids and offers for cabinet bonds are written out on cards and placed by employees of the Exchange in the appropriate cabinets. Colors of the cards indicate the time limits on the bids and offers. Bids are filed on one side of a panel with the highest bid at the top; offers are filed on the other, with the lowest offer at the top. A broker wishing to accept one of the bids or offers removes the card from the cabinet and steps into the ring for the cabinet crowd. He indicates his willingness to buy or sell; if no one else in the crowd (that is, no one other than the one who has placed the original card) responds, he completes the trade with the broker whose card he holds.

Once a bid or offer has been placed in the cabinet, it is considered firm until removed.

Listed bonds include rails, industrials (foreign and domestic), foreign government and foreign municipals, some U. S. Treasuries, and some obligations of New York City and New York State.

Market and Limit Orders

The two general types of orders to buy or to sell are *market orders* and *limit orders*. A market order must be executed as soon as possible at the best price possible at the time the order reaches the Floor. A limit order can only be executed at the stated price. However, there are modifying instructions in common use, and complete information must be obtained to handle the order properly.

On a market order to buy, no special information is needed. When a market order to sell is taken, however, it must be established whether the customer is "long" of the stock (that is, he is selling stock that he actually owns) or whether he is selling "short". . . this information must be given to the broker on the floor before he can execute the order. Short selling is discussed later in this chapter.

In accepting any limit order, it is important to know for how long the order is good. Is it good for today only? If so, it is a *day order*. It may be good only until a specified time . . . if it has not been executed by that time, it is treated as cancelled. An *open* or *G.T.C.* order is "good 'til cancelled." G.T.C. orders are automatically reduced when the stock sells ex-dividend. Since it is assumed that the stock is reduced in value when the dividend is paid out, the order drops by that amount on the ex-date of the dividend.

A *stop* order is given to protect a gain or to limit a loss. If a stock is currently selling at $45 a share, an order might be given to sell 100 shares "stop at 42". If the price drops, the order becomes a market order when a sale is made at 42. The stop order has limits as to its usefulness and does not always accomplish its purpose . . . on a rapid decline, the actual sale may be made well below the "stop" price.

A variation is the *stop limit order* which becomes executable as a limit order when a transaction has taken place at the stop price or at a price beyond it. The order is executable at the limit price or better.

A *fill* or *kill* order is a limit order that is automatically cancelled if the order cannot be executed right away in its entirety. If a "fill or kill" order is given to buy at $25 and the market is $25 or less when the broker reaches the trading post, the order is executed. If, on the other hand, the market is then above $25, the order is cancelled and a report is made back to the customer informing him of the cancellation and the present market price. This type of order is seldom used. A variation of this is the *immediate* or *cancel* order which may be executed in whole or in part with any portion not executed being treated as cancelled.

An *all or none* order is a market or limit order for bonds which is to be executed in its entirety or not at all, but, unlike a fill or kill order, is not to be treated as cancelled if not executed as soon as it is represented in the Trading Crowd. Bids or offers on behalf of all or none orders may not be made in stocks, but may be made in bonds when the number of bonds is fifty or more.

An *alternative* or *either/or* order is an order to do either of two alternatives, such as either sell (buy) a particular stock at a limit price or sell (buy) on stop. If the order is for one unit of trading and one part of the order is executed on the happening of one alternative, the order on the other alternative is cancelled. If the order is for an amount larger than one unit of trading, the number of units executed determines the amount of the alternative order to be treated as cancelled.

An *at the close* order, as the name implies, is an order that is to be executed at or as near to the close as practicable.

A market or limited price order which is to be executed at the opening of the stock or not at all is known as an *at the opening* or *at the opening only* order. Any such order or portion thereof not so executed is treated as cancelled.

In many cases, customers establish *discretionary accounts.* These are accounts in which the customers give the broker or someone else discretion, which may be complete or within specific limits, as to the purchase and sales of securities or commodities including selection, timing and price to be paid or received. A *discretionary order* from a customer empowers the broker to act on his behalf with respect to the choice of security to be bought or sold, the total amount of any securities to be bought or sold, and/or whether any such transaction shall be one of purchase or sale.

A *do not reduce* (DNR) order is a limited order to buy, a stop order to sell or a limit stop order to sell which is not to be reduced by the amount of an ordinary cash dividend on the ex-dividend date. A do not reduce order applies only to ordinary cash dividends; it is reduced for other distributions such as a stock dividend or rights.

When a customer wishes to give the broker on the floor time to evaluate a situation in buying or selling, particularly in cases of comparatively large blocks to be bought or sold, he may indicate that a market or limit order is *not held*. Other terms are *take time* and *disregard tape*. On a market order to buy, for example, this gives the broker on the floor the discretion to delay execution of all or part of the order if his evaluation of the situation indicates that the price will move down, or that by splitting the order and executing parts of it as the price moves up and down the net cost to the buyer will be lower.

An order, either market or limit, to buy or sell a stated amount of a stock after a fixed number of shares of the stock have traded is called a *percentage* order.

A *scale* order is an order to buy or sell a specified total amount of a security and the amount to be bought or sold at specified price variations.

A *switch* order or *contingent* order is an order for the purchase (sale) of one stock and the sale (purchase) of another at a stipulated price difference.

When an order is to become effective at a specified time, it is termed a *time* order . . . it may be either a market or a limit order.

Odd-lot Orders

Almost all round-lot orders are executed at the trading posts. The odd-lot orders are dealt with by the odd-lot dealers, who are obligated to accept all odd-lot buy and sell orders brought to them. The odd-lot dealer's activities are closely regulated. On market orders to buy, the odd-lot dealer fills the order at the same price as the next round lot trade (the *effective sale*) in that stock. On market orders to sell, the odd-lot dealer fills the order at the next round lot trade price. On market orders to sell *short*, the trade is executed on the next "up-tick" round lot trade price. In each case, the dealer applies an odd-lot "differential." On stocks selling at $55 a share or more, this differential is 25 cents a share; on stocks selling at less than $55 a share, it is 12½ cents a share. Thus, on market orders if the round lot price is $67, the odd-lot dealer would sell at 67¼ or buy at 66¾.

Limit orders are handled differently. For buy orders, the effective sale must be under the limit by the amount of the differential; for sell orders, the effective sale must be over the limit by the differential. Thus, the customer buys or sells at his specified price *including* the differential.

Although the customer receives a little less when he sells and pays a little more when he buys than the round lot customer, the difference is partially compensated by the fact that he pays $2 less in commission than for a round lot transaction of comparable value.

Through the purchase and sale of odd-lots, the odd-lot dealer either builds up an inventory of shares or he becomes "short" (has a minus inventory). When he wishes to dispose of an excess inventory or to cover his "short" position, he sells or buys a round lot for his own account. In conjunction with the differential on each odd-lot purchase or sale, the odd-lot dealer hopes to obtain a profit when he buys or sells a round lot. This is in return for the risk he assumes since he may be forced to buy or sell at a price disadvantageous to himself.

Commissions

Stock exchange commissions are extremely low for the services performed. The average commission change is about one per cent ($39 for 100

1–64

shares sold at $40). Following are usual commissions for stocks, rights and warrants selling at $1.00 or more per share.

Amount of Money Involved	Commissions
$100 to $399	2% plus $3
$400 to $2,399	1% plus $7
$2,400 to $4,999	½% plus $19
$5,000 and above	¹⁄₁₀% plus $39

Odd Lot......$2 less

There are exceptions to the above table in that:

(a) when the amount involved in a transaction is less than $100, the minimum commission shall be as mutually agreed;

(b) when the amount involved in a transaction is $100 or more, the minimum commission charge shall not exceed $1.50 per share or $75 per single transaction, but in any event shall not be less than $6 per single transaction.

On stocks selling at under $1.00 per share, the commission varies from a tenth of a cent per share to five and a quarter cents per share, depending upon the per share price. When the amount involved in a transaction is less than $100, the commission shall be as mutually agreed; when the amount involved is $100 or more, the minimum commission shall not be less than $6 or the rate per share, whichever is the greater.

Margins

When a customer buys a listed stock, he may either pay cash or he may buy on *margin*. Unlisted stocks cannot be bought on margin. Buying on margin simply means that the customer puts up part of the cost in cash and borrows the balance from his broker. The *initial margin*, the percentage of the total price that the customer pays, is set by the Federal Reserve Board. By expanding or shrinking sources of credit, such as loans for securities, the Federal Reserve hopes to keep economic conditions healthy. Since 1934, initial margin rates have varied from as low as 40 per cent to as high as 100 per cent (no borrowing allowed). Only at the time of a purchase is the initial margin rate involved. The *maintenance margin* requirements are set by the Exchange and can be considerably less than the initial margin rate. Margin is discussed extensively in chapter 10.

One reason advanced for the tremendous increase in stock prices in 1929 and the subsequent market "crash" was the then initial margin rate of only ten per cent. A customer could buy $1,000 worth of stock by only putting up $100 of his own money. This led to "pyramiding" and an actual shortage of stocks since the demand exceeded the supply. Because stocks react in price like any other commodity in relation to supply and demand, the excessive demand inevitably forced stock prices even higher. With so little of the customer's money actually at stake, a comparatively small drop in a stock price would wipe out the customer's equity which meant that the broker had to call for more margin from his customer. When stock prices sagged badly, an increasing demand for more margin, generally from people who didn't have any additional capital, was generated. As a result, their positions had to be sold out. The throwing of literally hundreds of thousands of shares on the market to clear up margin accounts drove prices down still farther and panic ensued.

Note that the only people who were forced to sell on that disastrously falling market were those who had bought on margin. People who owned their stocks outright sold at tremendous losses because they were frightened, but not because they had to sell.

Margin requirements are now kept so high that margin selling alone probably could not now create the type of panic selling that occurred in that period. The stock market break in May 1962 would have been far worse had margin requirements been less stringent.

While the initial margin percentage requirement is set by the Federal Reserve Board, the New York Stock Exchange requires a minimum deposit in a margin account of $2,000. No new purchase may be made unless there is an *equity* in the account of at least $2,000. However, a new purchase can be made when equity is less than $2,000 on a *cash* basis . . . that is, the purchaser pays in full for the new purchase. No member firm of the New York Stock Exchange can lower either the margin requirement nor the minimum equity, but any firm can set its own rules to require either more margin or more equity, or both.

Short Selling

Speculators who buy securities in the expectation that they can sell at a profit are termed *bulls*. Other speculators (*bears*) believe that the market is going down and sell securities in the hope that they can buy them later at a lower price. There are two ways in which a bear can do this. He can sell stock he already owns with the intention of rebuying it later at a lower price. This type of speculator, however, is not usually "long" (i.e., does not own) the securities in which he speculates. He is more apt to *sell shares he does not own*. By so doing, he is *selling short* or making *short sales*.

Obviously, the person who buys from this speculator expects delivery of the shares he has bought. But the speculator does not own shares he can deliver. How, then, is delivery effected? Certain firms and individuals specialize in the loaning of shares. Our speculator borrows the same number of shares as he has sold short, and makes delivery with these shares. At some time he is going to have to repay the loan—in shares. He hopes at a later date to buy at a price lower than his sale price, and then repay the borrowed shares with the lower-priced shares. There is always the risk for this type of speculator that the price of the shares continues to rise, and that he will be called upon to deliver the shares. In such circumstances, if he can not borrow from someone else, he must buy at the current market to effect delivery. He will then lose the difference between his sale price and his cost price. This corresponds to the loss taken by a speculator who bought in the expectation of a rise, only to have the security fall in value.

There is a technical short sale known as *selling against the box*. This consists of making a short sale when the seller is actually long of the stock sold. There are various reasons for this type of sale, most of them technical. But the important feature of such a sale is that the seller can always *cover* his short position by delivering his own shares.

Short sales may be made on margin. When a short sale is made, the cash received (net of commission) is transferred to the lender of the securities borrowed for delivery. The short seller must meet the same minimum margin requirement that applies to purchases. Also, the same $2,000 minimum deposit applies.

From time to time, the question has been raised as to whether the short seller does not, in fact, hurt the interests of the general public by forcing prices down. The Securities and Exchange Commission has ruled that short sales can only be made on a *rise* in the last sale price of a stock. In other words, if the stock starts falling in price and continues to do so, no short sales can be made. Therefore, short sales cannot be made just for the purpose of depressing the market.

From the previous discussion of the odd-lot dealer and the specialist, it is obvious that they must be permitted to make short sales to avoid difficulty in operating. Also, the short seller contributes to maintaining an orderly market since he offers shares for sale that might not otherwise be available.

In its booklet (which is recommended reading) *Understanding the New York Stock Exchange*, the Stock Exchange itself makes this statement:

A market in which people may buy in the hope of a rise but in which others expecting a decline may not sell would cease to be a true market. Such a market would give a distorted reflection of the public's opinion of values and could not function properly. A true market allows full freedom of expression.

Security Options

People generally are more familiar with real estate options than with security options. An *option* from the owner of a piece of real estate can often be bought to insure purchase of the real estate at a certain price during a certain period of time. The importance of the option is that for the stated period the owner of the property is committed to sell to the option holder and to no one else, but the option holder is not committed to buy. If the option is not *exercised*—if the property is not bought during the stated period—the option money is kept by the owner in return for his holding the property off the market.

Security options are similar. There are *two* general types. The option to *buy* (usually 100 shares) at a certain price within a certain period of time is termed a *call*. A *put* is an option to *sell* at a certain price within a specified period of time. A *straddle*, an option to buy and/or sell at the same price, is a combination of a *put* and a *call*. A *spread* is similar to a straddle except that it is "points away" from market price so that the put may be exercised at a specified price below the present market and the call at a specified price above it. A *strap* combines two calls with a put. A *strip* combines two puts with a call. Common time periods are 60 days, 90 days, or six months plus 10 days (to take advantage of capital gains taxes). The cost of an option depends upon the present market price of the stock, the amount of activity in the stock, and the time period involved. The higher the price and the longer the period, the higher the cost of the option.

Security options may be used speculatively or they may be used protectively.

Speculative Use. The percentage gain or loss can be very high with the risk greater than most people can tolerate. Suppose a speculator believes that PDQ is low-priced at $60 a share. He wants to buy 100 shares at this price so he can sell later at a profit. However, the 100 shares would require $6,000 (or a lesser amount on a margin purchase, depending upon the margin rate in effect). So the speculator buys a *call option* for 90 days for $500. If, at any time during the 90-day period the stock advances beyond the break-even point of 66 (allowing for two-way commissions of $91), he can exercise his call option at a profit. (He *calls* the 100 shares at $60 per share and then sells the shares in the market.) If the stock advances to $70 per share, his profit is $409 on the $500 investment, disregarding taxes. If the stock declines in price, his loss is limited to the $500 paid for the option. If he had bought the stock outright and he sold at 50, the loss would have been $1,089.

There are disadvantages, too. If he had bought outright and he sold on an advance to 64, he would have made $310. But if it had advanced only to 64 by the expiration date of his option, he would have lost $190.

Speculating with *puts* is similar, except that the speculator buys an option when he expects a decline in the market price. The put guarantees that he can sell 100 shares at a certain price regardless of any price decline. For the speculator, the greater the drop in price, the better. He can buy 100 shares in the market at the current low price and then exercise his put option to sell 100 shares at the guaranteed higher price. The possibility of loss is limited to the cost of the put, whereas if he had sold short, in the expectation of a fall in price, he would have a greater potential loss of an unknown amount.

The disadvantage of the put is that the stock must decline below the put price differential before a profit can be realized. A short sale would effect a profit at any decline (less commissions, interest costs on the borrowed stock, and taxes).

Protective Use. Assume that the owner of 100 shares of a stock would net a satisfactory profit were he to sell it at the current market price. He wants to protect that profit, but at the same time he would like to take advantage of a possible future rise in price. So he sells the 100 shares and at the same time buys a call option to buy 100 shares at the same price. If the stock shows a sufficient gain in price during the option period he can recapture his original position. His costs would be the option price plus brokerage and tax charges. He must also take into account, however, the effect of a capital gains tax on the original sale of stock.

Should he not wish to sell his shares and take a profit by hedging with a call option, he could use a put option to protect his paper profit. Expecting a decline in price, he buys a put option. If the price does decline, he exercises the option and takes the same profit he would have made through the outright sale (less the cost of the option). But if the price does not decline, he loses the cost of the put—but has protected his position during the interval.

Another use of call options is to limit losses on a short sale. With a loss in prospect, the owner could buy a call option to buy an equal number of shares at the same price. Thus, his possible loss during the option period would then be limited to the cost of the call.

Typical prices for a stock selling at 40 might be: 90-day put, $350; 90-day call, $400; six-month put, $475; six-month call, $550. Prices quoted for puts and calls are always for round lots.

Stock Rights

Stock rights are options issued as a pre-emptive right to stockholders in order that they may buy additional shares of stock at a set price during a specified period. They are issued by corporations as a means of raising capital from common stockholders.

Each stockholder receives one right, in the form of a subscription warrant, for each share of stock. The right can then be used as a "discount" in purchasing new shares from the company. If a stockholder should own 100 shares, and he needs, say, 20 rights for one new share, he may subscribe for five additional shares.

If he does not wish to exercise his option, he can sell the rights in the open market. Until mailed to stockholders, rights are traded on a "when issued" basis. After issuance, they are traded regular way.

Stock rights give the shareholder an opportunity to purchase additional shares of the company at a slight saving to prevent having his current holdings subject to the dilution which would otherwise result from the issuance of extra shares to new shareholders.

Deliveries

Under rules of the New York Stock Exchange, deliveries must be made on contracts for sale as follows:

Cash contracts state that deliveries are due the same day. This rule applies equally to stocks, U.S. Government bonds, convertible bonds, and other bonds. This contract, which calls for the fastest delivery of any of the four types of contracts, is used only when there is an urgent need to buy or sell a security. Cash delivery may be needed to take advantage of stock rights and conversion privileges or to register capital losses at the end of a tax year.

Regular Way is the standard type of contract. Delivery is to be made on the fifth business day following the day of the contract. U.S. Government bonds and odd-lot sales are exceptions to the five-day rule. Regular way for U.S. bonds means delivery is due on the first business day following the day of the contract. Odd lots are to be delivered on the fourteenth day via regular way.

Seller's Option transactions require the exchange of written contracts which specify the date of expiration of the option. In the cases of stocks and convertible bonds, the options may call for delivery in not less than six business days nor more than 60 calendar days. For U. S. Government bonds, the delivery may be not less than two business days nor more than 60 calendar days. The seller in each case may deliver earlier by giving written notice, on or after the day when delivery would have been due if the contract had been made the "regular way," of intention to make delivery on the next business day following the day of the notice.

Stock Clearing Corporation

Round lot transactions on the New York Stock Exchange must be cleared and settled through members or member firms who have applied to and been admitted as Clearing Members of the Stock Clearing Corporation.

From trade data submitted by the selling Clearing Members on the business day following the trade, the Corporation's computers produce purchase and sale contract listings for each Clearing Member. After adjustments are submitted and processed and all trades are confirmed in writing, the computer establishes for each Clearing Member the net balance of shares to receive or deliver of each security. The Corporation then matches firms having equal balances to receive and deliver and issues balance orders extended at settlement value to the respective parties. A uniform settlement price is established each day for each security (the closing price less any fraction) to permit the allotment of net balances to be made without having to maintain the original buyer-seller contractual relationship. This method results in the elimination of about 35 per cent of the physical delivery of securities.

On the settlement date, securities are delivered through the Corporation to the receiver in envelopes in accordance with the previously issued balance orders. The Clearing Member making the delivery is credited with the settlement value and the Clearing Member receiving it is charged with the same amount. After noon, when all deliveries have been completed, the Corporation computes, based upon all deliveries made and/or received, the net debit or credit balance in each Clearing Member's settlement account. This netting operation eliminates 85 per cent of the money which otherwise would have to be paid by check. A Clearing Member who has a net credit amount is paid by the presentation of a draft to the Corporation; a net debit amount is paid to the Corporation by check. At the end of each business day, as proof of the settlement, the payments disbursed must equal the payments received.

Stock Transfer

The process of recording the changing of title of securities from one owner to another is called stock transfer. Two elements essential to the transfer are the delivery of the certificates to the transfer agent and the recording of the delivery on the books of the corporation. Only after the second element is completed and the new and old certificates have been checked by the registrar, will the new owner receive his certificate and be entitled to all of the incidents of ownership in the eyes of the corporation.

Actual title passes upon proper endorsement of the assignment form printed on the rear of the stock certificate, commonly known as an "Assignment and Power of Attorney."

The name of the owner of a certificate must appear correctly on its face. Any errors should be corrected promptly by sending the certificate back to the transfer agent. In no case, should any changes be made by the individual owner.

To endorse a certificate properly for sale, the owner must sign exactly as his name appears on its face. If there is an error, the certificate can be endorsed by the owner signing as the certificate states and then signing correctly. If the certificate is endorsed "in blank," that is no transferee is named, it becomes negotiable paper and the holder of it for value is the owner. A certificate should never be endorsed unless a transfer is being made.

To protect themselves from fraudulent transfers, the corporation and the transfer agent usually require that the endorsement be guaranteed by a member of the New York Stock Exchange or a commercial bank or trust company. When a signature is so guaranteed, there is no need for it to be otherwise witnessed.

Some owners must provide additional documents to complete their endorsement. A corporate owner, for example, must provide the authorization of the endorser to assure the transfer agent that corporate officials are making only lawful transfers. Transfers by fiduciaries must generally be accompanied by a certificate of appointment signed by a proper court official and dated within 60 days.

A power of attorney is included on the back of the certificate to allow an agent or attorney to perform the actual transfer for the owner. This is left blank and is normally filled in at the office of the transfer agent.

Often an assignment is made on a separate form which is similar to that on the back of the certificate. By mailing the certificate and the form separately, the chances of both falling into the wrong hands are greatly reduced.

All companies whose securities are listed on the New York Stock Exchange must maintain a transfer agent and registrar. Each of these is usually a bank or trust company, but one company cannot do both. The transfer agent receives the old certificate and checks to be certain it is valid and is properly endorsed. If it is, the agent issues a new certificate and cancels the old. He then sends both certificates to the registrar whose sole concern is checking to be certain that the number of shares canceled is equal to those issued. This prevents any dilution of stockholders' equity.

Bond transfers are handled exactly as stocks if they are fully registered as to principal and interest. Many bonds, however, are bearer bonds and title to these passes by simple delivery.

If certificates are destroyed or lost, the corporation and the transfer agent will usually require the protection of a surety bond before they will issue replacements. The bond runs perpetually and its cost (usually 4% or less of value) must be paid by the owner of the certificate. To obtain a new certificate, the owner should first notify the transfer agent and issuer of the loss. Then he should file an affidavit with the issuer stating the circumstances of the loss. Lastly he will obtain a bond from a surety company and have it posted with the issuer.

The Uniform Commercial Code enacted in 1962 and adopted in more than 30 states as of 1966 has modernized somewhat the law of transfer with respect to securities. Basically it gives more extensive protection to a bona fide purchaser for value who is without notice of any adverse claim. With very few exceptions, such a person gets title to the securities against all third parties regardless of faults in transactions prior to his delivery.

Other Procedures

"When Issued" Securities. After effective registration of an additional stock offering, there is usually some delay before the rights or shares are actually issued. At this time, they may be approved for trading on one of the Exchanges on a *when issued* basis. In each transaction in when issued securities, there is a short side as well as a long side because there are no certificates actually available for delivery (the "when issued" refers to the delivery). Nevertheless, trading in such securities involves an actual commitment. The settlement date is set by the Exchange and is the settlement date for transactions that have occurred up to four days before the date.

When rights are being traded after issue, there may be two listings of the stock concerned on the Exchange. One is the old stock with *rights on.* The other is the new stock, which is without rights, and is traded on a when issued basis. This is indicated in the daily market quotations by "wi."

Buying In. When stock certificates are not delivered on time by the seller, the buyer notifies the seller and *buys in* under direct supervision of the Floor Department which sees that a fair market exists at the time for the execution of the order. There are specific rules as to times of notification to the seller and to the Exchange and as to times of executions of such buy ins.

Marking to the Market. The procedure is the same as in the over-the-counter market (page 1–44).

Give-ups. From the beginnings of the brokerage business, it has been customary for brokers to deal with each other on a preferential basis. However, this preference is restricted to those brokers who are members of a national securities exchange or a registered national association. Thus, members of the New York Stock Exchange must deal with non-members of the Exchange on the same basis as they deal with the general public.

As a part of this preferential treatment, a member of the New York Stock Exchange may *give up* all or part of his commission on a transaction to another member, whether or not the second broker performed any services in connection with the transaction. Thus, a customer may place an order for execution on the Exchange with one member and request that part or all of the commission be *given up* to another member. However, New York Stock Exchange rules do not permit a member to give up a non-member.

The question sometimes arises as to why one broker should give up to another. As an example, a bank's trust department might place all of its listed New York Stock Exchange business through one member as a matter of policy. At some time, the bank might request and receive from another member certain research material to be used by its trust officers. In return for this service from the second member, the bank would like that member to receive some of the commissions on its brokerage business. To accomplish this, the bank directs its own member broker to give up a certain amount to the second member. A second type of give-up occurs when one member acts on behalf of another and "gives up" the trade by giving the name of the second member at the time the trade is consummated on the floor.

Arbitrage. This may be defined as *a dealing in differences.*

The Federal Reserve Board defines arbitrage as:

> "(1) a purchase or sale of a security in one market together with an offsetting sale or purchase of the same security in a different market at as nearly the same time as practicable, for the purpose of taking advantage of a difference in prices in the two markets, or
>
> (2) a purchase of a security which is, without restriction other than the payment of money, exchangeable or convertible within 90 calendar days following the date of its purchase into a second security together with an offsetting sale at or about the same time of such second security, for the purpose of taking advantage of a disparity in the prices of the two securities."

As an example of the first type, there might be heavy buying of a certain security on the New York Stock Exchange. This would have the effect of raising the price. At the same time, there might be heavy selling of the same security on the Midwest Exchange. This would have the effect of depressing the price in Chicago. Seeing a differential, an arbitrager could sell short in New York, and at the same time, buy in Chicago.

Note that his actions would actually have the effect of stablizing the market in both locations. His sales in New York would tend to bring the price down there, while his purchases in Chicago would tend to raise the price on that exchange.

As an example of the second type, assume that the ABC Corporation has outstanding an issue of bonds each of which is convertible at any time into 20 shares of common stock. At a particular time, the bonds might be selling at $1100 and the common at $60. The arbitrager could buy five bonds for $5500 and sell 100 shares of the common short for $6000. Thus, for each unit of this type, he would have an apparent profit of $500 (less commissions and taxes). In a sense, he is short the common "against the box" because he can, if he must, convert the bonds to make delivery of the common. However, he might be bearish on the common, in which case he might wait for a drop in the common and then buy to cover his short sale. Since he would still be long of the bonds, he could again sell the common short if a suitable differential still existed. Again, the action of the arbitrager has the effect of eliminating the differential between the convertible and the common, and this tends to stabilize the market.

Arbitrage of both types is most often dealt in by members of the major exchanges for their own accounts. In most cases, the differentials dealt in are so small that they would be eaten up by normal commissions charged to the public. Also, because of the small differentials, arbitrage requires considerable capital to be conducted successfully.

Customers' Securities. For convenience, a customer may wish to have his broker/dealer hold his securities in safekeeping for him. Share certificates may be registered in the customer's own name or they may be registered in the name of the broker/dealer (in a *street name*). If registered in a street name, the securities may be sold by the customer by telephone order and no documents need be signed at that time. If registered in the customer's name and held by the broker/dealer, the customer may sign a *stock power* (a form of power of attorney) which removes the need for his signing the stock certificate itself.

In either case, a broker/dealer is under strict regulations requiring the segregation of customers' securities. Such securities must be kept separately (and appropriately marked as to ownership) from the firm's own securities and from each other. Customers' securities may be commingled (i.e. placed together) and pledged as collateral for loans under further strict regulations. Basically, the securities may only be used to borrow money to cover the firm's loans to its customers (margin accounts) and then only with the written consent of the owners of the securities. Further, the aggregate amount borrowed may not exceed the aggregate amount owed by the firm's customers to the firm. In other words, the firm may not use customers' securities as collateral for a loan intended to be used for the firm's own purposes.

The following paragraph about segregation is quoted from the rules of the Board of Governors of the New York Stock Exchange:

"In the general practice of brokerage offices, instructions for the segregation of customers' securities originate in the margin department and are carried out by the cashier. In the case of 'free' (fully paid) and excess margin stocks, the cashier places the stock certificates in a separate box and annexes to each certificate a small linen or paper tab giving the name of the specific customer as owner. If a customer having 'free' securities buys stock on margin or has a margin account which needs additional margin, the margin clerk directs the cashier to transfer from the box containing customers' 'free' and excess margin securities the certificates that are required as margin. These certificates are then placed in the box of the organization containing 'usable securities,' that is, securities which the organization may use as margin. In case a lesser amount of stock is required as margin or if the balance of a customer's margin account is paid in full, the margin department directs the cashier to release the shares from the box containing the 'usable securities' and they are returned to the box containing the customers' 'free' and excess margin securities."

Alternately, a NYSE Member firm may use a system of "bulk segregation" which does not identify each 100 share certificate because such certificates are fungible (equal to each other and so many be substituted for each other), but keeps the records as to ownership on cards.

Whether by individual identification or by bulk, segregation is a carefully controlled operation designed to protect the customers' interests.

Customers' Balances. When a customer pays money to a broker/dealer for the purchase of securities, at the present or in the future, the customer's account is credited with the payment. When securities are bought for the customer, the cost of the purchase plus commissions is debited (charged) to the customer's account. A customer who does not buy or sell short on margin (one who always pays in full) will not have a debit balance, but may have a credit balance. A customer who carries a margin account will usually have a debit balance, but may occasionally have a credit balance. A debit balance means that the customer owes the firm money; a credit balance means that the firm owes the customer money.

The relationship between a margin customer's debit balance and his equity is not static. His debit balance is what he owes the firm. His equity is the difference between the market value of his securities (held by the firm as collateral) and his debit balance.

In a new account, for example, a customer may deposit a check for $7,000 with his broker. He then purchases 100 shares of a listed security at a cost of $9,500, including commissions. His *debit balance* is $2,500. His *equity* is approximately $7,000. If two weeks later, the security is selling at $100 a share, his equity would be approximately $7,500 ($10,000 less his $2,500 debit balance). If, later, the stock declined to a market price of $90 a share, his equity would then be only about $6,500 ($9,000 less his debit balance of $2,500). The important thing to note is that his *equity* will change from day to day as the value of his stock changes on the market, but his *debit balance* will remain the same so long as he makes no further deposits nor further transactions in his account. Interest charges will increase the debit balance, of course. Both equity and debut balances are discussed extensively in chapter 10.

LISTING STANDARDS

New York Stock Exchange

Standards of eligibility for listing of securities on the New York Stock Exchange are the most stringent of any of our national exchanges.

General qualifications.—By reason of their nature and the necessity for flexibility, the qualifications for listing on the New York Stock Exchange can better be described in general terms than as exact formulae.

The company must be a going concern, or be the successor to a going concern, and must have substantial assets or demonstrated earning power, or both. While the amount of assets and earnings and the aggregate market value of the company's junior securities are considerations, greater emphasis is placed on such questions as degree of national interest in the company, its standing in its particular field, the character of the market for its products, its relative stability and position in its industry, and whether or not it is engaged in an expanding industry, with prospects of maintaining its position.

Minimum numerical standards. Effective April 15, 1965, certain standards were modified upwards. Present standards call for a minimum total number of stockholders of 2,000 with 1,700 owning, of record or beneficially, 100 shares or more. Minimum outstanding shares must total 1,000,000 with at least 700,000 of these being publicly held. In addition, the market value of the publicly held shares must be $12,000,000 or more. Net tangible assets should be $10,000,000 although greater emphasis is placed on market value.

Miscellaneous. Since 1926, the Exchange has refused to list non-voting common stock. Listing has also been refused in the case of voting trust certificates, except under certain circumstances. The Exchange also takes into account, when considering listing, the effect of concentrated holdings upon the voting position of the publicly-held stock, the proportionate distribution of voting power as between classes of stock, and unusual voting provisions which, in effect, tend to permit one class to nullify or veto the vote of another class.

Further, as a matter of policy adopted in 1940, the Exchange may refuse to list preferred stock not having certain minimum voting rights.

Before securities may be admitted to trading on the Exchange, they must be authorized for listing by the Exchange and, in addition, must be registered under the Securities Act of 1934.

Other Exchanges

Requirements for listing on other national exchanges, while less stringent as to capital, earnings and distribution of stock, are also designed to ensure that an adequate auction market in the securities will exist.

For example, the American Stock Exchange requires that the applicant for listing have a net equity of at least $3,000,000; have a demonstrated earning power of at least $300,000 annually after all charges, including Federal income taxes, with a reasonable prospect of sustaining this level; have a public distribution of at least 300,000 shares of a common stock issue (exclusive of the holdings of officers and directors and other concentrated or family holdings) among not less than 900 holders, of which not less than 600 must be holders of 100 shares or more, and an aggregate market value of at least $2,000,000 for all outstanding shares. In addition, shares of stock selling at less than $5 a share must be substantially in excess of the net equity requirement.

The American Exchange will not list non-voting stock unless the voting stock of the same company is listed. It will not list voting trust certificates. *Back-door* listings, which occur when a listed company has been acquired by an unlisted concern, will be listed only if the surviving company meets the regular listing standards and if the earnings and financial condition of the company will be improved.

REVIEW QUESTIONS

1. What is a "stock exchange"?
2. How is the New York Stock Exchange organized and managed?
3. On what most important objects are the programs and policies of the New York Stock Exchange based?
4. What are the purposes of "Trading Posts?"
5. What is meant by "bond crowd"?
6. Explain a "limit" order. How does it differ from a "market order"?
7. What is a "specialist?" State his responsibilities and functions. When does a specialist act as a broker? When as a dealer?
8. Name four other types of Floor members of the NYSE.
9. What is an odd-lot? A round lot?
10. Describe the execution of a typical transaction on the Exchange.
11. What is the basic difference between the quoted prices for o-t-c transactions and Exchange transactions? Who furnishes Exchange prices?
12. How does the auction market for NYSE bonds differ from that for stocks?
13. What are cabinet bonds? Free bonds?

14. What information is needed on a market order to sell that is not needed on a market order to buy?
15. What is meant by "long" of a stock?
16. What does "GTC" mean?
17. Describe a stop order and its function.
18. What are the functions of "odd lot dealers"?
19. What determines the prices of odd-lot executions?
20. How are commissions calculated on security transactions of the NYSE?
21. Distinguish between "cash" and "margin" transactions.
22. Distinguish between *initial margin* rate and *maintenance of margin* requirements.
23. Describe "selling short." How is delivery effected in a "short sale"?
24. What rule safeguards the public against a depressed market caused by short sales?
25. Explain "put," "call," and "straddle."
26. Explain the speculative use of security options.
27. What are stock rights? How can a stock right be used?
28. Explain regular way delivery of NYSE transactions.
29. What is the difference in the types of securities that may be sold for "delayed delivery" under NASD rules and those for "regular way, delayed delivery" under NYSE rules?
30. What is the function of a stock clearing house?
31. What is a "when issued" security? Why is there always a short side on a "when issued" security?
32. What is a "give-up?" What are the general rules concerning them?
33. What is arbitrage? Give examples of two different types.
34. What is the advantage of a security registered in a "street name"?
35. What are the general rules with respect to segregation of customers' securities?
36. When may a broker use a customer's securities as collateral for a loan?
37. Explain "equity" in a margin account. What is the relationship between a customer's debit balance and his equity?
38. What are the general qualifications which a corporation must have in order for it to be listed on the NYSE?
39. What are the minimum yardsticks as to earnings, net tangible assets, market value of stock, and distribution used by the NYSE in deciding eligibility of listing?
40. What are the corresponding yardsticks for the American Stock Exchange?

Chapter 5

Regulation
and
Registration

Direct regulation in the securities field existed on the State level long before it came into being on the Federal level. The first *Blue Sky Law* was enacted by Kansas in 1911. By 1919, 32 states had securities laws regulating either broker/dealers, the registration of securities, or both. It was not until 1933 that the first effective Federal law was passed . . . the Securities Act of 1933. It was quickly followed by the Securities Exchange Act of 1934. The Investment Company Act of 1940 was enacted at the request of the SEC to confer regulatory powers on that body over the investment company industry. All of these Acts were designed for the protection of the public by requiring full disclosure and by providing criminal and civil penalties for fraud and "manipulation" as defined in the Acts.

The famous 1929 collapse of the stock market was due in some part to speculative manipulations. Strict regulation was demanded by the public and by Congress during the Senate investigations of 1933 and 1934.

Before 1933 the stock exchanges were regulated by their own rules and by state civil and criminal law. Because of the earlier depredations of the "robber barons" of the late 19th century, the exchanges had promulgated regulations which drastically reduced fraudulent dealings in *already-issued stocks*. Prospective buyers of generally-held stocks could get definite information on past records and present financial conditions of companies whose issues were listed. Annual reports were required that gave complete information to present and prospective shareholders.

A serious gap in available information existed, however, in relation to *new issues*—of securities issued to finance new businesses. There was no set legal requirement on the information to be contained in a prospectus and there were no teeth in the Federal laws prior to 1933, which were vague and difficult to enforce. Until that year, the Federal Trade Commission was charged with the responsibility for administering the laws.

THE SECURITIES ACT OF 1933

In 1933, the first Federal legislative act designed to regulate the securities business on an interstate basis was passed. It was most recently amended in 1964. Its expressed purpose was:

"To provide full and fair disclosure of the character of (newly issued) securities . . . and to prevent frauds in the sale thereof."
There are three things to note:

1. It related to newly-issued securities, not to those already in the hands of the public.

2. It called for "full and fair disclosure."

3. It was designed to prevent fraud in the sale of these securities.

Named the Securities Act of 1933, the legislation contained within it a section (27) which led to the Securities Exchange Act of 1934 that established the Securities and Exchange Commission to administer both acts.

There are 28 sections to the Act:

Section 1. "This title may be cited as the Securities Act of 1933." Various court decisions have very liberally interpreted the meaning of "securities" as covered by the Act. One decision contains the following: ". . . that this statute was not a penal statute but was a remedial enactment . . .A remedial enactment is one that seeks to give a remedy for an ill. It is to be liberally construed so that its purpose may be realized." (*S.E.C. v Starmont*, (1940) 31 F .Supp. 264.)

Section 2. Definitions. This section defines many of the terms used throughout the other sections of the Act. Importantly, it contains definitions of "security," of "sale," of "offer to sell," and of "prospectus," among many others. Several important Rules of the SEC are directly derived from this section including Rule 134 (discussed under Section 5). In the definition of a security, the Act includes *investment contract*. Such a contract involves the concept that the investment will return a profit without any active effort on the part of the investor. Among other investment contracts that have been held to be securities as defined in the Act is *equity funding* which involves the periodic purchase of mutual fund shares, the pledge of all or part of these shares as collateral for loans, and the use of the proceeds of the loans to pay premiums on an insurance policy. The broad application of the definition of "security" is perhaps best exemplified by its inclusion of contracts for the sale of mated animals, such as chinchillas, to be kept on the seller's ranch with the buyers to share in the profits from the sale of the offspring.

Section 3. Exempted Securities. Some securities, such as those issued or guaranteed by the United States, are exempt from the registration and prospectus provisions of the Act. Securities specifically exempted are:

(1) Any security issued or guaranteed by the United States, i.e. Government securities.

(2) Any security issued or guaranteed by the District of Columbia or any State or Territory of the United States, including political subdivisions of any State or Territory, i.e. municipals.

(3) Any security issued or guaranteed by any national, state or territorial bank or issued by or representing an interest in or a direct obligation of a Federal Reserve bank.

(4) Commercial paper which has a maturity at date of issuance not exceeding nine months which are not intended to be marketed to the public.

(5) Any security issued by a person organized and operated exclusively for religious, educational, benevolent, fraternal, charitable, or reformatory purposes and not for pecuniary profit, and no part of the net earnings of which inures to the benefit of any person, private stockholder, or individual.

(6) Certain securities of savings and loan and farmers' cooperative associations.

(7) Any security of a common or contract carrier (e.g. railroads) the issuance of which is subject to provisions of the Interstate Commerce Act.

(8) Certificates issued by a receiver or by a trustee in bankruptcy, with the approval of the court.

(9) Insurance policies and annuity contracts.

(10) Any security exchanged by the issuer with its existing security holders exclusively where no commission or other remuneration is paid or given directly or indirectly for soliciting such exchange.

(11) Securities issued in reorganizations approved by court or Governmental authority.

(12) Intrastate issues—i.e. any security which is a part of an issue offered and sold only to persons resident within a single State or Territory, where the issuer of such security is a person resident and doing business within, or, if a corporation, incorporated by and doing business within, such State or Territory.

Section 4. Exempted Transactions. This section defines certain transactions that are exempt from the registration and prospectus requirements of Section 5 of the Act. Private offerings, where there is no true public distribution, come under this section. Court decisions have emphasized that the exemption from the requirements of Section 5 did not mean that any transactions were exempt from the anti-fraud provisions of the Act, specifically those given in Section 17. Basically, the exemption's afforded under Section 5 were provided to save unnecessary registration expense for securities that were not being offered to the general public.

Section 5. Registration Requirement. Both the offer to sell or delivery of a security after sale is forbidden under this section "unless a registration statement is in effect as to (such) security" where the offer or delivery is "by any means or instruments of transportation or communication in interstate commerce or of the mails." Further, any delivery of a security after sale may only be made when an effective prospectus has either preceded or accompanies the security. This effective prospectus must comply with the requirements of Section 10 of the Act.

There have been two important rules promulgated by the SEC under this section. Rule 134 defines the types of advertising and of letters or other communications which can be used without prior or concurrent delivery of an effective prospectus. Issuers, broker/dealers and representatives must adhere closely to the requirements of this rule so that they do not provide a prospective purchaser with an "incomplete prospectus."

In SEC Release 3844 of October 8, 1957, describes the creation of a prospectus in various forms and then states that they will not be deemed to be prospectuses when preceded or accompanied by a conforming prospectus.

"A prospectus is defined to include any notice, circular, advertisement, letter, or communication, written or by radio or by television, which offers any security for sale except that any communication sent after the effective date of a registration statement shall not be deemed a prospectus if, prior to or at the same time with such a communication, a written prospectus meeting the requirements of Section 10 of the Act was sent or given."

Thus, any letter, advertisement, or even telephone call that gives more information than that allowed by Rule 134 becomes itself a prospectus unless it is preceded or accompanied by the actual propectus. Such an abbreviated prospectus would be violation of Section 5 since it could not possibly comply with the requirements of Section 10.

The NASD requires that all letters, market letters, sales literature and advertisements used by all underwriters and dealers be filed with it. Correspondingly, members of a Stock Exchange must file such material with the Exchange. A dealer's representative must always have his dealer's approval of any letter he writes or any advertisement he intends to place. The dealer then takes the necessary steps to ensure that the lettter or material is properly filed.

Section 6. Registration of Securities. This section details what securities may be registered and how such registration is to be done.

Section 7. Information Required. This section gives the SEC broad powers in regulating what must appear in a registration statement. Information required is comprehensive and includes such items as the general character of the business; names and addresses of officers and directors with their business history for at least the past five years; salaries or other remuneration paid to officers and directors with the names of those receiving $25,000 or more a year; the amount of securities of the issuer owned by officers, directors and beneficial owners of more than 10%; capitalization and amount of funded debt; offering expenses of the issuer; and the specific uses to which the proceeds of the offering are to be put.

"Any such registration statement shall contain such other information, and be accompanied by such other documents, as the Commission may by rules or regulations require as being necessary or appropriate in the public interest or for the protection of investors."

Section 8. Taking Effect. Registration statements normally become effective on the twentieth day after filing, under this section. However, the SEC is empowered to determine whether or not the statement complies with the Act as to completeness and may refuse to allow the statement to become effective unless amended. If it appears to the SEC that untrue statements have been included, the Commission may issue a stop order.

Section 9. Court Review. As with any other act of Congress, provision is made so that any person who is aggrieved by an order of the administrative body (in this case the SEC) may obtain a review of the order in the Federal courts.

Section 10. Information Required in Prospectus. A prospectus must contain the same information as that contained in the registration statement. In addition, the SEC is given the authority to define the requirements for any additional material which that body considers necessary in the public interest. Red herring requirements and the manner and use of this type of preliminary prospectus are also detailed in this section. Prospectus requirements related to the registration statement are discussed in detail in Chapter 13, The Prospectus.

Note the application of Rule 134, discussed under Section 5, with respect to an "incomplete" prospectus.

One part of the section relates to the length of time a prospectus may be used (that is, be considered an effective prospectus).

Generally speaking, under SEC Rules, a Mutual Fund prospectus must be replaced with a new one within a period of not more than 13 months.

Under this section of the Act, the SEC issued Rule 425, which requires the statement at the bottom of the first page of all prospectuses "THESE SECURITIES HAVE NOT BEEN APPROVED OR DISAPPROVED BY THE SECURITIES AND EXCHANGE COMMISSION NOR HAS THE COMMISSION PASSED UPON THE ACCURACY OR ADEQUACY OF

THIS PROSPECTUS. ANY REPRESENTATION TO THE CONTRARY
IS A CRIMINAL OFFENSE."

Section 11. Civil Liabilities. It might be asked what a prospective
purchaser of a new issue could rely on in the light of the required statement
quoted above. Section 11 of the Act gives recourse to the civil courts for
recovery of an investment plus costs of the suit when a purchase has been
made pursuant to a prospectus that contains an untrue statement of a
material fact or is misleading because of the omission of a material fact. The
purchaser may sue every person who signed the registration statement, every
director or partner in the issuer, every accountant, engineer, appraiser and
other professional persons who participate in the preparation or certify any
part of the registration, and every underwriter with respect to the security.
Persons other than the underwriter have statutory defenses to such a suit
under certain circumstances such as reliance in good faith on information
furnished by others, resignation prior to the effectiveness of the registration,
and lack of knowledge as to the registration having been made effective.

Section 12. Further Civil Liabilities. If a broker/dealer or his representative offers to sell or does sell a security in violation of the registration
and prospectus requirements of Section 5 or uses any fraudulent method to
sell a security, he is liable to civil suit for damages including interest.

Section 13. Limitation of Actions. Specified are the time limits within
which civil suits may be instituted under Sections 11 and 12.

Section 14. Contrary Stipulations Void. Any provision in the sale of a
security that binds the purchaser to waive the provisions of this Act or of
the rules and regulations of the SEC is void. In other words, no one buying
a security can relieve the seller from complying with the Act and with the
rules issued under the Act.

Section 15. Liability of Controlling Persons. A dealer or broker is
liable to the same extent as his registered representative would be under
Section 12. Section 15 also extends liability under Section 11 to "controlling
persons."

Section 16. Additional Remedies. "The rights and remedies provided by
this title (the Act) shall be in addition to any and all other rights and
remedies that may exist at law or in equity."

Section 17. Fraudulent Interstate Transactions. As interpreted by
the SEC, this section might be referred to as a "catch-all" section. While
part of it has been incorporated in Volume 2, The Statement of Policy, it is
important enough to quote Section 17 (a) here:

"(a) It shall be unlawful for any person in the offer or sale of any
securities by the use of any means or instruments of transportation or
communication in interstate commerce or by use of the mails, directly or
indirectly—

(1) to employ any device, scheme or artifice to defraud, or

(2) to obtain money or property by means of any untrue statement of a material fact or any omission to state a material fact necessary in order to make the statements made, in the light of the circumstances under which they were made, not misleading, or

(3) to engage in any transaction, practice, or course of business which operates or would operate as a fraud or deceit upon the purchaser."

Both TV and radio have been included by the SEC as "communication in interstate commerce" because it is impossible to control their area of reception.

While Section 17 (a) refers only to the criminal courts in the term "unlawful," a court decision makes it clear that civil liability is incurred by violation of the section, in addition to criminal liability.

Court decisions also implement and amplify the language of the Act itself with respect to the phrase "or by use of the mails." It would appear that Section 17 only applied to interstate mailings. However, the courts have ruled that if one used the mails *within one State* on an *intrastate* offering, and violated any provision in Section 17 (a), he is as guilty as if he had mailed across a state line.

Subparagraph (b) of Section 17 makes it illegal for anyone to publish descriptions of securities when the publisher is paid for such publicity without his also publishing the fact that compensation has been, or will be, received for the publishing.

Section 17(c) makes the section applicable to those securities exempted under Section 3. In other words, fraud is fraud whether in connection with exempt or other securities.

Section 18. State Control. "Nothing in this title (the Act) shall affect the jurisdiction of the securities commission . . . of any State. . ." In other words, all the provisions of the Federal Act *and* all the laws of the State in which business is being conducted must be complied with.

Section 19. Special Powers of Commission. The Commission has the authority to make, amend, and rescind such rules and regulations as may be necessary to carry out the provisions of the Act. Commissioners or their representatives are also empowered to subpoena witnesses and to administer oaths.

Section 20. Injunctions and Prosecution. The SEC is empowered to make investigations and to bring criminal actions at law against persons deemed to have violated the Act. The wording of the section is interesting in that it gives the Commission power to act "whenever it shall appear . . . that the provisions of this title (the Act) . . . have been *or are about to be* violated . . ." (Emphasis added.)

Section 21. Hearings by Commission. "All hearings shall be public and may be held before the Commission or an officer or officers of the Commission designated by it, and appropriate records shall be kept."

Section 22. Jurisdiction. Jurisdiction of offenses and suits, and certain rules in connection with them, are defined in this section. Jurisdiction is given to the District Courts of the United States, the U.S. Court of any Territory, and the U.S. District Court of the District of Columbia.

Section 23. Unlawful Representation. Neither the fact that the registration statement for a security has been filed or is in effect shall be deemed to mean that the statement is true and accurate, or that it does not contain an untrue statement of fact, or that the Commission has in any way passed upon the merits of the security. It is unlawful to make any representations to the contrary. (See Section 10.)

In short, the words in the registration statement (*and* the prospectus) have been made under the penalties of fraud. The registrants are liable, even though the Commission has not certified the truth and accuracy of the statements or of the worth of the security.

Section 24. Penalties. "Any person who wilfully violates any of the provisions of this title (the Act), or the rules and regulations promulgated by the Commission under authority thereof . . . shall upon conviction be fined not more than $5,000 or imprisoned not more than five years, or both."

Section 25. Jurisdiction of Other Gov't Agencies. Nothing in the Act cancels anyone's obligations to make reports or other returns required by any other law.

Section 26. Separability of Provisions. If any one section of the Act is invalidated, such findings will not affect other sections.

Section 27. This section gave the effective date of the SEC and of the Act.

Section 28. This section directed the SEC to make a study and report to the Congress.

Sections 27 and 28 were actually Sections 210 and 211 of Title II of the Securities Exchange Act of 1934.

THE SECURITIES EXCHANGE ACT OF 1934

Whereas the Securities Act of 1933 sought to protect investors in the purchase of newly-issued securities, the Securities Exchange Act of 1934 sought to regulate trading in already issued securities.

The stated purpose of the '34 Act is "to provide for the regulation of securities exchanges and of over-the-counter markets operating in interstate and foreign commerce and through the mails to prevent inequitable and unfair practices on such exchanges and markets, and for other purposes."

The Act has been of immense importance in prohibiting abuses and manipulations through its creation of the SEC and later of the self-regulatory National Association of Securities Dealers, Inc.

The Act has 34 sections:

Section 1. Short Title. "This Act may be cited as the Securities Exchange Act of 1934."

Section 2. Necessity for Regulation. Citing that transactions in securities are affected with a national public interest, this section states that it is necessary to regulate and control such transactions and other matters "in order to protect interstate commerce, the national credit, the Federal taxing power, to protect and make more effective the national banking system and Federal Reserve System, and to insure the maintenance of fair and honest markets in such transactions."

Parts of Sections 2(3) and 2(4) are quoted directly because they actually explain the effects of "rigged" markets and manipulative practices:

"Frequently the prices of securities on such exchanges and markets are susceptible to manipulation and control, and the dissemination of such prices gives rise to excessive speculation, resulting in sudden and unreasonable fluctuations in the prices of securities which (a) cause alternately unreasonable expansion and unreasonable contraction of the volume of credit available for trade, transportation, and industry in interstate commerce . . . (c) prevent the fair valuation of collateral for bank loans and/or obstruct the effective operation of the national banking system and Federal Reserve System.

"National emergencies, which produce widespread unemployment and the dislocation of trade, transportation, and industry, and which burden interstate commerce and adversely affect the general welfare, are precipitated, intensified, and prolonged by manipulation and sudden and unreasonable fluctuations of security prices and by excessive speculation on such exchanges and markets, and to meet such emergencies the Federal Government is put to such great expense as to burden the national credit."

Section 3. Definitions. In addition to defining terms used within the Act, this section gave the SEC and the Federal Reserve Board, within their respective jurisdictions, authority to define technical, trade, and accounting terms so long as such definitions are not inconsistent with the provisions of the Act itself.

Certain of these definitions are important to a full understanding of the securities business:

"The term 'exchange' means any organization, association, or group of persons, whether incorporated or unincorporated, which constitutes, maintains, or provides a market place or facilities for bringing together purchasers and sellers of securities or for otherwise performing with respect to securities the functions commonly performed by a stock exchange as that term is generally understood, and includes the market place and the market facilities maintained by such exchange."

"The term 'member' when used with respect to an exchange means any person who is permitted either to effect transactions on the exchange without the services of another person acting as broker, or to make use of the facilities of an exchange for transactions thereon without payment of a commission or fee or with the payment of a commission or fee which is less than that charged the general public, and includes any firm transacting a business as broker or dealer of which a member is a partner, and any partner of any such firm." (Note: At the time of enactment, there were no corporate members of exchanges. The term "partner" has been extended to include an officer of a corporate member of an exchange.)

"The term 'broker' means any person engaged in the business of effecting transactions in securities for the account of others, but does not include a bank."

"The term 'dealer' means any person engaged in the business of buying and selling securities for his own account, through a broker or otherwise, but does not include a bank, or any person insofar as he buys or sells securities for his own account, either individually or in some fiduciary capacity, but not as a part of a regular business."

"The term 'issuer' means any person who issues or proposes to issue any security . . ." This definition has further explanatory statements with respect to who constitutes the issuer in the cases of certificates of deposit, voting-trust certificates and the like.

"The term 'person' means an individual, a corporation, a partnership, an association, a joint-stock company, a business trust, or an unincorporated organization."

Under its authority to make definitions, the SEC, in a release dated April 23, 1965, gave a later definition of "equity security" than that given in the Act. "The term 'equity security' is hereby defined to include any stock or similar security, certificate of interest or participation in any profit sharing agreement, preorganization certificate or subscription, transferable share, voting trust certificate or certificate of deposit for an equity security, limited partnership interest, interest in a joint venture, or certificate of interest in a business trust; or any security convertible, with or without consideration into such a security, or carrying any warrant or right to subscribe to or purchase such a security; or any such warrant or right."

Except for persons whose functions are clerical or ministerial, "The term 'person associated with a broker or dealer' means any partner, officer, director, or branch manager of such broker or dealer (or any person occupying a similar status or performing similar functions), or any person directly or indirectly controlling or controlled by such broker or dealer, including any employee . . ."

Section 4. SEC. This section established the Securities and Exchange Commission to be composed of five commissioners to be appointed by the President by and with the advice and consent of the Senate. Prior to the actual taking of office of the first three commissioners, the Securities Act of 1933 was administered by the Federal Trade Commission.

Section 5. Transactions on Unregistered Exchanges. Under this section, it became illegal for transactions to be effected by brokers, dealers, or exchanges on an exchange unless the exchange was registered under Section 6 of the Act. Exemptions could be allowed by the Commission for exchanges with very limited volume.

Section 6. Registration of Exchanges. Combined with Section 5, this section set up the requirement for exchanges to be registered (if brokers or dealers were to do business on them) and the method of registration. Exchanges file their rules and regulations with the SEC and must agree to take disciplinary action against any member who violates the Act or violates any of the rules and regulations issued by the SEC under the Act.

Section 7. Margin Requirements. The Board of Governors of the Federal Reserve System is given the power to set margin requirements for listed securities, which requirements may be changed from time to time at the discretion of the Board. Under this authority, the Board issued Regulation T and Regulation U. Regulation T governs the extension and maintenance of credit by brokers, dealers, and members of national securities exchanges. Regulation U governs loans by banks for the purpose of purchasing or carrying stocks registered on a national securities exchange.

Section 8. Restrictions on Borrowing. In four parts, this section (a) details from whom brokers or dealers may borrow money on listed securities, (b) lays the foundation for the SEC's "net capital rule" for broker/dealers (c) deals with pledging and commingling of customers' securities, and (d) states that no broker or dealer may lend or arrange for the lending of any securities carried for the account of a customer without the written consent of the customer.

Section 9. Prohibiting Against Manipulation. Both this section and Section 10 deal with manipulative practices which are intended to make money for those in the securities business at the expense of the general public.

Section 9 makes it unlawful to do certain things that constitute manipulation, such as: (a) creating a false or misleading appearance of active trading in a security, (b) giving of information to potential investors as to the likelihood of a rise or fall in price solely for the purpose of causing the market price to react to purchases or sales by such potential investors, (c) making false or misleading statements about a security, (d) "pegging" or "fixing" prices, (e) improper use of puts, calls, straddles, or other options to buy or sell. Transactions in which there is no real change in ownership are also specifically prohibited.

Note that all of these prohibited terms relate to outright fraud or the giving of false or misleading information. Creating active trading in a security, for example, is not prohibited. It is the creation of a false or misleading *appearance* of active trading that is forbidden. Indeed, the more actively a security is traded, the better the potential market for both buyer and seller. It is a broker/dealer's function to create or sustain an active market. Likewise, a broker/dealer would be prevented from giving his customers information to which they are entitled if he were prohibited from giving an opinion *based on facts* as to probable market action relative to individual issues. In fact, he is not so prohibited . . . he is forbidden to give such information *solely for the purpose of causing the market price to react to purchases or sales.*

Section 10. Deceptive Devices. Section 10 first forbids the use of short sales or stop-loss orders that violate any rules or regulations the Commission may set to protect investors. However, no such rules or regulations have been promulgated. This section then becomes much more inclusive in its language than Section 9 in that it forbids in general "any manipulative or deceptive device or contrivance . . ."

One type of deception was the creation of a false appearance of an active market through what were then known as *wash sales.* Two or more brokers or speculators would place buy and sell orders through other brokers at ever increasing prices. No securities nor money actually changed hands. As the prices climbed upward, members of the general public became interested and began to buy, forcing the price even higher. At a ripe moment, the manipulators would sell their own holdings to the public. With no further artificial support, the market for that particular security would collapse . . . and the public was the loser.

Today a wash sale usually means the completely ethical sale of one security at a loss (or gain) to offset the gain (or loss) and concomitant Federal taxes on another security.

Frequently, part of an issue of stock was sold to the public and the remainder was made available to "insiders" for nothing at all or for much less than the book (or real) value. The result was to reduce the actual book value of the publicly held shares. Such stock was called *watered stock*, or stock diluted from its real value.

At the present time, when new issues of stock are judged by their potential and current earnings, rather than by the book value, this idea of watered stock has very little meaning. While in some cases the public might perhaps pay in 80 per cent of the company's material assets for 30 per cent of the stock, the public is also buying the value of ideas which cannot be immediately translated into book value. Patents, salesmanship and advertising, and other techniques and new processes add to the worth of some companies with a small capitalization.

A *corner* occurs when the outstanding shares of a security have become concentrated in the hands of a speculative group. Often this group has manipulated a stock rise. Other speculators, not knowing of the controlling group's actions, believe that the stock is priced too high and will soon decline. They sell short. But the stock continues to rise, and the short sellers must cover by buying the stock at the market price. They then discover that the manipulators, who possess all of the stock there is to sell, have set their own price. The "cornered" short sellers must settle with the manipulators at a dictated price.

A *pool* was an agreement among market operators who combined resources for a stock manipulation. Often, in the speculative 1920's, a director or officer of a corporation was also involved. With a judicious combination of "inside" information, with perhaps the help of a specialist on the floor of a stock exchange, with publicity, wash sales, and other devices to show increased activity, the pool operators interested the public. The price of the stock was forced up even more by public buying. The Radio Pool of 1929, for example, showed a price rise from 93 to 109 in five days, primarily because of their own activities. At this point the pool operators were short 187,900 shares. Within two weeks the syndicate realized $4,900,000 in short sales as the stock dropped to 80.

The New York Stock Exchange and other exchanges already had stringent rules against such practices before the enactment of the '33 and '34 Acts, but it was considered in the public interest to make such manipulations actually illegal.

Section 11. Functions of Members, Brokers, and Dealers. Authority is here given to the Commission to set rules and regulations as to floor trading by members, brokers, or dealers for their own accounts and to prevent excessive trading off the floor of the exchanges. A part of this section deals with the roles of the odd-lot dealer and the specialist on the floor of the exchange. Further, the section places a limitation on certain customer credit extension in connection with underwritings.

Section 12. Registration Requirements for Securities. It is unlawful for any broker or dealer to effect transactions on an exchange in securities which have not been registered on the exchange. Information stating how such registration is to be accomplished is given here. The SEC is given authority to allow trading on one exchange in securities that are listed on another exchange (such securities are said to have "unlisted trading privileges"). As a matter of interest, the New York Stock Exchange does not extend any unlisted trading privileges. A 1964 amendment extended registration requirements to every issuer engaged in interstate commerce, affecting interstate commerce, or whose securities are traded by use of the mails or any means of interstate commerce.

Section 13. Reports. All companies whose securities are listed on a national securities exchange must file reports at such intervals and in such form as the SEC may require. The purpose of requiring such reports was to ensure that enough information was available on any company so that an investor could make an intelligent decision concerning the worth of its securities. This requirement was extended by the 1964 amendment to include companies of a specified size having unlisted securities outstanding.

Section 14. Proxies. Paragraph (a) of this section gives the SEC the authority to make rules and regulations as to the solicitation of proxies and makes it illegal to solicit proxies other than in accord with such rules and regulations. Several rules have been issued under this section which go into great detail as to the manner in which proxies may be solicited and the information that must be given to shareholders whose proxies are being solicited. All of these rules are designed to ensure that the recipient of a proxy solicitation will understand what it is that he is being asked to sign and to give enough background on the matter in question so that the shareholder can make an intelligent decision as to how he should vote.

Subparagraph (b) relates to the giving of proxies by brokers or dealers in connection with securities held for the accounts of customers. No rules have been issued under this sub-section. However, it is standard practice for broker/dealers to vote proxies for shares held in their names for customers directly in accord with the wishes of the customers themselves. In fact, if a broker/dealer implements proxy material with his own material, he is thereby placed in the position of "soliciting a proxy" and must conform to the requirements under sub-paragraph (a).

Section 15. Over-The-Counter Markets. It is mandatory that all brokers and dealers who deal in the over-the-counter market (on other than an intrastate basis) be registered with the SEC. Further, the section states that registration will be in accord with rules and regulations issued by the Commission. "Intrastate" means that the broker or dealer deals only in intrastate securities as well as doing business only within his state. Here, as elsewhere in the Act, the "use of the mails," even if within one State, places the user under the Act. An amendment to the Act in 1964 makes any act, practice or course of business that would be prohibited if the means of interstate commerce or the mails were used equally prohibited even when the means of interstate commerce or the mails are not used.

Section 15 also defines the grounds for denial of registration, for suspension, or for revocation of registration. Basically, these grounds are:

1. Making false or misleading statements in the application for registration or in other securities registrations or reports.

2. Having been convicted within the last ten years of a felony or misdemeanor involving the purchase or sale of any security or arising out of the business of a broker or dealer or any other business related to the investment field.

3. Being enjoined by a court from engaging in the securities or banking business.

4. Having wilfully violated any of the provisions of the '33 Act or of the '34 Act. (After the passage of the Investment Company Act of 1940, violation of that Act also became grounds for suspension or revocation.)

5. Having failed to supervise properly an employee who violated this Act.

Section 9 and 10 dealt with manipulation with respect to securities listed on a national exchange. Section 15 adds a prohibition against over-the-counter manipulation as defined by the Commission. Some of the practices that have been so defined are:

Excessive prices which are not fairly related to the market.

False representations to customer.

Taking of secret profits.

Failure to disclose control of a market.

Creating false impression of activity by dummy sales.

"Churning," or unnecessary sales in a customer's account.

Although the Act itself states that "manipulation" is as defined by the Commission, Rule 15(c)(1–2) issued by the Commission states "The scope of this rule shall not be limited by any specific definitions of the term 'manipulative, deceptive, or other fraudulent device or contrivance. . .' "

Another important rule of the SEC under Section 15 seeks to protect investors by forbidding certain practices in connection with pledging or commingling of securities held for the accounts of customers. This rule specifically applies to over-the-counter broker-dealers; a similar rule under Section 8 applies to broker/dealers who are members of or do business through members of a national exchange.

Section 15(c)(3) requires financial responsibility on the part of broker/dealers. The SEC "net capital rule" stems from this.

Section 12 and 13 as amended deal with registration and report requirements. Section 15(d) amplifies Section 13 with respect to unlisted securities.

Section 15A. Registration of National Securities Associations. Aided by the Maloney Act of 1938, which amended the original act by adding this section, the formation of associations like the NASD was authorized, but the NASD is the only national securities association incorporated under the Act.

Section 16. Directors, Officers, and Principal Stockholders. Requiring statements of ownership of stocks by "insiders" and other related information, including restrictions of types of trading and the like, this section is well explained by part of the House Committee report:

"A renewal of investors' confidence in the exchange markets can be effected only by a clearer recognition, upon the part of the corporate managers of companies whose securities are publicly held, of their responsibilities as trustees for their corporations. Men charged with the administration of other people's money must not use inside information for their own advantage . . . the most potent weapon against the abuse of inside information is full and prompt publicity. For that reason, this bill requires the disclosure of the corporate holdings of officers and directors and stockholders owning more than ten per cent of any class of stock, and prompt disclosure of any changes that occur in their corporate holdings. Short selling and selling against the box (Chapter 4) by insiders are prohibited."

The Wall Street Journal, among other papers, prints lists of changes of holdings by directors, officers, and stockholders holding ten per cent or more of a company's stock. Also, the SEC issues periodic compilations of such lists.

Section 17. Accounts and Records. Not only does this section require that all brokers and dealers maintain records in accord with such rules and regulations as the SEC may set forth, but it also authorizes the SEC to make examinations of any broker or dealer's accounts, correspondence, memoranda, papers, books, and other records whenever the Commission deems it in the public interest. Rules and regulations issued by the SEC under this section state the types of records that must be kept. In practice, an SEC examiner may walk into a broker/dealer's office and ask that all files and books be opened for his inspection. Under the law, no broker/dealer may refuse the examiner access to any and all correspondence and records. A broker/dealer can have his registration suspended or revoked by failure to keep copies of all correspondence or to keep books and records as required by the SEC.

Section 18. Liability for Misleading Statements. In a rather unusual statement of law, this section makes a person both criminally and civilly liable for any misleading statements made in connection with the requirements of Section 15 of this Act.

Section 19. Powers . . . Exchanges and Securities. The SEC has the power to suspend for 12 months or revoke the registration of any national securities exchange or of any security, if the Commission is of the opinion that such action is necessary or appropriate for the protection of investors. Further, authority is granted the SEC to censure, suspend or expel from an exchange or the NASD any member or officer who has violated any of the provisions of this Act. The intent of this Act, as well as the '33 Act, is to protect investors, not those in the securities business. Thus, Section 19 goes on to give the Commission authority to suspend trading in a particular security on an exchange or over-the-counter for a period not to exceed ten days, or to suspend all trading on an exchange for a period not more than 90 days (but this action requires the approval of the President).

Other provisions of this section give the SEC broad powers in supervising the rules of national securities exchanges, which the Commission may require to be changed or amended. In other words, the SEC supervises the members of an exchange through the exchange itself as well as on an individual basis.

Section 20. Liabilities of Controlling Persons. In effect, this section states that if A commits an illegal act under the direction of B, who controls A, then both A and B are equally liable under the law. Section 20 also makes it illegal for any "controlling person" to "hinder, delay, or obstruct" the filing of any information required by the SEC under this Act.

Section 21. Investigations; Injunctions and Prosecution. In the Securities Act of 1933, Sections 19 and 20 gave the SEC special powers in the areas of investigation, subpoenaing of witnesses, prosecutions of offenses and the like. Section 21 of this Act is similar in its provisions.

Section 22. Hearings. It is interesting to note the difference in wording with respect to hearings in the '33 Act and this Act. Section 21 of the '33 Act states that "All hearings *shall* be public. . ." Section 22 of the '34 Act states "Hearings *may* be public. . ."

Section 23. Rules and Regulations. Power to make rules and regulations under this Act is specifically given the SEC and the Board of Governors of the Federal Reserve System by this section. Both bodies are required to make annual reports to Congress.

Section 24. Information Filed. To protect those required to file under this Act, this section makes it possible for certain information, such as trade secrets, to be made confidential and not a matter of public record. This section also forbids any member or employee of the Commission to use information that is not public for his own benefit.

Section 25. Court Review of Orders. Like Section 9 of the '33 Act, this section reserves final judgment on any issue to the courts, rather than to the Commission itself.

Section 26. Unlawful Representations. It is unlawful to make any representation to the effect that the SEC or the Federal Reserve has passed on the merits of any issue. Also, the failure of either body to take action against any person cannot be construed to mean that that person is not in violation of the law.

Section 27. Jurisdiction. Jurisdiction of violations of this Act is given to the Federal courts.

Section 28. Effect on Existing Law. "The rights and remedies provided by this title (the Act) shall be in addition to any and all other rights and remedies that may exist in law or at equity. . ." The section also leaves jurisdiction of offenses against a State law with the State.

Section 29. Validity of Contracts. No one can avoid compliance with the provisions of this Act by getting someone else to waive the requirements in any contract. Any contract that seeks to avoid the provisions of this Act is automatically void.

Section 30. Foreign Securities Exchanges. It is unlawful to deal in securities on a foreign exchange in any manner other than that in which dealing in such securities would have to be handled in this country if the issuers are within the jurisdiction of the United States. In other words, the laws relating to U.S. exchanges cannot be circumvented by placing business through a foreign exchange.

Section 31. Registration Fee. Each national securities exchange is required to pay an annual fee to the Commission.

Section 32. Penalties. Individuals may be fined a maximum of $10,000 or sentenced to a maximum term of imprisonment of two years, or both, for violations of the Act.

Section 33. Separability. An escape section that states that if any one section of the Act is found to be invalid, such finding shall have no effect on the other sections.

Section 34. Effective Date.

OTHER REGULATORY LAWS

Investment Company Act of 1940

Between 1934 and 1940, the rapid increase in the number of investment companies with different objectives and many different methods of operation made it desirable to set a legal standard for this type of corporation or trust. After an extremely thorough study of existing companies by the SEC, working in close cooperation with the industry itself, recommendations were made to the Congress that resulted in the Investment Company and Investment Advisers Acts of 1940. Provisions of the Investment Company Act are summarized in Volume 2, Chapter 4.

State Regulations

Blue Sky Laws. Most of the states have their own laws regulating securities to prevent "speculative schemes which have no more basis than so many feet of blue sky." (Hall v. Geiger-Jones Co., 242 U.S. 539). From this statement the term "Blue Sky Laws" has been taken to apply to individual state securities laws.

The laws which may vary greatly from state to state, fall into two general categories.

The first is a simple one that prohibits the fraudulent sale of securities and prescribes penalties for such sales. The second general type, found in most states, regulates the sale of securities in detail and requires registration of the securities themselves as well as registration of broker/dealers and their representatives. There are variations of this second type. Maine controls broker/dealers and their representatives, but does not require registration of shares by the issuer. Wyoming requires registration of the securities, but not of the broker/dealer. There is enough variation between the laws of any two states so that no overall statement would suffice to give the requirements of a specific state. Licensing or registration in one state does not carry over to any other state.

"Prudent Man" Rule. In a Massachusetts court case involving the duties of a trustee, the court stated that the duty of a trustee "in investing other people's money is to observe how men of prudence, discretion, and intelligence manage their own affairs, not in regard to speculation, but in regard to the permanent disposition of their funds, considering probable income as well as probable safety of their capital." This rule has been widely accepted in other states. In those states in which it has been adopted into law, there is usually no obligation on the part of a trustee to get court approval for individual investments made on behalf of a trust. The Attorney General of Minnesota, for example, stated in 1949: "The Attorney General passes no opinion on whether in any specific case an investment should be made, as responsibility rests upon those who make the investment to determine whether or not the investment comes within the 'prudent man' rule."

"Legal List." In contrast to the states which apply the prudent man rule to investments made by court-appointed administrators or by trustees not given free investment choice by the trust instruments, there are states which have a "legal list." Except in cases in which a trust instrument or will specifically gives the trustees or executors the right to invest in accordance with their own judgment, the state requires that investments by trustees or executors be made only in those securities approved by the state. The list of such securities is generally known as the "legal list."

The restrictions do not apply to all investments made by a trustee or an executor under a trust or will. The state recognizes the right of a person to have investments made for him in accordance with his wishes. Therefore, when there is a specific delegation to the trustee or executor that permits him to invest in other than the legal list, he is not bound by that list.

Other than the application of legal list requirements to investments by trustees or executors, most states have special requirements as to investments by banks, insurance companies, and other types of fiduciaries. Like the Blue Sky laws, the rules and regulations with respect to investments by trustees, executors and other fiduciaries vary widely among the different states.

THE NASD

Background

The Securities Exchange Act of 1934, as originally passed, dealt with the regulation of members of registered national securities exchanges through the exchanges themselves. Section 15 of the Act required the registration with the SEC of all broker/dealers who dealt in the over-the-counter securities market. The effect of the combination of these requirements was to place one group (members of exchanges) under regulation both by the SEC and by the exchanges of which they were members. A second group, those broker/dealers who were not members of an exchange, were directly supervised only by the SEC. An overall regulatory body was required.

Recognizing that self-regulation was preferable to further regulation from without, representatives of the industry worked with the SEC over a considerable period of time to provide for such self-regulation. The result was the passage of the Maloney Act in 1938, which amended the '34 Act by adding Section 15A.

The Maloney Act allowed the formation of the desired self-regulatory body, the National Association of Securities Dealers, Inc. The NASD is the only organization registered under the Maloney Act to function as "a mechanism of regulation among the over-the-counter brokers and dealers operating in interstate and foreign commerce or through the mails."

It is extremely disadvantageous for a broker/dealer or a registered representative to lose his NASD membership or SEC registration. Loss of membership bars him from joint underwritings with NASD members. It also forbids payment of compensation by a member to an individual whose registration has been revoked or suspended. If an individual loses his SEC registration, he is prohibited from working for NASD members or in organizing a member concern . . . in effect, he is barred from the interstate securities business. As a practical matter, this usually results in his being barred from any intrastate securities business as well.

Section 15A

Section 15A(a) provides for the registration with the SEC of any association of brokers or dealers as a *national securities association*, under certain requirements of the section as interpreted by the SEC. A House Committee report on this section included the statement that ". . . the formation of associations and application for registration by them are matters of voluntary choice." The report goes on to point out that membership in a registered national securities association does not relieve the member from his obligation to register directly with the SEC under Section 15 of the Act.

Subsection (b) deals with the requirements for an association seeking registration and also with the rights of individual brokers or dealers to be admitted to the association. The House Committee commented: "The broad purpose of this paragraph is to make sure that all brokers and dealers who conduct an honest and responsible business shall be eligible for membership in some association."

Subsections (c) and (d) deal with Affiliated Securities Associations. Grant or denial of registration and withdrawal from registration are covered in (e) and (f).

A specific requirement that "the rules of the association provide that its members shall be appropriately disciplined . . . for any violation of its rules" is included in this subsection. Provisions are made in subsections (g) and (h) for SEC review of any disciplinary action taken by the association or denial of admission to the association.

Subsection (i) states in substance that a registered securities association may include in its rules a provision that its members may deal with non-members only as they would deal with the general public. Therefore, although one member may be able under the rules to charge another member lower prices, commissions, or fees than he would charge the general public, he may not give such lower prices or charges to a broker or dealer who is not a member of the association. If this were not so, members would be subjecting themselves to self-regulation not imposed on non-members and would not receive an important privilege of membership within the association. In fact, this subsection specifically states that there is nothing to prevent any member from giving another member "any dealer's discount, allowance, commission, or special terms."

Subsections (j) and (k) deal with changes in the rules of registered securities associations. Subsection (l) gives the SEC the right to suspend or revoke the registration of an association itself or of a member of an association under certain conditions.

History

The NASD Board of Governors met for the first time on January 22, 1940. In opening that meeting, its chairman, Benjamin Howard Griswold, Jr., said: "Today may be recorded as an unusual day in the history of the investment and securities business of our country. For it is today that the National Association of Securities Dealers begins its active functioning as a self-regulating organization under the Act of 1938 known as the Maloney Act."

Twenty years later, an article in *Barron's*, a leading financial publication, concluded with this statment: "On the one hand, the investing public must be protected; on the other, the business of Association members must be fostered. At times, this is a tight rope to walk. On the evidence to date, however, apparently the NASD has proved equal to the task."

What happened in those 20 years? An "experiment" became practical. After many court cases, some involving the Supreme Court of the United States, the position of the NASD relative to the SEC and to its members became quite clear. The Association became firmly established as the only trade organization in the country with regulatory powers. Some of the milestones since its founding have been:

1941. Drafted Section 26 of the Rules covering the distribution of shares of open-end management investment companies.

Developed the Uniform Practice Code.

Established uniform procedures for newspaper quotations on over-the-counter securities throughout the country.

Protected its members in the effective volume of their business by successfully opposing unlisted trading privileges for certain securities on the New York Curb (American) Exchange.

1942. With the help of letters from some 900 members, convinced the SEC to abandon a proposed rule that would have forced full disclosure of all profits by over-the-counter dealers. The proposed rule was finally dropped in 1947.

1943. Inaugurated a uniform nation-wide questionnaire examination program and an agressive enforcement of the standards of business conduct as set forth in the Rules.

Membership approved 27 amendments to the By-Laws, Rules of Fair Practice, and Code of Procedure. These included a proposed minimum capital requirement that was disapproved by the SEC, which then adopted its own net capital rule.

Adopted the 5 per cent mark-up policy for commissions on sales. (The mark-up policy serves as a guide to dealers in charging a fair price to customers. Generally, the mark-up should be about 5 per cent. Under certain conditions, such as with low-priced securities or with a security owned by a dealer which has appreciated in value over a period of time, more may be charged. Under other conditions, such as a customer's purchase of one security through the sale of another, a 5 per cent mark-up would be unfair. In this case, the NASD member dealer should act as if the purchase and sale were just one transaction. In 1963, some 82.4 per cent of mark-ups were 5 per cent or less.)

1945. Association was authorized by Federal Reserve Board to pass on applications for extensions of time for payment of cash account transactions under Regulation T.

Established requirement for registration of all salesmen, traders, officers and others in responsible positions. This established the Association's right to discipline salesmen and others responsible for violations in the same manner as the members themselves.

The Board of Governors, in company with major New York underwriters and other representatives of the business, met with the SEC. This meeting resulted in a new rule that permitted the use of the "red herring" prospectus.

1946. Issued an interpretation with respect to "free riding" that convinced the SEC to drop a proposed rule that would have prevented those in the business from investing in new issues. Enforcement of this interpretation has made unduly restrictive Federal action unnecessary.

1947. Staff examination of member's books and records replaced the questionnaire method.

1949. Discussions with Federal Reserve Board culminated in amendments to Regulation T that were particularly helpful to brokers and dealers distant from financial centers. The amendments made the 7 days referred to in the regulation "7 full business days" rather than 7 calendar days, and increased the exemption from a $50 balance in any transaction to $100.

1950. Establishment of Investment Companies Department. The work of this department in cooperation with the SEC resulted in the Statement ᵉ Policy. This department reviews sales literature (as defined in the Statement of Policy, Volume 2) for underwriters and dealers who are members the Association. This results in uniform application of the SOP and vance review prevents tremendous expense in reprinting of literature at might be found in violation of the SOP after publication.

1952. At Congressional hearings, the Association was able to convince nsors to drop a proposal that would have required an annual registra- fee of $50 for registered broker/dealers and $10 per individual for ain classes of employees.

Delegation of powers to the Association was challenged as unconstitu- l. A decision of the U.S. Court of Appeals (which the Supreme Court ed to review, thereby giving its tacit approval) made it clear that the ation of authority to the Association by the Maloney Act was constitu- . It also established that the Association in a proper case may expel 1 for improper activity in connection with the account of a single ner, and that an individual officer, partner, or employee may be l as a cause. Also, it was established that the Association had the to demand effective supervision of personnel in all dealings with ors.

954. Association efforts of several years finally resulted in amend- ᵣ to the '33 and '34 Acts that helped bring the statutes more in line actual practice.

Actively participated in protecting U.S. investors in German bonds through assistance to the U.S. Committee for German Corporate Dollar Bonds.

1955. Chairman of the Board and other officers of the Association appeared before the Fulbright Committee and presented evidence showing that punitive legislation was unnecessary.

Association started action in cooperation with the SEC to have variable annuities declared to be securities. In 1959, the Supreme Court declared that variable annuity contracts are, in fact, securities subject to Federal regulations.

1956. Established qualification examination as an admission requrement for new people entering the securities business. There has been a continuing effort made since that time to stiffen the qualification requirements as a part of the NASD's program to "up-grade" the industry.

1957. Adopted the "Uniformity of Concept" policy to ensure that District Committees of different districts would apply the same standards in determining disciplinary actions.

1959. Verified with the Board of Governors of the Federal Reserve System that no employee or director of a bank that is a member of the Federal Reserve System may be employed by a securities firm. Also, established with the Federal Deposit Insurance Corporation that no employees of an FDIC-insured bank should be in the securities business.

1960. Adopted a new "Free-riding and Withholding" Interpretation, expanding its scope and clarifying certain of the circumstances under which it is applicable.

Made effective a condensed memorandum covering the 5 per cent Mark-up Policy.

1965. Amended By-Laws to permit procedures against individuals without joining firms in proceedings. Amendments also established new qualifications and registration standards.

1966. Commenced supervising qualification examinations for SEC for non-members of NASD.

Implemented inter-dealer quotations on Local List stocks to conform to National List quotations on inter-dealer basis established in 1965.

1967 Amended By-Laws to provide for certain foreign personnel to be associated with the NASD as foreign associates.

Required members to submit statements of financial condition to other members on request in connection with a securities transaction.

Amended the By-Laws to include Puerto Rico, the Canal Zone, and the Virgin Islands in District 7.

Interpreted in detail the effect of suspension upon registered individuals.

Allowed members, under certain conditions, to use the Association's name on letterheads and other material.

Thus, the NASD serves as far more than a "self-regulating association". Its services to its members have been very important in the areas of public information, legislative action, and relations between its members.

Its Purposes

The Certificate of Incorporation of the Association gives the following as its purposes:

- To promote the investment banking and securities business;

- To standardize its principles and practices;

- To promote high standards of commercial honor and to promote among members observance of Federal and State securities laws;

- To provide a medium through which the membership may consult with governmental and other agencies;

- To cooperate with governmental authority in the solution of problems affecting this business and investors;

- To adopt and enforce rules of fair practice in the securities business;

- To promote just and equitable principles of trade for the protection of investors;

- To promote self-discipline among members; and

- To investigate and adjust grievances between members and between the public and members.

Organization and Administration

For administrative purposes, the NASD has divided the country into 13 districts with offices in major cities throughout the country. The members in each district elect the members of their own District Committee. This Committee, under the direction of the Board of Governors, administers broker/dealer affairs on the local level. The District Committee, or appointees thereof, sometimes sits as a District Business Conduct Committee in hearings upon alleged violations of the Rules of Fair Practice.

The District Committee, or its appointees, also constitutes the District Uniform Practice Committee for interpretations of the Uniform Practice Code.

In voting for members of the District Committee and for members of the Board of Governors, each member has one vote in the district in which its principal office is located. In addition, it has one vote in each district in which it has one or more branch offices. Regardless of the number of branches, no member has more than one vote in any one district.

Overall policy making and administration is provided by a 23-member Board of Governors. Some districts elect more than one Governor—all elect at least one. A total of 21 governors is elected by the membership. The Board itself elects the 22nd member from the underwriter members of the Association. The President is appointed by the Board and is *ex officio* the 23rd member of the Board. The term of office is three years for all the governors except the President, whose term is indefinite. One-third of the governors are elected each year so as to provide continuity of administration.

Rules of Fair Practice

As distinct from the Uniform Practice Code, discussed later, the Rules of Fair Practice deal with those aspects of the business which relate to *high standards of commercial honor and just and equitable practices* of trade. Indeed Section 1, Article III, of the Rules states "a member, in the conduct of his business, shall observe high standards of commercial honor and just and equitable practices of trade." The Uniform Practice Code, on the other hand, deals with the "nuts and bolts" of the business—covering such items as delivery dates, requirements for good delivery and the like.

From time to time the Board of Governors issues "interpretations" as to its own by-laws and rules as well as those of other regulatory bodies. Under Section 1 of the Rules of Fair Practice, there are two important interpretations:

Advertising. This interpretation sets standards for advertising, sales literature, market letters and recruiting advertisements. It requires any advertising to be filed for review at the Executive Office of the NASD in

Washington within five business days after its initial use (with certain exceptions). Members are required to maintain a separate file of such advertising material for three years from the date of each use.

Free-riding and Withholding. A bona fide public offering of a new issue is one, generally speaking, in which a dealer offers *all* of his allotment to the public. Failure to make such a public offering at the public offering price (the price stated in the prospectus) of a *hot issue* is known as *free-riding and withholding.* Such a failure when there is a great demand for an issue can be a factor in artificially raising prices. Not only is such a failure unethical in itself, but it impairs public confidence in the fairness of the securities business. A *hot issue* is one which on the first day of trading sells above (at a premium over) the public offering price.

Under the NASD's interpretation, if a member has:

1. Unfilled orders from the public for a security, or

2. Has failed to make a bona fide public offering of securities acquired by participation in the distribution,

it would be a violation of the Rules of Fair Practice to:

a. withhold any of the securities in the member's account;

b. sell any of the securities to any officer, director, partner, employee, or agent of the member, or to the members of the immediate family of any such person;

c. sell any of the securities to any senior officer of a bank, insurance company, or any other institutional type account, or to any person whose duties involve dealing in securities for such an institution, or to the immediate family of such persons;

d. sell any of the securities in which any person specified above has a beneficial interest;

e. sell any of the securities at or above the public offering price to any other broker or dealer.

There are certain exceptions under (d) and (e) above. A member may withhold for his own account, for example, part of an issue if he is prepared to demonstrate:

1. That the securities were withheld for bona fide investment in accordance with the member's normal investment practice (history of investment in an account), *and*

2. That the aggregate of the securities so withheld is insubstantial and not disproportionate in amount as compared with sales to members of the general public. Also, a member may sell part of the securities to another member to fill bona fide orders of public customers at the public offering price.

Recommendations to Customers. Known as the "suitability rule," Section 2 requires that in recommending to a customer the purchase, sale, or exchange of any security, a member shall have reasonable grounds for believing that the recommendation is *suitable* for such customer upon the basis of the facts, if any, disclosed by such customer as to his other security holdings, and as to his financial situation and needs.

(Under SECO [registration solely with the Securities and Exchange Commission], the "suitability" requirement extends to the obtaining in written form, and filing in the broker/dealer files, a statement by the customer as to his other security holdings and as to his financial situation and needs.)

Fair Dealing with Customers. An NASD policy statement under Section 2 points out several types of selling practices which have resulted in NASD disciplinary action against members and member salesmen. These include such activities as:

1. Recommending speculative low-priced securities in such a manner that certain investors with limited funds may be influenced to buy;

2. Excessive trading (defined as "churning") in a customer's account;

3. Trading in mutual fund shares. These securities, particularly on a short term basis, are not proper trading vehicles;

4. The setting up of fictitious accounts in order to execute transactions which otherwise would be prohibited;

5. Abuse of discretionary authority, unauthorized transactions, and misuse of customers' funds or securities;

6. Transactions by registered representatives which are concealed from their employer, or made outside their regular employment;

7. Recommending purchase of securities in amounts which are inconsistent with the customer's financial capacities.

Arranging Loans. The effect of the Securities Exchange Act of 1934 and of Regulation T of the Federal Reserve Board is to prohibit a broker/dealer from granting or arranging for credit to enable customers to buy or carry open-end investment company shares, because such shares are both *new issues* and are *unlisted.* Also, the arranging of loans or granting of credit appears to result in excessive activity (churning) in accounts of customers who borrow money to purchase investment company shares using the shares as collateral.

Charges for Services. Section 3 requires that any charges for services performed for customers be reasonable and not unfairly discriminatory between customers.

Fair Prices and Commissions. An interpretation under Sections 1 and 4 states "it shall be deemed conduct inconsistent with just and equitable practices of trade for a member to enter into any transaction with a customer in any security at any price not reasonably related to the current market price of the security or to charge a commission which is not reasonable."

This section deals with the broker/dealer in his two capacities: as a dealer (principal), his price to customers must be reasonably related to current market prices; as a broker (agent) he may not charge an unreasonable commission.

As an aid to broker/dealers in establishing reasonable mark-ups or commissions, the NASD promulgated what is known as the "5% Policy" as a guide. In successive interpretations it has been pointed out that:

1. The 5% Policy is a guide, not a rule;

2. Mark-ups may not be justified on the basis of excessive expenses;

3. The mark-up over the prevailing market price is the significant spread from the point of view of fairness of dealings with customers in principal transactions;

4. Determination of the fairness of mark-ups must be based on consideration of all relevant factors—percentage mark-up is only one of such factors.

Relevant Factors:

a. Type of security involved. For example, a higher percentage mark-up customarily applies to a common stock transaction than to a bond transaction of the same size.

b. Availability of the security in the market. In the case of an inactive security the cost and effort of buying or selling the security may have a bearing on the amount of mark-up justified.

c. Price of the security. The percentage mark-up generally decreases as the price of the security increases.

d. Amount of money involved. A small transaction may warrant a larger percentage mark-up to cover handling expenses.

e. Disclosure. While disclosure to the customer before the transaction does not of itself justify a mark-up or commission which is unfair or excessive in the light of all other circumstances, it is, nonetheless, a factor to be considered.

f. Pattern of mark-up. Each transaction must stand on its own. However, when reviewing transactions of a member, attention is paid to any apparent pattern of mark-ups.

g. Nature of member's business. There are differences among members in the services provided customers. To some degree the costs of these services and facilities are properly considered in determining fairness of mark-ups.

The 5% Policy applies to all securities handled in the over-the-counter market in these types of transactions:

1. A "riskless" or "simultaneous transaction." That is, a transaction in which a member buys a security to fill an order previously received from a customer for the same security.

2. A sale to a customer from inventory. Here the amount of mark-up should be determined on the basis of the prevailing market. The amount of profit or loss to the member due to market appreciation or depreciation of his inventory does not ordinarily enter into determination of the amount of fairness of the mark-up.

3. Purchase of a security from a customer. The mark-down must be reasonably related to the prevailing market price of the security.

4. Agency transactions. The commission charges must be fair in the light of all relevant circumstances.

5. Sale to or through a member, the proceeds of which are used to purchase other securities from or through the member. This is viewed as one transaction. In such cases the profit or commission on the liquidated securities must be taken into consideration in computing the mark-up on the securities purchased by the customer.

The NASD mark-up policy does not apply to the sale of securities where a prospectus or offering circular is required to be delivered and the securities are sold at the specific public offering price. Thus, the sale of new issues and of open-end investment company shares are not covered by the policy.

Under Section 5 members are prohibited from publishing or circulating fictitious quotations and fictitious reports of transactions in securities. *If nominal quotations are used or given, they shall be clearly stated or indicated to be only nominal quotations.*

Quotations released to the NASD for publication must be interdealer quotations, reflecting a representative interdealer spread, under the Quotations Policy of the Board of Governors. Quotations may not be released on a "no bid, asked only" basis—a bid price only may be released when appropriate in the judgment of the National Quotations Committee. Nominal quotations shall not be released. (The conditions under which nominal quotations may be used relate to material published or circulated by a member rather than through the NASD Quotations Committee.)

Under Section 6, members who furnish quotations must identify the nature of their quotations, if they do not represent firm prices. In some instances a dealer's quotations reported firm were found to be so qualified upon further inquiry as to constitute "backing away." Such backing away disrupts the normal operations of the market and is in violation of the Rules of Fair Practice.

Section 7 states "selling syndicate agreements or selling group agreements shall set forth the price at which the securities are to be sold to the public or the formula by which such price can be ascertained, and shall state clearly to whom and under what circumstances concessions, if any may be allowed."

It sometimes happens that a member of a selling syndicate or a selling group takes other securities in trade for the securities of the new issue. Section 8 requires such a member to purchase securities so taken in trade "at a fair market price at the time of purchase." Alternatively, the member may act as agent.

When a member is a paying agent, transfer agent, trustee or acting in any other fiduciary capacity, he may receive information as to the ownership of securities. Section 9 prohibits the member from making use of such information for the purpose of soliciting purchases, sales or exchanges except at the request and on behalf of the issuer.

Among other things, the Rules of Fair Practice are designed to protect each member from unethical practices on the part of another member. Section 10 prohibits a member from giving anything of value to any employee of another member without the latter's knowledge and consent. The term "giving" includes the meanings "permitting to be given" and "offering to give."

Section 11 prohibits the giving of anything of value to any person in connection with the publication or circulation of any matter which is intended to have an effect upon the market price of any security.

A broker/dealer is required to send a confirmation of a purchase or sale to his customer not later than the first business day following the date of the transaction. Section 12 requires that such confirmation indicate whether the member has acted as a broker (agent) or as a dealer (principal). If he has acted as a dealer, no further information need be given, except the net price to be paid to or received from the customer. However, when the member acts as a broker, he must show not only the price but the source and amount of his commissions or other remuneration received or to be received in connection with the transaction. Also, he must either furnish or offer to furnish the name of the other party to the transaction and the date and time of the transaction.

In "third market" transactions, the third market firms sometimes confirm to the retailing member plus or minus a differential. The retailing member may absorb this differential in his own commission. If he does so, he must disclose this to his customer in some such language as the following, "This security was purchased from a dealer who confirmed the transaction at a price of 20 plus $\frac{1}{8}$. However, the $\frac{1}{8}$, or $12.50, is paid by us out of our commission." Of course, if the retailer does not absorb the differential he must reveal this fact as well.

A member may be controlled by, may control, or may be under common control with the issuer of a security. When such is the case, Section 13 requires that the member buying or selling the security disclose in writing to his customer the existence of such control before the completion of the transaction.

A member participating or otherwise financially interested in a primary or secondary distribution is required to give his customer written notification of the extent of such participation or interest in any dealings in that security.

A discretionary account is one in which the customer gives the broker/ dealer discretion, either complete or within specified limits, as to the purchase and sale of securities, including selection, timing, and price to be paid or received. Section 15 provides that no member or registered representative shall exercise any discretionary power in a customer's account unless such customer has given prior written authorization to a stated individual or individuals and the account has been accepted in writing by the member. Discretionary orders must be reviewed at frequent intervals to detect and prevent transactions which are excessive in size or frequency in view of the financial resources and character of the account. Discretionary orders must be approved promptly and in writing. (Note: Transactions which are excessive in size or frequency constitute "churning," whether in a discretionary account or a regular account. "Excessive" is the key word—a trading account might have many transactions within a short period of time but this would not necessarily represent *excessive* activity.)

Sections 16 and 17 pertain to members participating in or who are financially interested in primary or secondary distributions. When such a distribution is of a security not traded on a national securities exchange, the member may make no representation that the security is being offered "at the market" unless there is an actual market independent of the dealer's own operation. To prevent the false appearance of a market, a member is specifically prohibited from arranging for a transaction in a security on a national securities exchange which would seek to establish a market price for a security in which the member is involved in a primary or secondary distribution.

Section 18 bans the use of manipulative, deceptive or other fraudulent devices to induce the purchase or sale of securities.

Section 19 refers to prohibited practices in the dealings of a member with a customer. Members are forbidden to make improper use of a customer's securities or funds, to lend a customer's securities without written authorization from the customer, or to pledge or hypothecate more of a customer's securities than is fair and reasonable in view of the indebtedness of the customer to the member unless the customer specifically authorizes it and designates the securities to be loaned. In addition, this section prohibits guarantees against loss and indicates the extent to which a member may share in the profits or losses in an account with a customer.

Hypothecation is the pledging of customers' securities as collateral for loans to brokers and dealers. SEC rules of hypothecation adopted under the Securities Exchange Act of 1934 have a number of important provisions which can be summarized as follows:

a. A broker or dealer may not hypothecate or pledge securities carried for the account of his customers in such a way as to permit the securities of one customer to be commingled with the securities of other customers unless he first obtains *the written consent of each such customer.*

b. A broker or dealer may not hypothecate or pledge securities carried for the account of his customers under a lien for a loan made to the broker or dealer in such a way as will permit such securities to be *commingled with the securities of any person other than a bona fide customer.*

c. A broker or dealer may not hypothecate securities carried for the account of his customers in such a way as to permit the liens or claims of pledges *to exceed the aggregate indebtedness of all such customers* in respect of securities carried for their account.

No member or person associated with a member shall guarantee a customer against loss either in the customer's account or in any specific transaction. Further, no member or person associated with a member shall share directly or indirectly in the profits or losses in a customer's account without prior written authorization from the member, and then only in direct proportion to the financial contributions made to such account by the member or person associated with a member (the direct proportionate share limitation does not apply to accounts of the immediate family).

Under Section 20 instalment purchases of securities by customers are prohibited.

Record Keeping. Each member is required, under Section 21, to keep and preserve books, accounts, records, memoranda, and correspondence in conformity with all applicable laws, rules and regulations of the SEC and the NASD.

Customer accounts must show at least the following:

1. name and address of the customer;

2. whether the customer is legally of age;

3. the signature of the registered representative introducing the account; and

4. the signature of the member, partner, officer, or manager accepting the account for the member.

If the customer is associated with or employed by another member, this fact must be noted.

In discretionary accounts the following is required in addition to the items given above:

1. the age (or approximate age) of the customer;

2. the occupation of the customer; and

3. the signature of each person authorized to exercise discretion in the account.

Each member is required to keep and preserve in each Office of Supervisory Jurisdiction a file of all written complaints of customers and the actions taken by the member on each complaint. A complaint is defined as "any written statement of a customer or any person acting on behalf of a customer alleging a grievance involving the activities of those persons under the control of the member in connection with the selection or execution of any transaction or the disposal of securities or funds of that customer."

A customer means any person who, in the regular course of a member's business, has cash or securities in the possession of the member. Section 22 requires a member to make available to inspection by any bona fide regular customer, upon request, its most recent balance sheet. Also, any member who is a party to an open transaction with another member (or who has on deposit cash or securities of another member) must furnish that other member a statement of its financial condition as disclosed in its most recently prepared balance sheet upon written request. (There is no requirement that either a customer or another dealer be given information about or access to a member's income [profit and loss] statement.)

Sections 23-25 are very important because they contain the provisions limiting discounts, concessions, and allowances to transactions between members. This means that *no NASD member is permitted to deal with any non-member broker or dealer or with anyone not engaged in the investment banking or securities business except at the same prices, for the same commissions or fees, and on the same terms and conditions as are accorded to the general public by the member.*

An interpretative memorandum, Transactions Between Members and Non-Members, expands on Sections 23, 24 and 25. The important point for the registered representative is that, with certain exceptions, members must deal with non-members on the same basis as they would deal with the public. The interpretation also indicates the extent of dealing permitted with foreign non-members and with members who have been suspended from the Association.

Section 26 applies exclusively to the activities of members in connection with the securities of open-end investment companies. There are a number of important restrictions of which the registered representative should be aware:

a. No member may purchase open-end investment company securities at a discount from the public offering price from the underwriter of the securities unless the underwriter is also a member.

b. No member who is an underwriter of the securities of an open-end investment company shall sell any such securities to any broker or dealer at any price other than the public offering price unless the broker or dealer is also a member and there is at the time of sale a sales agreement in effect between the parties.

c. The minimum price at which a member may purchase open-end investment company shares from the issuer is the net asset value.

d. The public offering price for open-end investment company securities normally is calculated twice daily, at 1 p.m. New York City time, and at the closing of trading on the New York Stock Exchange.

e. No member shall withhold placing customers' orders so as to profit the member from the withholding.

f. No member shall purchase open-end investment company securities from the underwriter other than for investment except for the purpose of covering purchase orders already received. This means that a dealer may not buy shares from the underwriter to hold in his inventory for resale at a profit.

g. Conditional orders may not be accepted by an underwriter except at a specific definite price.

Section 27 provides that each member shall establish, maintain, and enforce written procedures so as to supervise properly the activities of registered representatives and associated persons. In addition, each member must designate an Office of Supervisory Jurisdiction to be responsible for the review of the activities of registered representatives and associated persons of the member. A partner, officer, or manager must be designated in each OSJ to be responsible for this function. Each member is responsible for maintaining the records necessary for carrying out the member's supervisory procedures.

Each member must review and endorse in writing all transactions and correspondence pertaining to the solicitation or execution of any securities transaction. A member must review the activities of each office, periodically examine customer accounts to detect and prevent irregularities or abuses, and make annual inspections of each Office of Supervisory Jurisdiction.

Each member should ascertain by investigation the good character, business repute, qualifications and experience of any person prior to certifying his application to the Association.

Section 28 requires that if a registered representative seeks to open an account with another member that member must notify, promptly and in writing, the employer member. An employer member may require duplicate copies of confirmation or monthly statements of the executing member.

Code of Procedure

The Code of Procedure for Handling Complaints describes how complaints for alleged violations of the Rules of Fair Practice shall be handled. It makes clear that first jurisdiction is with the District Business Conduct Committee and that the role of the Board of Governors is that of an appellate and review board. It also gives the detailed procedures and practices to be observed in holding hearings.

Complaints may be filed (on forms provided by the Committee) by a customer, by another broker/dealer or by NASD examiners, through the District Business Conduct Committee. When a complaint is filed it is referred to the complained-against member for comment. The member must reply in writing within ten business days. Either he or the complainant may request a hearing or the District Business Conduct Committee may order a hearing on its own motion.

Upon a finding of a violation the District Business Conduct Committee may impose sanctions which include censure, fines, suspension or expulsion.

The National Business Conduct Committee reviews the proceedings of the District Committees and may recommend hearings before the Board of Governors. Also a member against whom sanctions have been imposed may appeal for a hearing before the Board. Unlike Review Courts, the Board of Governors has the authority not only to mitigate but also to increase sanctions imposed by a District Committee. The decision of the Board of Governors may be appealed to the SEC, and from the SEC to the Federal Courts.

In any case in which a District Business Conduct Committee is of the opinion that the facts are not in dispute, that a violation has occurred, and that the regular complaint procedure does not appear appropriate, the Committee may offer the respondent an opportunity to waive the hearing and accept summary complaint procedures. Under this procedure the penalty for all violations alleged cannot exceed censure and/or a fine of $500. The respondent may either accept the offer within 10 business days, or he may reject it. In the latter case, the regular complaint procedure will be followed.

Uniform Practice Code

As mentioned earlier, the Uniform Practice Code reflects the nuts and bolts of the business. It is designed to make uniform the customs, practices, and usages of trading techniques employed in the investment banking and securities businesses.

All over-the-counter transactions in securities *between members* are subject to the Uniform Practice Code, with two exceptions:

a. Transactions in exempt securities such as Government bonds and municipals, and

b. When the parties agree that certain or all sections of the Code shall not pertain.

Importantly, refusal to abide by rulings of the Uniform Practice Committee is considered conduct inconsistent with just and equitable practices of trade and therefore constitutes a violation of the Rules of Fair Practice.

Important provisions of the Uniform Practice Code deal with the following:

a. Deliveries. See page 1-42.

b. Transactions in stocks ex-dividend and ex-rights. It is important to know the definitions of delivery date, settlement date, record date and ex-dividend date and ex-rights date (see Glossary).

c. Confirmations must be exchanged on the day of a cash transaction or on or before the first full business day following any other type of transaction. This does not apply to transactions cleared through the National OTC Clearing Corporation.

d. Units of delivery (see page 1-43).

e. Assignments. Any registered security, to be a good delivery, must be accompanied by an assignment and a power of substitution (see page 1-43).

f. Due bills. When the transfer procedure occurs close to an ex-dividend date it frequently happens that the dividend is distributed to the wrong party. The due bill is a demand for payment to the other party, who should have it. When a security is sold shortly before it trades ex-dividend, ex-interest or ex-rights and is delivered on or before the record date it must be accompanied at delivery by a due bill for the distribution to be made.

g. Transfer fees. The party at whose instance a transfer of securities is made shall pay all service charges of the transfer agent.

h. Marking to the market. See page 1-44.

i. Buying-in, selling out. These sections deal with the procedures to be followed when a contract between a buyer and seller is not completed according to the original terms of the contract. When the seller is at fault, the buying-in procedure is initiated; when the buyer is at fault, the selling-out procedure is used. See "Buying-in," page 1-44.

j. Rights and warrants (rights to subscribe and stock purchase warrants). Unless otherwise specified, the unit of trading in rights is 100 rights, one for each share of issued stock. The unit of trading in warrants is 100 warrants, that is, warrants to purchase 100 shares of stock.

k. In addition:

1. Any endorsement, alteration or erasure on a certificate shall bear a guarantee acceptable to the transfer agent or registrar.

2. The certificate with either the assignment or power of substitution witnessed by a person since deceased is not good delivery.

3. A certificate executed by a person since deceased is not a good delivery.

REVIEW QUESTIONS

1. Contrast the definition of the term "wash sale," as once used in the speculative sense and as used now.

2. What was the expressed purpose of the Securities Act of 1933? What are the three elements in this purpose?

3. Do the provisions of the '33 Act apply to securities issued by or guaranteed by the Federal Government?

4. What is the requirement in the '33 Act as to registration of securities offered for sale?

5. When must a prospectus be delivered?

6. What is a "red herring" prospectus and how is it used?

7. What requirement of the NASD must be met with respect to correspondence?

8. What information must be contained in a prospectus?

9. Is a representative liable to civil suit for violation of rules in offering securities?

10. What liabilities are involved in interstate violation?

11. What does the '33 Act have to say with respect to the jurisdiction of the securities commission of a state?

12. When can injunctions and prosecutions under the Act be instituted by the SEC

13. If a registration statement and prospectus are filed with the SEC and allowed to become effective by the SEC does this imply SEC approval?

14. State the general purposes of the Securities Exchange Act of 1934?

15. What is meant by a "rigged market"? What are the results on a national scale of "rigged markets"?

16. What is a registered exchange?

17. Who establishes margin requirements?

18. What is the distinction between regulations T and U?

19. Before a dealer or broker may lend any of the securities held for a customer, what must the dealer do?

20. What is the purpose of corporate reports required by the SEC?

21. What are proxy rules? How do brokers vote proxies for shares held in their names for customers?

22. Must all brokers and dealers register with the SEC?

23. What is the purpose of the SEC's "net capital rule"?

24. Why are statements of ownership of stocks by "insiders" required?

25. What powers of suspension and revocation are granted to the SEC concerning registration of an exchange, its members and officers, or of a particular security?

26. Is a broker or dealer liable for the illegal act of his representatives?

27. What are Blue Sky laws?

28. What is the prudent man rule?

29. In a state with a legal list, does the list affect all trusts? Explain.

30. What are the important registration features of Section 15A (a) (relating to the NASD) of the SEC?

31. What are the effects of the loss of NASD registration?

32. Indicate the significant differences of dealers trading with members of an association and dealing with non-members.

33. What is the 5% mark up policy?

34. What is meant by "free riding"?

35. What are the purposes of the NASD as stated in its certificate of incorporation?

Chapter 6

Money
and
Capital

Economic
Trends

THE BASIS OF MONEY AND CREDIT

The Money System

Money is the "unit of value" by which goods and services are measured and the "medium of exchange" through which business is transacted. Money in use is more than the dollar bills and change commonly carried. It includes any generally accepted method of payment. In fact, well over 80 per cent of all money daily used in the United States consists of checks and drafts drawn on commercial banks. Such checks, which usually transfer money from one account to another, are actually an order and a promise to pay—and this "promise to pay" is the basis of the banking and credit system by which the government, banks, and the average citizen make their expenditures.

The three kinds of money now in circulation are all issued from different sources. The smallest amount, about two per cent of the total, is Treasury currency. This includes both coins and the "United States Notes" issued by the Treasury Department. Federal Reserve notes are released by the Federal Reserve System through commercial banks. And the commercial banks themselves create money by making loans on money deposited in them.

Such personal and business deposits are in the form of checking accounts and are called *demand deposits*, because commercial banks are the only banking institution which accepts deposits for withdrawal on demand.* The sum total of demand deposits becomes a pool from which a bank lends money. As the loans are repaid, or as the loan money is deposited in another bank, more money becomes available for other loans.

The money supply in the United States is always limited to some extent and Treasury currency is limited by statute. In addition, commercial banks are required by the Federal Reserve Board to keep on hand a varying reserve sum. The amount of the reserve (called the *required reserve*) depends on local and national economic conditions. It roughly varies from 11 to 20 per cent of time and demand deposits.

There are sources of loans other than commercial banks. Savings and loan associations, insurance companies, and savings banks, all of which transmit funds to borrowers from the accumulation of money deposited by savers, are part of the elaborate banking system. Like commercial banks, they pay interest to savers for the use of their money; all savings institutions actually lend money to borrowers from the sums they themselves have borrowed.

When used for short-term business loans, usually one year or less, the money (or credit) is called *commercial credit*. Long-term credit, carried over a longer period and required by businesses for the procurement of capital goods, is called *investment credit*.

The Money and Capital Markets

The interrelationship of money, credit, and banking exists every day everywhere in the United States. There are, however, a few square city blocks which contain the most concentrated business area in the country. From these blocks in the financial district of New York City known as Wall Street come decisions which affect, at least indirectly, the entire country. Most banks and financial institutions in the United States, as well as the Federal Reserve Bank of New York, are represented here.

Wall Street is the center of the *money market* which deals in all forms of short-term business debt obligations. Although these obligations are generally for five years or less, all such loans are broken down into periods

---

* Strictly speaking, other savings institutions such as savings banks and savings and loan associations *may* require advance notice of withdrawals. Practically speaking, they ordinarily do not. Such a requirement would be an admission of financial weakness.

of one year for formal accounting and amortizing purposes. *Current* assets or liabilities are these receivable or payable within twelve months.

The money market itself includes the *customer market* and the *organized market.*

The short-term business loans in the customer market are arranged directly with the lender, usually a commercial bank.

The organized market is more complicated. It encompasses a greater variety of short-term obligations including well-known governmental and corporate units of the very best credit standing. For example, the Federal government may require temporary loans of short duration or loans for refunding (refinancing) three-month bills (debts which mature after three months) or one-year certificates. Securities brokers and dealers may need funds for "inventories" of securities or to make margin loans to customers. The largest domestic corporations issue notes of up to six months duration for seasonal needs known as *commercial paper* which are really promissory notes without collateral that are issued in denominations or multiples of $5,000. (This form of lending has increased greatly since 1945.) State and local governments, awaiting periodic tax receipts, often issue *tax anticipation notes.* Banks who are temporarily short of their reserve requirement and exporters and importers also enter the organized market as borrowers.

Most of these funds are supplied by commercial banks. Other suppliers are financial corporations, business corporations, sometimes state and local governments who have excess funds for a short time, and foreign banks. All are either in the business of investing or may have surplus funds to invest. Last, and the most important, is the Federal Reserve System which enters the money market to expand or diminish the supply of money in commercial banks. As we shall see, the Federal Reserve exerts a powerful influence on the flow of money and hence on the contraction or expansion of business.

Unlike the money market, which deals only in short-term obligations of debt, the *capital market* deals in longer-term security issues of both debt and equity. The capital market includes bonds and preferred and common stocks, whether purchased by individuals or financial institutions. It also includes mortgage loans. In the capital market, what are called intermediate term funds (with a maturity of one to ten years) may best be had from government agencies, commercial banks, insurance companies, other corporations, and finance companies. Long-term funds (those with maturities in excess of ten years) may be secured from banks, insurance companies, pension funds, and sale and leaseback arrangements.

The demand for funds within the money and capital markets is highly competitive. Borrowers and lenders alike may choose among many debt and equity issues with respect to the length of time, purpose, and interest or yield. Competition for funds arises because money is fluid in the sense that it can easily flow from one form of investment into another. So, despite the distinctions between the markets, the money market alone closely interacts with:

(1) The capital market for *new issues* of stocks and bonds.

(2) The stock and bond markets, or *secondary capital market*, which comprise the stock exchanges, brokerage houses, and all the other agencies accessory to the securities markets.

(3) The foreign exchange market which includes all international financial dealings between the United States and the rest of the world.

(4) The commodity markets, such as the cotton and sugar exchanges.

(5) The insurance market.

(6) The shipping market.

Most financial institutions are rather limited in the types of investment they can make, or the sort of contracts they can accept in return for the surrender of their funds. They have fixed obligations to their depositors, policy holders, or pensioners. Because they cannot assume much risk they must place safety of principal before the possible rate of return. Thus their investment policies often are a stabilizing influence on business expansion. They will undertake conservative investments in business, agriculture, governmental obligations, and residential housing. Such institutions are:

(1) Commercial banks.

(2) Life insurance companies.

(3) Mutual savings banks.

(4) Fire, casualty and marine insurance companies.

(5) Corporate pension funds.

(6) State and local government retirement funds.

(7) Savings and loan associations.

Consumer financing has a higher element of risk—and therefore higher interest rates are charged by lending institutions. These are:

(1) Sales finance companies.

(2) Consumer finance companies.

(3) Credit unions.

(4) Industrial loan companies.

(5) Consumer credit departments of commercial banks.

Even though there are many financing agencies, there is one basic point to be understood about the money and capital markets. Through them the lifeblood of the economic system is transmitted: money and credit figuratively make the world go round.

Brokers' Loans

Brokers' loans are the loans made to securities firms. They should not be confused with the loans made by the firms to their customers. Normally the need for loans is caused primarily by demands for credit on margin accounts, but they are also required to carry inventories while making a market in a security or for participating in a distribution of securities.

The demand for brokers' loans is determined by the conditions of the securities markets. Generally, there will be increased borrowing in market rises and decreased borrowing in declines. This is caused to some degree by the increased number of margin accounts during a rise and vice versa.

Although there are many types of loan arrangements available (the number is limited only by the ingenuity of the parties), the principal one utilized is the call loan. This type is payable upon demand of either party. Most money for call loans comes from New York banks and trust companies, but an increasing amount is now coming from cities within the U.S., from Canada, and from individual corporations. Although these loans are payable on demand, they are rarely called and are usually renewed daily.

THE GOVERNMENT AS A BANKER

There are many factors which affect the money and capital markets. The variable influences of general economic conditions such as consumer prices and the rate of business failures, as well as the effect of Federal and state tax laws, combine with numerous other indicators to act on the money and capital markets.

Because of fluctuations in business and consumer spending and consumption, the aggregate demand for goods falls and rises. Thus investment spending, mostly based on the expectation of sales and profits, declines and rises. Also affecting the general state of the economy are the technological changes which may create new industries or make old ones obsolete. The 100-billion dollar Federal budgets, and the year-by-year shift and changes of amounts into defense, space, welfare, agriculture, veterans aid and other programs have had a very marked effect since the New Deal days of the 1930s.

All these forces, which combine to make up the general direction of the economy, have been likened to a train moving on a track which is not always smooth. Sometimes the going gets so rough that the train may be derailed and require major assistance to get started. At other times the train may slow down, and more power is needed to keep full steam. At all times, a watchful eye must be kept on the roadbed.

The Government attempts to ease the slow, rough passage of the low points of the business cycle by its monetary and fiscal management of the economy. *Fiscal management* refers to management of the national debt and to financing by the Federal government; these operations are under the Treasury Department. Changes in *fiscal policy* are made through revised tax laws and in the amount and direction of government spending.

Changes in *monetary policy* are made by the Federal Reserve System, which influences the flow of money and credit in the economy.

The Federal Reserve Board

The key to our managed economy is the Federal Reserve Board, a non-political body set up by the Federal Reserve Act of 1913 which reformed the banking and monetary system. By that time, the United States had over-grown the centralized financial structure that had developed since the Civil War. A flexible system to finance nationwide business was needed to move funds quickly and to use most efficiently all the monetary resources of the economy.

Consequently, 12 Federal Reserve Districts, most of which now have one or more branch offices for a total of 24, were established in the 12 most important business centers of the country. A Board of Governors, composed of seven members appointed by the President and confirmed by the Senate, governs the system. Members are appointed for 14 years with one term expiring every two years. One of the seven governors is named chairman.

Each Federal Reserve bank operates as a central bank and supervises the member commercial banks (totalling 14,000 throughout the country) in its district. Although each Federal Reserve bank has its own board of directors and its own group of officers headed by a president, its policies are largely determined by the Federal Reserve System's Board of Governors.

Basically, the Federal Reserve Board attempts to control the supply of currency and credit so that the amount of each is correctly proportioned to effect the best money and credit conditions for a stable, growing economy in which, as far as possible, the business cycle has been smoothed out.

Reserve Requirement

The Federal Reserve has the power to operate directly on the financial and money markets through its influence on the commercial banks. The total of their loans can be quickly affected by the Federal Reserve, since the "Fed" regulates their *reserve requirement*.

The reserve requirement for Federal Reserve member banks is an amount which must equal specified percentages of a bank's demand and time deposits. It must be kept on deposit with the district Federal Reserve bank. While the percentage of demand deposits is usually higher for New York and the larger money centers and lower for small city banks, the average is abount 16 per cent. To say this another way, every $6 demand deposit must be backed up by about $1 of reserve money.

The required reserve is a check on the ability of banks to create money (which is a power delegated by the Constitution). As banks increase their demand deposits, they can so increase their loans: but no more than is dictated by the reserve requirement. An increase in the required reserve results in a decrease in loan capacity with a consequent reduction in credit and a slowing of the economy.

As money is created by a loan, and as deposits, perhaps in other banks, are made with the loan money, there is a multiplying effect in that money gives birth to more money. If a $1,000 loan from a bank is deposited in another bank, this second bank may lend the deposit money less the reserve requirement. At 16 percent, then, the bank must keep $160 and may lend $840. If the $840 goes into a third bank, the additional bank must keep $134.40 on reserve and may lend $706.60. The process theoretically can continue through many banks and several times the amount of the original loan is added to available credit.

Regulation of Credit

There are five methods used by the Federal Reserve to regulate credit. Often more than one is used at a time.

(1) The Federal Reserve can change the *reserve requirement*. If indicators reveal that the growth of the economy is slowing, it lowers the required reserve and allows banks to lend a greater proportion of their dollars. By expanding the money supply, this action has the effect of lowering interest rates. Money becomes "easy." Through the multiplying effect, even a small change in the percentage of required reserve can result in a manifold percentage change in credit expansion. Similarly, the Board can raise the required reserve and contract credit.

(2) By its *lending to member banks*, the Reserve Bank creates additional reserves. Borrowing from the Reserve can be accomplished quickly but, like all borrowers, the member banks must pay interest which is *rediscounted*, or deducted in advance. Money is ordinarily borrowed because the funds of the borrowing bank are falling below the reserve requirement. The borrowing rates vary in order to make credit "elastic." By raising rates even the smallest fraction say from 3 per cent to $3\frac{1}{8}$ per cent, the Federal Reserve forces member banks to increase interest rates to their own customers. The consequent rise tends to discourage borrowing and, consequently, business activity. A decrease in the rates encourages borrowing and business activity. To simplify borrowing procedures, member banks usually use Government securities for collateral.

Paradoxically, member bank borrowing shows an inclination to rise when the discount rate is increased. Because credit is restricted, more banks need money. Nevertheless, changes in the discount rate, which are coordinated with general money operations in the open market, affect short-term loan rates. The discount rate is reviewed every fourteen days, sometimes more frequently, by the Board of Governors in Washington.

(3) *Open market operations* are the third major method by which the money supply can be expanded or contracted through Federal Reserve action. The Federal Open Market Committee will buy Government securities in the open market to combat a recessionary tendency in the economy. Its check to the securities dealer, when deposited in a bank, becomes money that has been directly pumped into the banking system and is available for loans. With the supply of loanable funds increased, interest rates are expected to go lower. The supposition is that business expansion and consumer buying are encouraged. By selling Treasury bonds directly to banks, or on the open market, which takes money out of the banking system, the supply of loanable funds is decreased; interest rates are expected to go up, and potential borrowers are expected to be discouraged.

Open market operations are carried on daily. They have become the most effective monetary control because their direct, unpublicized, continuous action has an immediate effect on the money supply.

(4) *Changes in margin requirements* are made by the Federal Reserve Board to exercise some degree of control over speculative activity in the stock market. If the Board believes that speculation is having an unwholesome effect on the market, it dampens such activity by raising margin requirements to as high as 100 per cent—or no margin lending at all. The Board lowers margin requirements when warranted by the economic climate. This power is given to the Federal Reserve by Section 7 of the Securities Exchange Act of 1934.

(5) *Moral suasion* is used by the Federal Reserve to "suggest" its attitude through warnings and speeches by Board members. Such pronouncements are usually directed at the officers and directors of member banks in the hope that corrective measures will be taken by them without the necessity of more direct action by the Federal Reserve.

The "defensive" functions of the Federal Reserve require constant reappraisal. Every three weeks the seven Board members and the twelve Reserve Bank presidents meet to determine monetary policy. The Board constantly projects several alternative courses of action (or, perhaps, inaction) into the future, and decides how to implement its decision through one or more of the methods outlined in the previous paragraphs.

The Federal Reserve Board sees the money market as more than a debt and credit institution. "Quite the reverse . . . it is primarily an aggregate of liquidity—an aggregate changing each day, and flowing into, out of, and across closely interlinked but competing alternative uses. From Liberty Street (office of the Federal Reserve Bank of New York) the market appears primarily as a mechanism for effecting a day-to-day balance in the demand

and supply of liquidity, in turn closely related to the demands and supplies of longer-term credit in the economy."*

ECONOMIC TRENDS AND THE BUSINESS CYCLE

The Inconsistent Economy

Over the course of decades, the American economy has fluctuated through periods of prospering businesses, full employment and production, rising consumption, and inflation. It has also undergone years when business failures have shown alarming increases, unemployment has been high, and deflation and lower price levels resulted from production unconsumed. The latter periods, the "recessions," are evidenced by five declines since 1945. They occurred in 1949, 1953-54, 1957-58, 1960, and 1962. For various reasons, the recessions have been of different lengths and severity and have affected differently the segments of the economy.

From 1962 through 1965 there was relative stability in the economy, with wages, prices, employment, and production all showing upward tendencies. Despite a great increase in the money in circulation, the cost of living increased only slightly; inflation and deflation do not always result immediately from changes in the business cycle.

However, the costs of the war in Vietnam coupled with the "guns and butter" approach resulted in a consumer demand in excess of production in late 1965. The expanding economy put such a demand on capital that money and credit were in short supply—money was "tight." Despite increased reserve requirements and increased interest rates, with a consequent reduction in loanable funds, employment continued at high levels. Labor demands on industry for higher wages were successful beyond certain "guide lines" set by the administration. Decrease in the purchasing power of the dollar in 1966 was greater than it had been for many years. With the increase in interest rates, bond prices declined and new bond issues carried ever-increasing yields. Uncertainly as to the war situation and taxes was reflected in marked decreases in stock prices, despite the inflationary trend. In many areas economic indicators, such as *housing starts*, showed sharp drops usually associated with a recessionary trend due to the "tight money" situation while the national income continued at record high levels. The period demonstrated, as many others have done, that economics is still far from being a science.

The errant business cycle in recessionary periods affects the men and women who cannot find jobs, the factories working at only 50 per cent capacity, and the farmers who receive less for an overabundance of crops. In addition, changes in the business cycle affect money markets in the rest

---

* *The Money Side of "The Street,"* Carl H. Madden, Federal Reserve Bank of New York, September 1959, page 80.

of the world and, just as directly, the attitude of our international friends, enemies, and the nations we seek as friends.

The problems of the business cycle are based on the classical law of supply and demand. When consumers are buying goods and services, when production is rising to meet consumer demand, and when Federal, state, and local governments are contracting for goods, we say that the aggregate demand is rising. A fall in the aggregate demand usually means that prices decline somewhat, farm surpluses increase, factories are idle, and fewer people are working.

Consequently, aggregate demand is limited by income which, in turn, is determined by the rate of production. Aggregate demand is further limited by the restrictions imposed upon income by taxes and by personal and business decisions not to invest and spend money.

The investment level of business is one of the most important factors influencing demand. It tends to fall when the businessman does not think investment will provide an adequate return. His lack of spending thus further curtails spending. On the other hand, business expansion will generate purchasing power which, in turn, will stimulate other purchasing.

Demand is also enhanced by technological changes. The use of plastics and frozen foods, for example, created new industries. New techniques in marketing, such as supermarkets, also increase demand.

The habits of consumer spending influence the type and amount of goods produced. An example is the automobile industry, which produced "finny" cars when large vehicles were the fashion but engineered and built compacts when the public showed a demand for foreign small cars.

Spending by the consumer is dictated by the level of "disposable" income—his pay after taxes have been deducted. Spending by the Government has a different type of effect than consumer spending. It is subject to decrease or increase at the will of the administration which can direct the method and timing of its expenditure. While consumer spending has been influenced by the course of the economy, government spending has in great measure influenced that course. Certainly, since New Deal days, a most important part of government domestic policy has been to attempt to keep the economy on an even growth level.

General Economic Indicators

The best efforts of the Federal government have not always kept the economy on the track. Fortunately, though, there are many statistical devices which are extremely sensitive to our changing economic system. Called *economic indicators*, they are enlisted to constantly measure the complicated trends of business.

Among the broadest of the economic indicators are the *national income and products accounts*. These figures attempt to answer: How much has been produced? Where does it go? How much is due to consumer spending? How much is due to government spending?

The sum of all incomes received by the people of the United States including indirect business taxes and depreciation of capital equipment is the *gross national product* or GNP. A rising or declining GNP is a gross measure of the increasing or decreasing total output of goods and services. The GNP is either spent and used up, invested to increase the number of goods and services, or exported abroad. The GNP is broken down as follows:

- Personal consumption expenditures (used up).
- Gross private domestic investment (invested).
- Net export of goods and services (exported).
- Government purchases of goods and services (used up).

Subtracting depreciation and indirect business taxes (such as those on alcohol and tobacco) from the gross national product gives another indicator known as *net national product*. When this is further reduced by the subtraction of sales taxes, the result is termed *national income*. This is a measure of income received by individuals and business. It includes:

- Compensation of employees.
- Proprietor's income.
- Rental income of persons.
- Corporate profits and inventory valuation adjustment.
- Net interest.

National income can also be classified by industry and by the sector of the economy in which it originates (e.g. manufacturing, government, agriculture).

Personal income is the national income *less* corporate profits and inventory valuation adjustments *plus* certain government payments to individuals such as social security and veterans pensions. Still another indicator is *disposable personal income* which is derived by subtracting personal tax payments to all governmental sources from personal income. This figure is extremely useful in analyzing mass purchasing power. For one thing, a significant part of disposable personal income does not go into the purchasing stream. It is deposited in savings accounts or invested in properties and securities. The per capita distribution of personal income and disposable personal income is obtained by dividing their totals by the total population.

All of these figures may be broken down in great detail and can be used to shed light on specific areas of the economy. They are published regularly by the U.S. Department of Commerce in its *Survey of Current Business*. They are also reported in the financial sections of the leading newspapers.

Statistical data on financial changes are published in the *Federal Reserve Bulletin*.

Specific Economic Indicators

Some other widely used economic indicators include:

● The Federal Reserve Board Index of Industrial Production. This index, published monthly, measures the amount of manufacturing and mining output. It is widely used to measure the trend of business conditions.

● The Bureau of Labor Statistics—Consumer Price Index. This monthly index measures the change in the price level of items bought by average white collar and blue collar employees living in certain large cities. It is widely used in studies in labor economics and in discussions of the "cost of living."

● Average workweek in manufacturing.

● Gross accession (hiring) rate in manufacturing.

● Layoff rate in manufacturing.

● New orders for durable goods manufacturing industries.

● Housing starts.

● Commercial and industrial building contracts.

● Net change in number of operating businesses.

● Business failures.

● Corporate profits after taxes.

● Changes in business inventories.

● Industrial raw materials spot market price index.

● Employment in non-agricultural establishments.

● Unemployment rate.

● Bank debits outside New York City.

● Retail sales.

● Plant and equipment expenditures.

● Manufacturers' inventories.

● Consumer installment debt.

● Bank interest rates on business loans.

Up-to-date figures covering most of the above indicators are found in *Economic Indicators*, a monthly publication of the Council of Economic Advisors. It is available at a nominal subscription rate from the Superintendent of Documents in Washington, D.C. It can be found in many business reference libraries. Charts of one or more of these and many other indicators are included almost daily in the financial sections of most large newspapers.

ECONOMIC CHANGES

The Three Types of Changes

All these data are valuable when they are compared over seasonal, yearly or longer periods. Retail sales show variations during seasons of the year; Christmas and Easter are periods of buying spurts, whereas the summer months usually show declines. Such changes are known as *seasonal changes*.

Over the course of years in the United States it is natural that data on steel production, farm products, oil, and other growth factors will show general trends. These are changes that occur over long periods of time and usually show significant growth when averaged over a period of years. Because of the long time span by which these indicators are measured, they are known as long-term changes or *secular* changes.

By eliminating seasonal variations and statistically averaging growth factors over the course of years, the economist is left with a graph of advances and declines in the economy. These are *cyclical* changes, commonly called the business cycle.

From a historical viewpoint, measurement of economic changes can shed light on economic behavior in the past—although, as we have indicated, all such changes differ and are often caused by differing forces. Theoretically speaking, however, the reasons for each upswing or dip in the cycle when known can help develop governmental policies to avoid crippling economic changes. This exactly is the purpose of the Federal Reserve System and the other governmental rules and regulations.

Long-Term Changes

The investor who purchases a security or property is interested in increasing, or at least conserving, its value. His investment future is equated with the future of the economy. He is interested in four basic factors: economic growth of the economy, inflation and deflation, population growth and trends, and the impact of government spending.

Economic Growth. Rising levels of output and consumption are an indication of growth which is measured by rising *real* levels of output and consumption and may be reflected in such figures as rising gross national product, industrial production, corporate profits, dividends, and stock prices.

The span of American history from the colonial days to the present is one of the greatest stories of economic growth on record. In the eighteenth century, the American colonies were little more than an economic backwater, with most of the population engaged in agriculture and trade. Today, the United States is the richest and most economically developed country on t¹ face of the earth.

The reasons are many. The United States is blessed with a more than ample supply of natural resources. There has always been a good supply of labor which possesses a level of productivity second to none. One good reason for American productivity is the amount of capital stock or equipment and machines for each industrial worker, which far exceeds the amount in other industrial nations. There have always been the resources for inexpensive natural power. And there are savings and investments: corporations reinvest part of their earnings in added facilities and research; individuals invest and save, and their money (in securities, savings and loan associations, and bank accounts) provides capital for business loans and investments.

In many parts of the world, where economic activity has been static because of lack of natural resources or their development, the problem of growth has become a key political and economic issue. The emerging nations of Africa, Asia, and Latin America know that without development, their relative position vis-a-vis the richer nations will decline.

Our potential for future growth is measured by the increasing population, technological changes, and growth of the saving and investing rate. It is limited by the strenuous demands placed on our natural resources and the possibility that such vital minerals as tin may require increasing import. And of course, a general war with or without a nuclear catastrophe, an economic disaster which the government with all its forces cannot avert, or just a change in the economic attitudes of the American worker are all possibilities which could put a sudden stop to economic growth. Countries all over the world look to the economic status of the United States. Our country no doubt has more influence on world economy than any other country, and its economic quiverings are quickly felt in world capitals.

Inflation and Deflation. There are many definitions and explanations of inflation. In general, inflation refers to a period of rising prices with a related decline in the buying power of the dollar. Deflation, by contrast, refers to a period of falling prices, which enhances the dollar's purchasing power.

The root cause of inflation and deflation lies in the change of total money spending in relation to the amount of goods and services offered for sale.

In the 1930's the United States was in a period of severe deflation. But by 1940, as the United States built up its war production, the cycle turned. More people were at work and their spending dollars forced up the price of goods and articles. During the war, because manufacture of consumer goods was severely cut back, the excess purchasing power had no place to go and so the government, to forestall a rampaging inflation, instituted price controls, high taxes, and sales of war bonds. These controls continued until the government felt it safe to relieve them.

During periods of inflation those with goods or claims on goods generally have a hedge against price rises. For example, stock prices will rise in value and in general keep pace with rising prices. This does not hold true for all stocks, however, nor does it hold true for all periods of inflation. On the other hand, holders of dollars or claims on fixed dollars (e.g., creditors such as bondholders) will not fare well because of the decline in the *purchasing power* of their holdings. Common stocks are one of the most widely used hedges against inflation. During periods of deflation, fixed dollar holdings rise in purchasing power.

Most economists feel that inflation will be with us for a long time to come. Some of the factors making for a high (and rising) price level include:

- Increasing population.
- High level of defense spending.
- Price supports, subsidies and tariffs.
- Inflexible or rising wage rates.
- Inflationary government monetary and fiscal policies.
- Escalator clauses in union contracts.

Population Trends. Population trends are significant factors in determining the business potential of many industries. For many types of goods and services, for example, foreseeable growth may occur only as a result of increased population.

In addition to the size of the population, it is important for many industries to know the age composition of the population and how it is changing. A company producing products for teenagers, for example, will be vitally interested in the present and projected size of the group. A company in the baby foods business will look to its particular age group and a company making geriatric products will carefully follow the trends of the senior age groups.

Of course, population in itself is not enough to guarantee a growing market. The population must also have the money to spend on various products and the desire to buy at the prices offered.

Nevertheless, in analyzing various types of consumer products, the potential investor would do well to take note of the relevant population trends.

Government Spending. There was a time when the government was looked upon as a far-off entity which engaged in delivering mail, collecting a few minor taxes and sending seeds to school children. As unreal as this image was half a century ago, it is even less real today.

Today, the Federal government is the largest single economic force in the land. It spends some 15 per cent of the gross national product, it employs a significant portion of the labor force, and it controls many varied aspects of business activity.

Much of the spending of the Federal Government goes for defense. These expenditures alone amount to almost 10 per cent of what the nation produces . . . the percentage rises in times of actual armed conflict. In addition to its direct impact on defense-related industries, it has been argued that defense spending stimulates other non-defense businesses by injecting money into the economy. It is argued also that technological innovations in defense have a "fall-out" effect similar to the ripples of a stone thrown in a pond, and thus stimulate non-defense businesses. It is said that a reduction in defense spending must lead to a major decline in overall economic activity.

Recent experience has shown that this is not the case. The 1963 and 1964 cutbacks in defense, mild as many economists claimed they were, did not lead to a business decline. Increased consumer spending, tax cuts and the projected use of the tax dollar for more public works and welfare programs had a beneficial effect on the economy.

Short-Term Changes

Business Cycles. Business cycles according to Burns and Mitchell, two of the leading students of the subject, are defined as:

". . . a type of fluctuation found in the aggregate economic activity of nations that organize their work mainly in business enterprises; a cycle consists of expansions occurring at about the same time in many economic activities, followed by similarly general recessions, contractions and revivals which merge into the expansion phase of the next cycle; this sequence of changes is recurrent but not periodic; in duration, business cycles vary from one year to ten or twelve years.

Burns outlines a business cycle as follows:

"Let us then take our stand at the bottom of a depression and watch events as they unfold. Production characteristically rises in the first segment of expansion, so do employment and money income; and so do commodity prices, imports, domestic trade, security transactions. Indeed, every series moves upward except bond yields and bankruptcies. In the second stage the broad advance continues, although it is checked at one point—the bond market where trading begins to decline. Bond prices join bond sales in the next stage; in other words, long term interest rates, which fell during the first half of expansion, begin to rise. In the final stretch of expansion, declines become fairly general in the financial sector. Share trading and stock prices move downward; the liabilities of business failures, which hitherto have been receding, move up again; security issues and construction contracts drop; the turnover of bank deposits slackens; and bank clearings in New York City, though not as yet in the interior, become smaller.

"These adverse developments soon engulf the economic system as a whole, and the next stage of the business cycle is the first stage of contraction

Production, employment, commodity prices, personal incomes, business profits . . . decline. Of course, the liabilities of business failures continue to rise which merely attests the sweep of depression. Long term interest rates also maintain their rise, but in the next stage the downward drift of bond prices ceases, that is the rise in long term interest rates is arrested. By the middle of contraction, bond sales join the upward movement of bond prices. More important still, the liabilities of business failures begin declining, which signifies that the liquidation of distressed business firms has passed its worst phase. These favorable developments are reinforced in the following stage. Share trading and prices revive; business incorporations, security issues and construction contracts move upward; money begins to turn over more rapidly; even total money payments expand. Before long the expansion spreads to production, employment, prices, money incomes and domestic trade. But this is already the initial stage of general expansion—the point at which our hurried observation of the business cycle started."*

No two business cycles are the same. Each cycle requires separate study since it behaves differently.

There are many theories which purport to account for the business cycle. A list of the leading theories includes:

- Monetary theories.
- Innovation theories.
- Psychological theories.
- Under-consumption theories.
- Over-investment theories.
- Sunspot and weather theories.

INTERNATIONAL ECONOMIC POLICY

The last two decades have seen a general loosening of the obstacles to trade between nations. High tariffs, trade quotas, restrictions on currency movements between countries, and independent economic and monetary policies that have divided countries have taken second place—in most instances—to a feeling of outward cooperation. The success of the European Common Market is the prize example of such amity.

The result has been to increase trade among the economically mature industrial countries. Unfortunately, the underdeveloped countries who have not been able to exploit fully their natural resources themselves, have suffered often. The policy of the United States has usually been to offer economic aid to such nations in an attempt to put them in the mainstream

---

* The above quotations are taken from *Business Cycle Indicators*, Vol. I, edited by Geoffrey H. Moore.

of world trade. Our success or failure is a matter for discussion by the experts.

It is essential for the stability of the world that the United States maintain its economic growth and power. A heavy depression here could reduce imports drastically and immediately affect foreign exporters. They in turn will produce less, and harm the economies of their own countries. Their people will, in turn, purchase less from the United States. Without doubt, the United States more than any other country has the power to make the world prosperous or poor.

As mentioned in Chapter 2, our international trade picture has been unbalanced for many years now. The difference of the excess of imports, foreign aid, and other capital outflows have been made up by gold from our gold reserves. Normally, the export of gold often indicates that a country is living beyond its means. It may have to restrict imports through tariff walls or devalue its currency (making its money worth less in relation to other currencies). It may also expand its exports of goods and services by lowering costs. This is often accomplished by devaluation which has the immediate effect of reducing the prices of goods sold in other countries.

Gold outflow makes the currency of a country less highly regarded. It often induces foreigners to dispose of investments, thus further limiting the import of money and goods. The entire depressing effect is felt in the sensitive barometers of the stock and bond prices of securities in the gold exporting country.

Countries with a weak financial structure now have several aids. The International Monetary Fund, founded at the end of World War II to establish a payments mechanism for countries with limited gold supplies, and the International Bank for Reconstruction and Development (the World Bank) which was later founded to supplement the IMF, have helped both the developed and underdeveloped countries.

The Export-Import Bank of Washington, "an independent agency of the United States," has since 1934 fostered trade of many nations on a strictly business basis.

REVIEW QUESTIONS

1. What is meant by the term "money"?
2. What kinds of money are in circulation?
3. What are "demand deposits"? How does their use expand the supply of money?
4. Name three types of organizations (in addition to commercial banks) which are part of the overall banking system of the United States.
5. Define: Commercial credit; investment credit.
6. Describe what is meant by "money market."
7. Distinguish between the "capital market" and the "money market."

8. Define: short-term funds; intermediate term funds; long-term funds.

9. Discuss different methods of borrowing equity capital.

10. State the sources of funds for short-term, intermediate term, and long-term borrowings.

11. Why must banks and insurance companies put safety of principal ahead of rate of return?

12. What are the sources of funds financing: a. business, b. agriculture, c. government, d. residential housing?

13. What are the sources of funds for consumer financing?

14. Discuss some of the general factors which can affect the money and capital markets.

15. Distinguish between the responsibilities and policies relating to fiscal management and to monetary management.

16. Why was the Federal Reserve Board organized? What are its objectives?

17. Describe briefly the organizational set-up of the Federal Reserve Board?

18. What methods are used by the FRB to regulate money and credit?

19. Define and discuss the purpose of the reserve requirement.

20. How often does the FRB meet to decide on changes of policy?

21. Discuss the factors which influence the demand for goods.

22. What are the statistical devices called which are used to measure the economic health of business?

23. What do the "national income and product accounts" measure?

24. Define "gross national product."

25. Distinguish between gross national product and national income.

26. What is a "sector of the economy"?

27. Distinguish among national income, personal income, and disposable personal income.

28. Where are national accounts figures published?

29. Name several additional economic indicators?

30. Define secular, seasonal, and cyclical changes.

31. What are some of the reasons for the industrial growth (or lack of industrial growth) of a country?

32. What is the root cause of inflation and deflation?

33. Give examples of hedges against inflation and against deflation.

34. What are the factors making for high and rising price levels?

35. Discuss the effects of population trends.

36. Describe the effects of government spending on GNP. What percentage of GNP does the Federal government spend?

37. Describe a business cycle.

38. What has been the result of the decreasing trade barriers among nations?

39. How can changes in U.S. economic growth and power affect the world?

40. What is the significance of international trade and gold flows?

Chapter 7

Market Analysis

INTRODUCTION

Any businessman knows from his daily experience whether business is good, bad, or indifferent, and whether the outlook is favorable or unfavorable. Many people in the securities business have a similar "feel" for near-term stock prices and trends, and attempt to read a meaning into the daily and weekly trading patterns and up-and-down behavior of the stock market.

An analysis of such internal stock market behavior which takes into account neither the long-range economic behavior of the economy nor the differing investment qualities of individual securities is called *market*, or *technical analysis*. To the market analyst, the most important consideration in the buying and selling of stocks is the daily—perhaps hourly—changes which develop within the market itself, and which he believes to cause the daily fluctuations in stock prices.

He is primarily a short-range trader who hopes to make a profit on small changes which appear insignificant to the investor who buys for the future. His approach to the stock market is geared to *when* to buy and sell, not *what* to buy and sell. Timing, not value, is the most important factor. He makes his profit (or loss) by trading securities at what he feels is the opportune moment. He may find many such moments to take small profits during a general upward trend because, in any period of rising prices, the increases will be highly irregular and will not occur every day. The pattern always zig-zags, with many small declines and advances superimposed on an advance of many months. The daily trend of a rising stock for a period of four weeks may look like this:

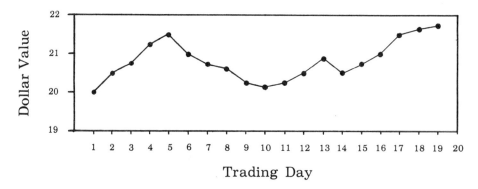

Theoretically, he has several opportunities to buy at the bottom of each small downward trend and sell at the top of the upward trend. If he can correctly forecast or guess the exact time to trade he may reap a larger profit than the man who holds the stock for the long run.

Needless to say, the odds of forecasting correctly are very, very low. Even the most astute floor trader can guess wrong, and in a period of declining prices, where the highs are never as high as the preceding high, and the lows are always lower, he could sustain consistent losses unless he halted trading in time and foresaw the beginning of the up-trend.

There have been a great many technical market theories developed over the years. Most appear to have been failures. Some, despite inherent weaknesses, have been successful. This chapter explores the better-known technical thories, the tools used in their analysis, and criticisms which have been advanced of them.

Market analysis is entirely different from *fundamental analysis*, which is for the long-term or lifetime investor. Fundamental analysis is based upon study of the fundamental economic, political, and sociological forces which are projected into an interpretation of current and future stock market activity. Such a study, more properly called *security analysis* when it analyzes *individual issues*, is discussed in the following two chapters.

TOOLS OF MARKET ANALYSIS

The most popular method which measures the trend and level of stock prices is a stock *average*, which is simply the average price of a group of representative stocks in various fields of industry and business. In recent years there has also been increasing use of the stock price *index* which is a more statistically refined method of determining the level and trend of prices. The market analyst follows both methods closely as he measures overall market action.

Stock Price Averages

All stock price averages have certain similarities. The representative issues included are usually subdivided into categories. Industrial stocks and rail stocks are the most common groupings. The more complex averages, such as the Dow-Jones Average, include a category for public utilities.

The Dow-Jones average is computed hourly while most of the other averages are computed daily. Adding the prices of the last hourly or daily sale of each stock and dividing the total by a standardized divisor gives the average. The average closing price of the day and usually the high and low extremes of the trading range are published.

Averages also face problems in computation. The most serious is the need to adjust for stock splits. For example, assume an average of three stocks, X, Y, and Z:

Stock	*Price*
X	25
Y	20
Z	45
	90
Average	30

If stock Z were split three-for-one, its price would fall to 15. The total of the three stocks would then be 60. Dividing by three results in an average of 20—or a decline of 33⅓ percent. Yet the average has not really lost 10 points.

Two acceptable adjustments are used to overcome this inconsistency. The first uses a *multiplier* to bring the new price of stock Z to its prior ratio in the average. Here stock Z is multiplied by three. The New York Times averages began using this system in 1925. Its one drawback is that it leads to rather large multipliers—du Pont's price is currently being multiplied by 14.

The second (used by the Dow-Jones average since 1928) is called the *constant divisor*. This method changes the divisor of the average so that its level remains unchanged. The constant divisor is the figure which divides into the new aggregate of prices to yield the same level as that reported on the old on the day before the new divisor was put into use. The formula is:

$$\text{Constant Divisor} = \frac{\text{New Price Aggregate}}{\text{Old Average Price}}$$

This formula applied to our example results in a constant divisor of two.

$$\text{Constant Divisor} = \frac{60}{30} = 2.$$

The new price aggregate of 60 does not change the new average price of 30 which is the same as the pre-split level. The trend is uninterrupted by the three-for-one split. Until another split occurs, the same (constant) divisor will be used . . . the divisor is "constant" only between changes.

Other problems are involved in computing averages when the size of the list is changed and substitutions are made. Occasionally, an average will drop one stock and add another. The issue eliminated may have been absorbed in a merger or consolidation, or have declined in importance to such an extent that it is no longer considered a representative issue.

There are two solutions for making substitutions. One is to select another stock in the same industry which sells at the same price as the old issue. Any price differential can be adjusted by adding to or subtracting from the average a certain number of dollars. This is not sound statistical procedure but it is satisfactory for rough accuracy. The second method is to adjust the divisor. Few averages have changed the size of their list and so this problem seldom arises; however, when it happens, either the entire average must be recomputed or a new divisor used.

The Dow-Jones Averages are the most widely used. Their existence extends back as far as 1884. They are widely quoted in the press and enjoy the best distribution of any averages in use today. Their acceptance stems also from a favored position, not enjoyed by any other averages. They are associated with the Dow Theory, a well-known theory of market analysis which is discussed in greater detail later in this chapter. Followers of the theory feel that only the Dow-Jones averages can be used for its interpretation.

The original Dow-Jones Averages were the handiwork of Charles Dow, who founded the Dow-Jones Company which publishes the *Wall Street Journal*. Its first list consisted of 11 stocks. Almost all were rails, the leading stocks of the time. In 1897, the original 11-stock average was converted into a 20-stock rail average. This number has been retained to the present. Today's rail average consists of the following stocks:

Atchison, Topeka & Santa Fe
Atlantic Coast Line
Baltimore & Ohio
Canadian Pacific
Chesapeake & Ohio
Chicago, Rock Island & Pacific
Delaware & Hudson
Erie-Lackawanna
Great Northern
Illinois Central
Kansas City Southern
Louisville & Nashville
New York Central
New York, Chicago & St. Louis
New York, New Haven & Hartford
Norfolk & Western
Pennsylvania
Southern Railway
Southern Pacific
Union Pacific

In 1897, the first Dow-Jones *industrial* average of 11 stocks was published. In 1916, a number of changes were made and the list was increased to 20 stocks. Between 1916 and 1928, the average was expanded to 30 stocks, the number it now has. The current Dow-Jones industrial average includes:

Allied Chemical	International Nickel
Alcoa	International Paper
American Can	Johns-Manville
American T. & T.	Owens-Illinois Glass
American Tobacco	Procter & Gamble
Anaconda	Sears Roebuck
Bethlehem Steel	Standard Oil of California
Chrysler	Standard Oil of New Jersey
Du Pont	Swift & Co.
Eastman Kodak	Texaco
General Electric	Union Carbide
General Foods	United Aircraft
General Motors	U.S. Steel
Goodyear	Westinghouse
International Harvester	Woolworth

The first *utility* average was published in 1928. It consisted of 18 stocks, which was later increased to 20. It was reduced to its present level of 15 in 1938. Following are the stocks in the Dow-Jones utility average:

American Electric Power	Niagara Mohawk Power
Commonwealth Edison	Pacific Gas & Electric
Cleveland Electric	Panhandle Eastern Pipeline
Columbia Gas System	People Gas
Consolidated Edison	Philadephia Electric
Consolidated Natural Gas	Public Service Electric & Gas
Detroit Edison	Southern California Edison
Houston Light & Power	

Significant criticisms have been leveled against the Dow-Jones averages, especially the industrial average.

The first is that the samples of stock used are too small to be truly representative. The 30 stocks in the industrial average are only about two per cent of all industrial issues traded on the New York Stock Exchange.

Second, the issues which are used are themselves not representative of the overall types listed on the Exchange today. The industrial average is composed entirely of high-grade, high-priced stock. Yet since the end of World War II there have been cycles in which low-priced issues or so-called growth companies dominated the market to the exclusion of the higher grade stocks. Critics claim that the industrial average does not truly represent a greatly expanding, widely-diversified number of listed companies.

Another widely quoted criticism of the Dow-Jones averages and indeed, of all averages, is their lack of weighting. The higher-priced a stock, the more weight it carries in an average. This factor also does not take into consideration either the size of the company or its importance, since a small company with a high-priced stock whose high price is entirely due to a small capitalization is accorded more importance than a lower-priced giant company with a large capitalization. Many critics contend that a sounder method of measuring stock prices would weigh each stock on the basis of its relative importance in the market.

A fourth criticism is that the averages are inflated. In December 1966 the industrial average was over 800, approximately twice as high as it was at the end of 1957, and many times the price of the average stock in the index. On a point basis it would appear that small percentage changes in the industrial average result in unrealistic movements in the average. An eight-point drop is just a one per cent drop in value.

A final criticism is that the averages are subject to unfortunate influences because of stock splits. Each time a stock is split, its influence on the overall average drops in direct ratio to the split. This situation tends to minimize the gains made by the more successful companies which split their stock frequently. Over a period of time, therefore, the average fails to rise as rapidly as it might otherwise. The divisor corrects for a split at the time the split occurs, but does not adequately compensate thereafter for the reduced per-share value.

The New York Times Averages consist of a rail average of 25 leading railroad stocks and an industrial average of 25 high-grade issues including one utility, the American Telephone & Telegraph Company.* These averages have many of the same advantages and weaknesses as the Dow-Jones averages. The only major difference is the multiplier system to adjust for stock splits.

The New York Herald Tribune Averages offered a wider sampling of issues than either the Dow-Jones or New York Times Averages. They were composed of nine separate sub-groups of industrials and two sub-groups of rails. The industrial average contained 70 industrials which were broken down into the following sub-groups:

15 Manufacturing issues	4 Equipments
10 Oils	5 Stores
8 Public Utilities	10 Motors
6 Steels	5 Foods
7 Coppers	

The rail average contained 30 issues broken down into 20 grade A rails and 10 grade B issues. The paper also had a separate aircraft average of ten stocks. This newspaper is no longer published.

---

* Note that this utility is also included in the Dow-Jones industrial average.

Although these averages can be criticized on the same general basis as the Dow-Jones averages, they still give a more comprehensive sampling of the stocks on the Exchange.

Somewhat similar to the Dow-Jones averages are the *Associated Press Averages* of 60 stocks, containing 30 industrials, 15 rails, and 15 public utilities.

The 200-stock *Moody Average,* compiled by the Moody Service, is one of the most inclusive averages. It is composed of 125 industrials, 25 public utilities, 25 rails, 15 banks, and 10 insurance stocks.

All these services compile similar statistics for bonds.

Stock Price Indexes

Stock price indexes, a statistically more refined method of measuring changes in stock price levels than averages, are not used as frequently nor are they given as much publicity as averages.

There seems to be very little difference in the way indexes or averages reflect market changes. For the short run, both demonstrate market changes, although the indexes, with a much larger sampling of stocks, will give a truer indication of long-term market moves. They differ from averages in four basic ways.

(1) They employ a base period from which price changes are measured. The base period used varies from index to index. Standard & Poor's index, for instance, uses a base period of an average of the years 1941-43 which is given a value of 10.

(2) They are weighted by various methods. A common one is the number of shares outstanding for each stock multiplied by the market value per share.

(3) They usually include a larger sampling of issues than the averages. Standard & Poor's index, for instance, includes 500 stocks.

(4) They employ precise statistical formulas to eliminate the statistical weaknesses found in averages.

Standard & Poor's Index is one of the best known and statistically refined index in use today. It is based on 500 stocks—425 industrials, 25 railroads, and 50 utilities. This broad sampling is about 90 per cent of the value of New York Stock Exchange issues held by investors. For that reason, as well as its statistical accuracy, it has been considered by many to be the most comprehensive and well-designed index available. Since 1957, this index has been reported hourly.

NYSE Common Stock Index. To provide the investing public and the Exchange Community with a comprehensive measure of NYSE market price trends, the Exchange, on July 14, 1966, inaugurated a new investor service—the NYSE Common Stock Index.

Developed by Exchange research, the Index covers price movements of all common stocks listed on the Big Board—reflecting the trend in stock prices day-to-day, hour-to-hour and even minute-to-minute. To provide historical continuity, the Index has been calculated on a daily basis back to May 28, 1964—and on a weekly basis back to January 7, 1939, based on the Index of 300 stocks published between those dates by the SEC.

Point changes in the NYSE Index, which are printed on the ticker tape each half-hour, are also converted to dollars and cents, providing a readily understandable measure of the changes in the average price of listed stocks. The Index is also readily available on all leading stock interrogation devices.

The Exchange's Market Data System is programmed to compute the composite index plus a separate index for each of four groups of stocks: industrial, transportation, utility and finance. In November, this information was supplemented by the addition of daily and weekly high and low data on the composite index and the four sub-groups.

The Exchange continues to believe that investors should concern themselves primarily with the prices of individual securities. However, computer technology has now made possible, for the first time, an all-inclusive, official NYSE market index. This is becoming increasingly useful to Exchange Community personnel—to research analysts seeking to evaluate the market's performance, and to registered representatives dealing with the public. Beyond the Exchange Community, a number of professional publications have begun carrying the Index.

There are two other indexes available to investors. The *SEC Index* was introduced by the Securities and Exchange Commission in 1951 and is composed of 300 stocks broken down into five main classifications: manufacturing; transportation; utilities; trade, finance and service; and mining. The *Merrill Lynch Index* publishes an index of 540 stocks which is broken down into 112 classifications.

FORECASTING METHODS

The Dow Theory

An index or an average is a tool of the market analyst. Neither has any inherent interpretive value although they can be used as the basis for theories which attempt to forecast. The best known is the Dow Theory which is based on its interpretation of the Dow-Jones industrial and rail averages.

The foundation for the Dow Theory was a series of editorials written for *The Wall Street Journal* by Charles Dow between 1900 and 1902. These editorials dealt with the movement of security prices but did not attempt to define an absolute theory.

After Dow's death in 1902, William P. Hamilton, who succeeded Dow as editor of the *Journal*, and S. A. Nelson, a financial reporter in Wall Street, evolved Dow's original editorials into a cohesive theory. In 1902, Nelson wrote a book entitled *The A. B. C. of Speculation* in which he stated the principle of "Dow's Theory" (later changed to the Dow Theory). Hamilton wrote editorials for the *Journal* clarifying the theory and, in 1922, he incorporated his studies into a book, *The Stock Market Barometer*. After Hamilton's death, a third Dow Theory scholar, Robert Rhea, wrote an exhaustive study called *The Dow Theory*. These three books, as well as Dow and Hamilton's original editorials, form the cornerstone of the theory. The *Journal* no longer carries editorials interpreting market action in the light of the theory and, while there are several services which purport to forecast on the basis of the theory, none has added to previous concepts of the subject.

There are several important points to bear in mind while studying the theory. Dow never intended it as a means of forecasting stock prices. Both he and Hamilton believed, rather, that it could be used to forecast changes in business activity. While Hamilton seems to have been convinced that the theory could forecast changes in the trend of stock prices, he cautioned against people considering it a "get-rich-quick" scheme. The prime objective of the Dow Theory is to tell when either a bull or bear market has terminated. It was not meant to forecast how long that market would last since Hamilton, in particular, believed that the duration of cycles is irregular.

The system of interpretation worked out by Dow and his followers falls into several parts: the theory of the *three movements of the market;* the theory of *corroboration of the averages;* the theory of *confirmation* by either "lines" or by new highs and lows.

Three Movements. The theory is based on the premise that there are three movements present and operating simultaneously at all times in the market. These are:

(1) The *primary movement*, which is the long term trend of a major bull or bear market. This is the most important movement. The purpose of the theory is to forecast a change in the direction of this movement. According to the theory, the primary movement of stock prices continues in the same direction until there is an indication of a change. Dow believed that the length of this trend could continue anywhere from one to four years. Hamilton concluded that the average bull market ran 27 months and the average bear market ran 15.

(2) The primary trend is interrupted periodically by *secondary movements*. These are major rallies in primary bear markets or major reactions in primary bull markets. These movements are both normal and necessary. Dow believed that they normally run from two weeks to a month or more and retrace about three-eighths of the preceding rise or fall of the primary trend. Rhea, on the other hand, concluded that these reactions usually run anywhere from three weeks to three months and that they retrace from 33 to 66 per cent of the primary price change of the last preceding secondary reaction.

(3) The third movement is *daily fluctuations* in stock prices. Dow theorists regard this as inconsequential.

Corroboration of Rails and Industrials. A basic premise of the theory is that a primary movement in the industrial average is never established until there is a similar move in the rail average. The theory held that the averages are an index of stock market movements which are, in turn, the sum of every influence that plays on the market. When all fundamental forces are strong, both the industrials and rails averages will advance together.

Confirmation. A primary trend remains intact as long as both the industrial and rail average confirm it by either (1) breaking out of a *line* or (2) making *new highs and/or lows*. According to the theory, the primary trend is still in force when each rise in a bull market or decline in a bear market exceeds the previous peak or trough. In other words, if the industrial average advances from 700 to 800 and at that point a secondary reaction sets in, which takes the average back to 760, the next move upward must exceed 800 for the primary uptrend to be confirmed. This action must also be corroborated by the rail average. It also frequently happens that for weeks at a time, after a long rise or decline in the market, the fluctuations in the averages are confined to a very limited range. On the chart there is neither an upward or downward trend. The theory holds that this "line" signifies either accumulation or distribution and that if the averages break out on the upper side of the narrow zone, the market will advance strongly before its direction is reversed. On the other hand if the average breaks on the downside of the zone, and is corroborated, then the downward trend will continue for a relatively large number of points in the averages.

Evaluation Of The Dow Theory

There have been many criticisms of the Dow Theory. Most are based on the fact that vast economic changes which have taken place in recent years have out-moded the theory. Rails, once dominant in the stock market and in 1900 the strongest industrial group in the country, have lost their signficance. Because their price movements may no longer corroborate the industrial average, some traders use only the industrial average as an indicator.

One of the most famous of all studies of the Dow theory by an economist, Alfred Cowles III, showed that the Dow forecasts from 1904 through 1929 had less than a 50 per cent chance of being right.

Probably the greatest success of the Dow theory came in 1929 when on October 25 Hamilton forecast that a bear market was beginning. An investor who had immediately followed the theory and sold all his holdings would have lost only 22 per cent of the total final industrial loss and only 12 per cent of the final decline in the rail average.

In October 1957, after an already considerable decline, the industrials confirmed the bear market signal sounded by the rails in August. The Dow theory then did not forecast a bull market until November 1958, when the industrials had climbed about 75 per cent towards the next high mark.

In March 1960 the industrial and rail averages verified a bear market. However, even though the industrials had risen almost 30 per cent by the end of the next year, the Dow had not forecast a bull market.

Other criticisms revolve about the slowness and uncertainty of the theory. It can not say when a top or a bottom has been reached. Just what the yardsticks are that indicate confirmations of trends are vague.

It must be remembered, however, that Dow's work was a pioneering effort which stimulated others to examine the functioning of the market. To a degree, a great deal of Dow's original work is incorporated in much of later theory, such as the chart theory, which we discuss in this chapter. In any event, there is still no market theory which is as widely followed and quoted as is the Dow theory. For this last reason alone, it deserves attention.

TECHNICAL FACTORS

The technical analyst, who is interested in the short run, looks to the actions of the market itself for his decisions. The technical factors he closely follows determine the relative short-term strength or weakness of the market. There are many such factors:

Breadth of the Market refers to the number of issues traded. At the end of each trading day, the total number of issues traded, the number of issues that advanced, declined, and remained the same are reported. Many technical analysts devise statistical measures from these raw figures which are supposed to measure the trend of the supply and demand for all stocks, rather than for just a handful of high quality issues. These measures are known as breadth indexes.

An increase in the number of issues advancing in a bull market is considered a favorable sign. Conversely an increase in the number of issues declining in a bear market is considered an unfavorable situation. The technical analyst attempts to measure these forces over a period of time and to correlate breadth with other technical indicators.

Volume is perhaps the most popular technical yardstick. Its importance lies in the market axiom "volume goes with the trend." Expanding volume in a primary bull market and declining volume in secondary reactions is considered a strong sign. In a bear market, volume should increase on strong downward trends and contract on rallies. An upward trend is technically weak when volume fails to expand on the upside and increases on reactions. Heavy volume after an extended price movement is supposed to indicate the end of a trend and a turning point in prices. The market term *selling climax* stems from this phenomenon.

Short Interest, or the activity of short sellers, is watched by many technical analysts. The theory is that a large short interest makes the market technically strong because short sellers must eventually cover their positions and thus bring a buying emphasis back into the market. Conversely, a small short interest makes the market weak because there is no underlying support from short covering.

There are three main criticisms leveled against the adherents of the short interest theory. First, the amount of short sales is quite small in relation to total volume. Second, a great deal of short selling is not speculative. Last, and most conclusive, the amount of short selling and the movements of stock prices seem to have very little in common.

Odd Lot Behavior refers to the buying and selling of the odd-lotters, usually the small investor, who deal in units of less than 100 shares. Each morning the odd-lot figures are reported for the previous trading day. The raw data consist of odd-lot purchases, sales, short sales and total odd-lot shares traded. Garfield A. Drew has done more than any other technical analyst to promulgate this theory.

Drew stated that the market can be forecast by watching for trends in odd-lot buying on balance and selling on balance. Drew's theory is not based on the axiom that the public is always wrong, but on the theory that the small, non-professional investing class will be selling on balance more than they will be buying at market bottoms and buying on balance more than they are selling at market tops. From a technical analyst's standpoint one particular day's action is not significant. It is the trend that is indicative of odd-lot sentiment.

Low and High-Priced Stocks. The movements of low-priced stocks compared or contrasted with those of high-priced stocks have given rise to still another theory. In a rising market, low-priced stocks will show better percentage gains than will the higher-priced issues because stocks selling at low prices offer more temptation to the speculatively-inclined public.

Several services regularly publish indexes of low-priced stocks which the technical analyst can compare with the better grade stock indexes. Others watch the average price of the ten most active issues each day which are reported by most newspapers.

There seems to be some validity to this theory. During market rises of the last 40 years the low-priced stocks of good quality have a better performance record than similar high-priced stocks.

New Highs and Lows are reported at the end of each day. These totals represent the number of stocks which have achieved new high or low prices over the year's trading. Because they indicate a trend of technical strength or weakness for the entire trading list—as does market breadth—many analysts watch these figures closely.

Reaction to News. Often, but not always, the market will be influenced by national or world events. Good news should buoy the market, bad news should deflate it. When the averages do not point upward after good news it is thought that the market is technically weak. When the averages do not decline after bad news, the market is technically strong. That such technical reactions do not always occur is demonstrated by the fact that the market very often discounts expected news far ahead of its actual happening.

Seasonal Movements. The summer months bring a "traditional" rise in stock prices. Then there usually is a decline in the fall. For a majority of years, these movements are more or less true. There is one seasonal movement which is true nine years out of ten: the stock market advances between Christmas and New Year's Day . . . it did not do so in 1965.

Technical Analysis of Individual Stocks

The isolation of particular stocks which might show changes from the general behavior pattern of the stock market is most difficult. It can be most confusing to the uninitiated in chart and tape reading. To the technical analyst, charts revealing daily stock behavior and the small price fluctuations in each stock revealed by the ticker tape are principal methods.

By watching and analyzing the short-term patterns traced, the analyst hopes to see an indication of future movements and to be able to pick the correct stocks to buy and sell. He may possibly use the Dow-Jones average for an overall behavior pattern but, unlike the long-term Dow theorist, he will not stand aloof until the rails and industrials have indicated a market primary trend. The chart reader will attempt to isolate individual stocks that are acting much better or worse than the market, without regard for the signs of overall price action.

Tape Reading. The tape reader spends all of his time watching and analyzing the fluctuations of prices on the tape. For the most part, he picks the active market leaders and confines his trading to them. He perfers to close out his trades at the end of each day. He limits his losses to a minimum and is always ready to make a turn if the tape gives the signal that the market is about to reverse itself. His aim is for small profits, smaller losses and a large turnover. He is interested in the longer 5 to 15 point swings only as giving the general framework within which he must operate. His theory is identical to that of the chart reader because he believes that the price of a stock is dependent solely upon the law of supply and demand and that no other facts or information are necessary in forecasting prices since they themselves contain all the knowledge of all people operating in the market. He believes implicitly in the theory that the tape immediately records transactions of those who know the facts before the news is generally available. In short, the tape reveals everything.

Chart Reading. The principle difference between the simon-pure tape reader and the chart reader is that the tape reader follows the course of the market mentally. The chart reader, on the other hand, records in a regular fashion the fluctuations in the price of a stock, and interprets and forecasts from these charts. Because of this, the tape reader can only concentrate on a handful of issues at any one time. A chartist, on the other hand, may make and compare hundreds of charts in a day. While this is more time consuming, it gives him a potentially broader trading scope.

A chart is merely a graphic history of a stock's price action. It can be kept on a daily, weekly, or monthly basis. Weekly and monthly charts are available in several modestly priced services but the general rules of chart interpretation have not concentrated on their usage. Daily charts are more frequently used by traders and it is upon these that most students concentrate. It must be pointed out that each trader has his own preferences as to methods. There are no hard and fast rules applicable to interpreting price movements by the use of charts. This section concentrates, however, on some of the widely used and accepted terms of chart reading rather than detailed explanation of the many ramifications involved in the subject. For further study, R. D. Edwards and John Magee's *Technical Analysis of Stock Trends* is comprehensive.

There are two basic types of stock charts—*line charts* and *point and figure charts*. A line chart is constructed on an arithmetic or semi-logarithmic scale. More sophisticated investors prefer the latter since they show rates of change instead of differences in size. When arithmetic paper is used, absolute values are represented by equal spaces. In other words, on equidistant horizontal lines one would find stocks priced at $10, $20, $30, etc. The value of semi-logarithmic charts is that they place price movement in a more valid perspective. The percentage change from $10 to $20 is 100 per cent just as a change from $1 to $2 or from $100 to $200 is. On semi-log paper the distance from $20-$40 is the same as from $40-$80 since both represent changes of 100 per cent. On arithmetic paper these percentage differences are obscured.

Point and figure charts are viewed with favor by certain analysts. A point and figure chart differs from a line chart in that rather than plotting prices over a given period in the form of a continuous line, changes are plotted by a series of x's. The theory of point and figure charting is to ignore all minor fluctuations and to concentrate on the development of patterns indicating major price movements. This is accomplished by rounding off digits to ignore fractions and only plotting prices when significant changes have occurred.

By itself, a chart, whether point and figure or line, is nothing but a graphic representation of a stock's price history. As such it tells where the market has been. It does not necessarily tell where the market is going. There are endless chart patterns and many excellent books which describe various theories of chart interpretation. These interpretations usually illustrate various formations which have presaged certain movements in the past. Some of the more common of these are head-and-shoulders tops and bottoms, double and triple tops and bottoms, rectangles, ascending and descending triangles, and gaps.

Two commonly used terms are *support* and *resistance*. A *support level* is a price at which traders believe a decline will stop. When a stock sells between two prices for an extended period of time and "breaks-out" into new high ground, the upper part of the previous trading range is usually considered a support level when and if the stock declines. A *resistance area* on the other hand is a price or price range where an upward move is expected to be halted. As an example, if a stock trades within a narrow range and then drops below the bottom part of the range and falls to new lows, a rally is usually expected to run into resistance when it reaches the bottom part of the previous trading range.

Formula Investing

To the formula investor, it is equally important to know *what* to buy as *when* to buy and *what* to sell as *when to* sell. Supposedly the astute Bernard Baruch answered the question of how to make money in the stock market with the classic "Buy low, sell high." He knew the problem always is that no one ever knows what is low and what is high.

The usual methods of market analysis are extremely complicated and demanding. Careful study of technical factors and judgment are necessary. Few individuals have the time or knowledge to utilize market analysis in the timing of purchases or sales of securities. Neither are most individuals successful in keeping their emotions out of investment or speculative decisions.

The psychology of the average man in the securities market is to do usually the exact opposite of what is most desirable. Unable to restrain his feelings and to examine the market picture with the calculating eye of the professional trader, he usually hurts himself during market crises. Typically, he is optimistic during bull markets and is inclined toward buying when prices are high. During bear markets he becomes pessimistic, and is inclined to sell when prices are low.

An answer to his problem might be *formula investing*, a mathematical approach to investing that eliminates emotion. Its mathematical principles are designed to reduce inherent risks or increase potential gains or both. No formula, of course, will assure a profit. There is none that will protect absolutely against loss in a declining market. But the use of a formula will frequently produce better results than amateur judgment. There are many formulas.

Dollar-Cost-Averaging calls for a fixed number of dollars to be invested in a selected security at regular fixed intervals for an extended period. Payments may be spaced monthly, quarterly, or yearly without taking the daily price level into account. For this formula to be successful, the investor must be able to continue his payments during all phases of the market, especially at the lower price levels. Unless he does so he is not dollar-cost-averaging and he will lose the gain he would have received after the price level rises. The effect of dollar-cost-averaging is to insure that *the average cost is less than the average price*. It is a mathematical certainty that, over the long run, he will save regardless of market variations because he buys fewer shares at high prices than at low prices. This fact is demonstrated by the difference in the number of shares bought and the average price of the shares under the following two situations:

(1) Purchase of 100 *shares* each of a stock at $2 per share, at $4 per share, and at $6 per share.

(2) Purchase of $400 *worth* of shares at $2 per share, $4 per share, and $6 per share.

In the first situation, a total of 300 shares cost $1200. Both the average cost and average price per share is $4.

In the second situation, the investor would have bought a total of 367 shares (to the nearest whole share). He would have ended up with 67 additional shares because he bought equal dollar amounts at each purchase rather than an equal number of shares at different prices. His 367 shares would have cost an average of $3.27, whereas the average price was $4 per share. This investor was dollar-cost-averaging.

The effect of dollar-cost-averaging on purchases in a declining market is marked. Had the stock declined from $6 per share to $4 per share to $2 per share, the investor would still have acquired 367 shares at an average cost of $3.27 per share. After the last purchase, the total market value of the 367 shares would have been $734. Since he paid $1200 he would have had a $466 loss had he sold all his shares at the $2 level. Thus, dollar-cost-averaging cannot protect the investor from loss in a declining market. However, a return of the stock to a market price of $4 a share (the average purchase price) would give him a value of $1468 for a gross profit of $268.

The investor who purchased by shares, not by dollar averaging, would have had no profit whatsoever when the stock returned to $4. In fact, he would have lost because of the commissions on the stock purchases.

Whether in an advancing or declining market the average cost of shares is always less than the average market price. In addition, the dollar-cost-averaging plan is simple. Assuming a constantly growing economy, the investor's money will show satisfactory growth over the long term.

But there is always the danger that the investor will sell out when stock prices are low and thus incur a loss. Or worse, the possibility exists that the investor might have to curtail his purchases during a recession period when his own income might be reduced. In addition, if his purchases are limited to only one or a few securities he may not do as well as the market averages.

Dollar cost averaging is the basis on which many purchasers acquire mutual funds. It is also the basis of the Monthly Investment Plans of the New York Stock Exchange which are discussed in Volume 2.

Constant Dollar. Some investors who already have an established portfolio use the constant dollar formula for determining the timing of their purchases and sales of stock. The intention is to "buy low, sell high" by gradually selling stocks on a rising market and by gradually buying them on a falling market. The term "constant dollar" arises from the attempt to keep the market value of the portfolio at a fixed dollar amount.

The method requires periodic review of the market value of the stock portfolio. Some investors review annually, others quarterly or even monthly. Some make it a rule to review on a certain percentage change in one of the stock averages or indexes, such as the Dow-Jones or Standard & Poors. Regardless of the timing of the review, the method is the same.

EXAMPLE: Mr. Sampson has a portfolio that is valued at the current market at $100,000. He reviews his holdings every three months. After each review, he adjusts his holdings to maintain the market value at $100,000. If the stocks have increased in value to a total of $115,000, he sells $15,000 worth of stocks and puts the money into a cash account. If the value of his portfolio, on the next review, has declined to $93,000, he buys $7,000 worth of stocks to add to it. Thus, he is selling as prices rise and buying as prices fall.

This plan is also a simple one, and its big advantage is that by "selling high" the investor will not buy when stocks are over priced. But this advantage can turn into a disadvantage during an extended bull market when Mr. Sampson will accumulate an increasingly large cash account that is not working for him. The unused proportion of his money during any bull market becomes larger and larger, and consequently he is not increasing his capital during the period of increasing stock prices. His results will be much less than if he had bought stock on a purely "buy and hold" basis. All these possibilities should be considered by an investor who wishes to employ the constant dollar formula.

Constant Ratio. Two different funds are involved in the constant ratio formula. As in the constant dollar method, there is a stock fund. Instead of a cash account, however, there is a bond fund. A periodic review is made to determine the current market value of both funds. Purchases and sales of both bonds and stocks are made to keep a constant ratio of stocks to bonds.

EXAMPLE: Mr. Queen has a bond fund with a market value of $30,000. He also owns a group of common stocks with a market value of $70,000. He wishes to maintain this 30/70 ratio.

At one review period he determines that his bond fund has a market value of $26,000 and his stock portfolio a market value of $80,000 with a total market value for the two funds of $106,000. Applying this ratio, Mr. Queen determines that the market value of his bond fund should be $31,800 (30 per cent of $106,000) and that of his stock fund should be $74,200. He therefore sells approximately $6,000 worth of stocks and buys $6,000 worth of bonds. With his bonds then having a market value of $32,000 and his stocks a value of $74,000, his 30/70 ratio has been restored.

This ratio, like the constant dollar method, causes the sale of stocks as their prices advance. Because the theory assumes that bonds follow a pattern which is the opposite of stocks, Mr. Queen will buy bonds at their low. Theoretically, he will then obtain a high rate of return on the bonds. Then, as the bond and stock market interest rates start to equalize, i.e., as stocks decline and pay a proportionately higher interest rate and as bond prices advance with a consequently lower percentage return, Mr. Queen will again adjust his portfolio to keep a 30/70 ratio.

There are several weaknesses to the constant ratio formula. First of all, stocks and bonds have not really shown their "traditional" ratio for many years. Government supports and props to the economy and the overall growth rate have tended to destroy the stock-bond relationship which might have held true 40 years ago.

Even though the method does use all profits from sales in its operation, it is still less favorable in a long bull market than a "buy and hold" situation.

One more criticism: even if the formula be valid and the plan started when the market is very high or very low, the investor may never obtain the proper proportion of stocks and bonds for maximum profit unless he can properly adjust his portfolio to the always indeterminate optimum.

Variable Ratio. There are several variable ratio formulas which are all based on the concept that the higher stock prices are the riskier they are, whereas bond prices tend to be steadier. Therefore, the ratio of stocks to bonds is decreased as the market level rises and is increased as the market level falls. During a lengthy and very strong bull market, the application of such a formula will remove the investor almost entirely from common stock investments long before the market reaches its peak. The extent to which the investor switches from stocks to bonds depends on what stock market levels have been predetermined as high.

Such plans require complex computations. There are many variable factors which must be used in computing the so-called normal value of stock prices. The danger always exists that the "normal" value is too high or too low.

Percentage Approaches. Whether the "reserve" fund used in conjunction with the stock fund is held in cash or in bonds, the percentage approach is a simple one that calls for the selling of stock when the market level advances a fixed percentage (say 10 per cent) and calls for the buying of stock when the market level declines a fixed percentage from its previous high. There are many variations of the percentage approach, but again the concept is to sell gradually on a rising market and to buy gradually on a declining market.

REVIEW QUESTIONS

1. What is market analysis?
2. Distinguish between market analysis and fundamental (security) analysis.
3. What is the most popular and widely used method for measuring trend and level of stock prices?
4. What is the purpose of the use of a multiplier or a divisor in computing a stock average?
5. Why are substitutions made from time to time in a stock average?
6. When and in what connection were the Dow Jones averages begun? How many different stocks are in the present Dow Jones averages?
7. What are stock price indexes? Explain the differences between an index and an average.
8. What are the three basic theories of Dow and his followers?
9. Describe: a primary movement; a secondary movement; a daily fluctuation.
10. What are meant by "corroboration" and "confirmation" in the Dow Theory?
11. Discuss stock and bond yields as a basis for forecasting.
12. Explain what is meant by "formula" investing?
13. What is "dollar cost averaging"?
14. What is the advantage and purpose of a "constant dollar" formula?
15. What "funds" are involved in investment in the "constant ratio" method?

16. What are the advantages and disadvantages of constant dollar and constant ratio investment formulas?
17. What is the basic concept of the "variable ratio" formula?
18. Describe what is meant by "breadth of the market."
19. Explain "short interest."
20. Discuss and criticize the "odd-lot behavior" theory of forecasting.
21. What is the theory relating to interaction between low-priced issues and high-priced issues?
22. Explain the principal difference between tape and chart readers.
23. Compare presentations in arithmetic and semi-logarithmic charts.
24. What is a "support level"? A "resistance area"?

Chapter 8

Securities Analysis

... the Fundamental Approach

THE VALUE BASIS FOR SELECTION

S*ecurities analysis* is the selection and appraisal of individual securities on a *value* basis. It seeks to determine the long-range suitability of a security for the investor's investment objectives. From the information available about a corporation, an analysis is made of its stability of capital, current income, long-term growth, and any special gains which the future could hold.

Such a study is known as the *fundamental* (or *valuation*) *approach* because it is based on the conditions which have and which probably will exist within a class of business or industry, the firm itself, and the security itself.

Each major industry has problems peculiar to itself. Some of them are discussed in the next chapter. But all companies, regardless of industry, follow standard accounting procedures. Their balance sheets and income statements reveal the basic condition of each company.

Earnings

An investor who is considering the purchase of a bond issue is interested in determining whether earnings will cover the cost of the indebtedness and whether the issuer will be able to redeem the principal when due. The prospective stock purchaser is interested in an increasing earning power for payment of regular (and perhaps increased) stock dividends.

Earnings are so important that many analysts have believed that stock prices primarily fluctuate because of anticipated earnings changes. Since changes in the economic conditions which influence earnings precede any actual earnings increase or decrease, these conditions are applied in determination of probable future earnings so that investment buying and selling may anticipate actual changes in reported earnings. Such anticipation is sometimes referred to as *discounting the future.*

This theory of the interrelationship of prices and earnings has long been given as a basic explanation of the cause and effect of stock price changes. The rising and falling patterns of stocks often do anticipate fundamental business changes that affect earnings. A violent example occurred in 1929, although the hysterical effect of tumbling stock prices probably influenced the business decline of the 1930s.

At any time, a corporation has a *market position* based on its volume of stock trading, relative strength, popularity among investors, and history. Of great importance is the history of earnings and the ratio of the price of the stock to earnings. This is called the *price-earnings ratio.* A high and rising price-earnings ratio is a sign of strength. A low price-earnings ratio, which might appear to indicate a good dividend, could merely indicate bad economic conditions or bad conditions within an industry or within the company itself.

Adherents of conservative market theory consistently use the price-earnings ratio as their guide. During the past few years, however, the price-earnings ratio has often been discounted in stock valuation. The rush of investment money from institutions and individuals has caused the so-called "glamour" stocks in electronics and aerospace issues to sell at many times the ten-to-one ratio that was once a standard measure. Buyers became more interested in the golden future than the realistic present.

The price-earnings ratios vary during bull and bear markets. During an inflated market, the average ratio may rise to as high as 23 or more to one. When the market is deflated, as in 1949, the average may be as low as seven to one.

Dividends

Dividends represent dollars which are paid out of current income or surplus to stockholders. Dividing the annual dividend of a stock by the market price gives its *yield,* or *return.* At bull market highs, yields are low and may average less than three per cent. At bear market lows, yields are much higher.

An investor can also express yield as a percentage of his original investment. If his common stock was purchased for $24 a share some time ago and now pays $1.08 annual dividends, the rate of return on his investment is 4.5 per cent ($1.08/$24=4.5 per cent.) If the stock is currently selling for $36, the dividend based on present market value is three per cent.

The word "dividend" has several meanings. For a preferred stock, it is generally a fixed amount to be paid out of earnings. The dividend of a common stock usually represents a distribution from earnings. However, a company's directors may elect to pay a dividend on either preferred or common stock from surplus, even if the company did not have sufficient earnings that year to cover the dividend.

A company's dividend is normally expressed as a *rate*. It is an *amount per share*. Thus, of the total dividends paid, each shareholder receives his proportionate share based on the number of shares he owns. Some companies pay dividends quarterly; others pay semi-annually, annually, or irregularly.

Companies that are expanding rapidly may wish to retain all of their earnings as working capital or for buying additional facilities. Such companies may either pay no dividend at all or they may pay a dividend in the form of additional shares of stock to its present shareholders. A distribution of this type is called a *stock dividend*. All shareholders receive the same pro rata extra stock from a stock dividend. After the distribution each holder still has the same percentage ownership of the company he had before the dividend.

A company sometimes pays a *property* dividend from securities it holds for investment. It may be in the form of shares of a subsidiary corporation; this type of dividend is known as a *spin-off*.

Return on preferred stock is sometimes expressed differently from the usual rate applied to common stock. For example, a preferred stock of the ABC Company might be described as "ABC par $50 four per cent" or it might be called "ABC $2 par 50." In either case, the dividend each year should be $2 or four per cent on the par value of the stock. Its yield on a current basis, however, would be computed on the basis of its market value, not on the basis of its par value.

Par value has no real meaning with reference to common stock, except that it places a lower limit on the price at which new shares may be issued. It is a dollar amount assigned to the share by the company's charter. "No par" stock (i.e. without an assigned value) is usually carried on the books at what is called a stated value. Actual *book value* reflects the theoretical value on liquidation of the company. Low-par stock ($1 to $25) is sometimes used for tax advantages over no-par or high-par stock. (In at least one state, no-par stock is treated for tax purposes the same as $100-par.) Neither par value nor book value has any real significance with respect to the *market value*, which is the current trading price of the stock.

Bond yield is figured in the same manner as stock yield. A 4 per cent bond that is selling at $1,000 gives an actual return of 4 per cent. The interest paid on a bond is always stated interest rate times the face value of the bond.

If investors do not have full confidence in the issuer, the 4 per cent bond might be selling at $800 (at a *discount*). At that price the current return would be 5 percent ($40/$800=5 per cent). On the other hand, if interest rates generally are low and this particular bond is considered to be very high grade, the bond might be selling on the market *at a premium* (at a price above its face value). If the bond were selling at $1230, the current return or yield would be 3.25 per cent ($40/$1230=3.25 per cent).

Yield to maturity is a term frequently used in connection with bonds. This per cent return is based upon the actual interest of the bond adjusted for the change in its value from its selling price to its maturity price. A bond selling at a premium will show a lesser return "to maturity" than its stated yield because the holder will receive only the face amount of the bond when it matures. In the example given above, at a selling price of $1,230, the bond was selling at a premium of $230. Because the holder will receive only $1000 when the bond is retired, he will lose that $230 premium over the period of time between his purchase and redemption of the bond by its issuer. On the other hand, an investor who bought a bond at a discount would show a gain at maturity. This gain or loss is applied to the interest rate to determine yield to maturity. The calculation is not simple and bond yield tables are customarily used.

The yield from a corporate or other bond that is not exempt from Federal taxes must be considerably higher than the yield on a tax-free municipal bond to provide the same net income to the holder. To determine the yield needed from a non-emempt security to give the equivalent of a tax-exempt, divide the tax-exempt yield by 100 minus the top percentage bracket of the taxpaper. For example, to equal 4% from a tax-exempt bond, a corporate bond must pay 4 divided by 100 minus 60 for an individual in the top bracket of 60%. Thus, the corporate bond would have to yield 10% for equivalence.

Sources of Financial Information

There are many sources of data for the information required to analyze a stock.

The primary source of information is the company itself. Most companies with stock publicly traded issue annual financial reports, as well as other periodic reports, on a quarterly or semi-annual basis. The annual report includes not only the income statements and balance sheet, but will often give detailed information about the company's products, management and future plans.

Many companies issue special news releases discussing important developments. These often—but not always—are reported in the newspapers.

Companies whose stocks are traded on national securities exchanges are required to file periodic statements with the SEC and to furnish stockholders periodic reports. Recent amendments to the '34 Act now require similar statements and reports by companies whose stocks are traded over-the-counter. These are available for inspection at the SEC offices in Washington and in various regional offices of the SEC. They are also available at the exchanges on which they are listed.

Quotations of securities traded on exchanges and over the counter may be found in the financial sections of leading newspapers. In addition to quotations, the leading newspapers publish information on trading volume, odd-lot volume, change in price since the previous day, number of new highs and new lows, and indexes of general market prices. These include the Dow-Jones averages, New York Times averages, Standard & Poor's indexes, etc.

When companies sell new securities publicly, they are required to register with the SEC. To do this they must submit a lengthy document known as a *registration statement* which is kept on file at the SEC's Washington office. A condensation of this document, the *prospectus*, is issued for the general public. The prospectus often contains information not available from any other printed source. The prospectus will usually discuss the company's business in some detail. It will present detailed financial information as well as background material on the management of the company.

The financial news ticker, which prints up-to-the-minute news, is an excellent source for "spot" information. This is expanded in the financial news coverage in the newspapers and in a number of magazines which carry detailed business information. There are numerous trade journals which cover various industries or aspects of industries. Virtually every industry and trade has several trade journals which carry news of interest to those concerned with the industry. Trade journals often carry more detailed information about an industry then is found in the more general publications. They often disclose information before it becomes widely known outside the industry.

Another source of general economic information is provided by the various Federal Reserve banks. Each of these banks issues a monthly newsletter discussing business and economic conditions in the area in which it operates. The Federal Reserve Bank of New York's monthly letter covers national and international financial trends.

There are many publishing services. Some are the lowest form of "tipsheet," and their information is suspect. Others elaborately analyze securities and publish considered recommendations. Still others are concerned with general investment advice and the state of the market. Statistical services, such as Standard & Poor's and Moody's issue reports on almost all large domestic corporations.

Distinct from these publications are the market letters and studies mailed regularly to clients by many brokerage houses. These range from short summary-type reports to detailed operating and financial studies.

The Federal government publishes several general business and economic surveys which may be of assistance to investors.

But the company itself is the prime reference source. Of all the literature a company might furnish, the company's balance sheet and income statement which reveal the dollars-and-cents standing are the most important. From these two tallies come the basic data for investments because they are an unbiased accountant's evaluation of the position of the company.

FINANCIAL STATEMENTS

The Balance Sheet

The *balance sheet* is a picture of the financial condition of a company on a specific date. It is a static statement because it does not show how the company got into that particular condition or whether the condition is relatively good or bad. The profit and loss or *income statement* tells the story of the company's activities for an annual, semi-annual, or quarterly period of time. The balance sheet is static; the income statement is dynamic. Neither is complete by itself. To determine the financial health of a company, both the balance sheet and the income statement for the period preceding the date of the balance sheet must be used. Comparative statements, which show figures for more than one period, help to show whether the company is operating more effectively or less effectively with the passage of time.

Because of difficulties of inventory right after the Christmas season, the need for public accountants in tax work (who cannot be available to everyone in the period from January 1st to April 15th), and other reasons, many companies prefer to end their accounting years on dates other than December 31st. Whether the accounting year ends December 31 or on some other date, the year is referred to as a *fiscal* year.

A typical balance sheet is shown on following pages. Numbers in parentheses refer to the following notes. These notes are purely explanatory. Footnotes appended to most financial statements explain in detail any items that are not self-explanatory in themselves.

(1) *ASSETS.* Assets include all items of value a company owns and all monies owed to it.

(2) *Current Assets.* These include all cash and all items easily converted into cash within the next 12 months. Because accounts receivable (money owed to the company for goods or services) are 30-, 60-, or 90-day obligations, they are a part of current assets.

(3) *Cash on hand and in banks.* This item includes petty cash, cash kept in the company safe, and all bank deposits. Sometimes people ask why a corporation dealing in millions of dollars shows a balance sheet with figures shown to pennies. It is important to establish that no errors have been made in bookkeeping to "balance" accounts. This can only be done if all items are

carried out to the pennies. "Rounding" is sometimes done in annual reports, but the firm's own books are usually balanced to the penny.

(4) *U.S. Government securities.* Because they can be readily converted into cash, many companies keep a substantial amount of money invested in Treasury notes or other U.S. Government paper. Interest on these obligations adds to the company's income while money deposited in a checking account does not usually draw interest. Even when the interest rate on Government notes is low, companies generally prefer them to savings account deposits with banks because of the 30- to 90-day withdrawal notification usually required by banks on very large savings accounts, which are usually in the form of *time deposits.*

(5) *Notes receivable.* These represent loans made to others; they may be demand notes, payable on demand by the company, or they may be payable at stipulated times.

(6) *Accounts receivable.* These are amounts owed to the company for goods or services. Because these accounts are usually payable in 30 days, sometimes in 60 or 90 days, they are properly included as a current asset. Accounts that are to be carried for longer than 90 days are frequently in the form of "notes receivable" rather than as accounts receivable.

(7) *Inventories.* If the total of inventories of goods is less than a normal year's sales, which it usually is, the inventories are properly classified as a current asset. It is standard accounting practice to be as conservative as possible in valuing inventories so as to understate rather than overstate a company's financial strength. Inventories include not only finished goods for sale but also work in process and supplies to be used in the manufacture of finished goods.

There are several methods of valuing inventories. The most common are:

● The standard method—inventories are carried "at cost or market, whichever is lower."

● FIFO—"first in, first out."

● LIFO—"last in, first out."

Valuation at the lower of cost or market ensures that inventory is conservatively valued. "Cost or market" is a method that can be applied to the entire inventory on an average-cost base, or it can be applied to either FIFO or LIFO.

The differences between FIFO and LIFO may be illustrated by a company's coal pile. If the coal bought is piled on top and the coal used is taken from the bottom, we have a case of first in, first out. Since the old coal is used up first, the remaining stock is valued at the most recent price paid. If, however, the coal used is taken off the top we have a case of last in, first out. The coal on hand at the inventory date represents some old or original purchase and it may be valued at an unchanging price from year to year.

BALANCE SHEET
Constructive Company, Inc.
as at December 31, 19—

(1) **ASSETS**

   (2) *Current Assets*

      (3) Cash on hand and in banks ....$ 7,434,326.11

      (4) U.S. Gov't securities 745,000.00

      (5) Notes receivable 100,000.00

      (6) Accounts receivable 17,906,210.47

      (7) Inventories 44,800,462.59

      Total Current Assets ....$ 70,985,999.17

   (8) *Other Assets*

      (9) Cash value of life insurance ....$ 484,900.00

   (10) Prepaid charges 606,492.18

      Total Other Assets ....$ 1,091,392.18

   (11) *Fixed Assets*

      Buildings, machinery, equipment—cost ......$ 78,497,516.78

   (12) Less depreciation 16,322,643.22

                   $ 62,174,873.56

      Land (at cost) 167,500.00

      Total Fixed Assets ....$ 62,342,373.56

   (13) **TOTAL ASSETS** $134,419,764.91

(14) **LIABILITIES & STOCKHOLDERS' EQUITY**

   (15) *Current liabilities.*

   (16) Note payable (due Feb. 28) ....$ 500,000.00

   (17) Current maturity of Long-term debt 1,333,333.33

   (18) Taxes payable 12,600,219.23

   (19) Accounts payable 4,767,310.42

   (20) Accrued liabilities 3,494,363.36

   (21) Dividends payable 8,800,890.45

Total Current Liabilities ....$ 31,496,116.79

   (22) *Reserves* ....$ 2,567,432.19

   (23) *Long-Term Debt*

      5% Mortgage Bonds due July 1, 1980 ....$ 20,000,000.00

      5½% Sinking Fund Debentures

         due July 1, 1975 .... 10,000,000.00

      Total long-term Debt ....$ 30,000,000.00

(24) *Stockholders' Equity*

      $2.25 Cum. Preferred Stock ($50 par)

         300,000 shares ....$ 15,000,000.00

      Common Stock ($1 par) 7,500,000 shares 7,500,000.00

   (25) Capital surplus 12,750,000.00

   (26) Earned surplus 35,106,215.93

Total Stockholders' Equity ....$ 70,356,215.93

      TOTAL LIABILITIES $134,419,764.91

During a period of sharply rising prices, the effect of FIFO is to mark up inventories to about current replacement costs. The LIFO method serves to hold down the value of inventories and so exclude inventory profits from reported earnings.

(8) *Other Assets.* These are assets that are not readily converted to cash but which cannot be classified as fixed assets, such as certain investments in subsidiaries and intangibles such as patents.

(9) *Cash values of life insurance.* Many corporations carry considerable life insurance coverage on their key personnel. The cash values of these policies are an asset of the company, but they are not usually considered as a part of current assets.

(10) *Prepaid charges.* Such items as rent and insurance premiums are frequently paid for a year in advance. If the entire payments were charged as an expense in the month in which they were made, a distorted picture of expense to sales would result. Therefore, these payments are "capitalized;" they are added as an asset at the time the payment is made (they are the equivalent of cash in another form) and monthly charges are made against them

(11) *Fixed assets.* These are assets that could only be converted into cash by reducing plant facilities or by going out of business. They are sometimes referred to as "frozen" assets. These include land, buildings, equipment, trucks, office furniture, tools and machinery.

(12) *Depreciation.* Except for land, fixed assets become less and less valuable through use. Because these assets must be replaced when they are worn out, some account must be taken of their declining value (depreciation) to give a true picture of total expenses when computing profit and loss. An amount is charged each month to expense to reflect this. *Depletion* refers to the loss of an actual asset through removal, such as in oil and mining. *Obsolescence* refers to the loss due to a technical change that makes the asset less valuable. *Amortization* either may refer to the writing-off of an asset over a period of time, through depreciation for example, or it may refer to the reduction of a debt through periodic repayments.

(13) *TOTAL ASSETS.* This is the total of all items owned by or owing to the company. The difference between this figure and total liabilities is the *Stockholders' equity* or *net worth*. The net worth divided by the number of shares outstanding gives the *book value* per share. Again, note that this represents the net value per share of the company as a "going concern" and has very little bearing on the market value of the shares or what the shares might be worth on liquidation of the company.

Some assets cannot be measured in money and are either not shown on a balance sheet or are given a nominal value. These are intangible assets, such as good will. While this may have real value in any sale of a business, it has no real value in its credit structure.

(14) *LIABILITIES.* The direct opposite of assets, liabilities are all the debts or obligations of a company. The sum of the liabilities and the stockholders' equity is exactly equal to the sum of the assets. It is for this reason that ownership interest (stockholders' equity) is shown with liabilities, even though the amount is not "owed" by the company.

(15) *Current liabilities.* These are the total of those items that are now due or will become due and payable within the next 12 months. It includes interest on bonds but not dividends to shareholders. It also includes that part of the firm's long-term debt that is payable within the year.

(16) *Note payable.* Notes have preference over accounts payable. The note listed here might represent the balance of payments to be made on equipment purchased or it might represent a cash borrowing from a bank. Notes differ from debentures in that no issue of a security is involved.

(17) *Current maturity of long-term debt.* This is the amount of either or both of the bonds and debentures listed below that becomes due and payable within the next 12 months, and includes the money that must be set aside in accord with the terms of the trust indenture of the sinking fund debentures.

(18) *Taxes payable.* These are taxes of whatever nature, including income tax, that are now due and payable. In order to give as true a picture as possible of financial conditions, when income tax will become due shortly but final computations have not been made, a company may list a "reserve" item representing its best estimate of what the tax will be. While not actually payable at the time of the statement, this "reserve" effectively removes that amount of money from total net assets and stockholders' equity.

(19) *Accounts payable.* Usually due in 30 to 90 days, these are what the firm owes to others for goods or services. The monthly bill from the electric company is an account payable by the recipient for the electricity used during the preceding month.

(20) *Accrued liabilities.* These represent money that the company must pay within the next 12 months, but has not yet become payable. An example can be found in the payroll. If the accounting period ends on a Wednesday and pay-day is Friday, the amounts earned by employees up through Wednesday are accrued liabilities. Interest on bonds from the last payment date to the date of the statement is also an accrued liability.

(21) *Dividends payable.* These are dividends that have been declared by the board of directors but which have not yet been paid to the company's shareholders. On some balance sheets, this item is shown separately for preferred stock and common stock.

(22) *Reserves.* These include items that will not necessarily become payable but that must be included as a liability to avoid giving too optimistic an outlook. Sometimes *contingent liabilities* are included here. A contingent liability is one that will become an actual liability should a certain event

occur, though the actual amount of such liability may not be known. For example, should someone bring suit against the company which may be successful, it is good practice to add an amount equal to that of the suit to the liabilities of the firm. If the suit is successfully defended, the amount is removed from liabilities and added to stockholders' equity. Reserves are also used to show amounts earmarked to retire bonds, debentures, or preferred stock.

(23) *Long-term Debt.* This item includes all of the debt owed by the company that is not payable within the next 12 months. Such long-term debt is referred to as *funded debt*.

(24) *Stockholders' Equity.* This represents the net ownership value of the stockholders' both preferred and common. Stockholders' equity is also known as *owner's capital* . . . it includes paid-in capital, paid-in surplus, and earned surplus. Note that the number of shares is multiplied by the par value of the stock to give the stated value of the total stock outstanding. In the case of the preferred stockholders, this may constitute their entire equity. However, some preferred stock participates in the liquidating value of the firm and some of the surplus may accrue to them.

(25) *Capital Surplus.* This represents the amount in excess of par value paid by the shareholders into the corporation for their stock. In this case, the shareholders paid $3 a share for the 7,500,000 shares. The underwriter kept 30¢ a share for his services in selling the stock. The balance of $20,250,000 that went to the company makes up the $7,500,000 par value plus $12,750,000 capital surplus.

(26) *Earned Surplus.* This is the total of accumulated earnings, all the money after dividends held in the business since its beginning. It is frequently referred to as *retained earnings*.

The balance sheet also shows the *capitalization* of the corporation, which is the total dollar amount of all the securities (bonds, preferred stock and common stock) issued by it. When bonds and preferred stocks form a large part of the capitalization, earnings on the common stock per share will vary more than the total earnings vary, hence this type of *capital structure* is known as speculative. (See Leverage Analysis, page 1–178.) When most or all of the securities issued are common stock, the capital structure is conservative.

Many ratios and other indicators are derived directly from the balance sheet. Useful both to the investment analyst and to potential lenders, these are discussed later under "Balance Sheet Analysis."

The Income Statement

The neatly totaled balance sheet does just what it calls itself. It balances the assets against the liabilities. By so doing it shows the condition of the

STATEMENT OF INCOME
Constructive Company, Inc.
Year Ended December 31, 19—

(27)	**SALES**	$115,835,436.52

Cost and Expenses

(28)	Cost of goods sold	$ 74,213,229.00
(29)	Selling and administrative expense	13,927,104.61
(30)	Depreciation	3,427,741.22
		$ 91,568,074.92
(31)	Operating Profit	$ 24,267,361.60
(32)	Interest Charges	1,550,000.00
	Earnings before Taxes	$ 22,717,361.60
(33)	Provision for Federal and State Income Taxes	11,813,028.03
	Net Income for the Year	$ 10,904,333.57
	Dividend on Preferred Stock @ $2.25 per share	675,000.00
		$ 10,229,333.57
(34)	Dividend on Common Stock @ $1.08 per share	8,100,000.00
	Balance to Earned Surplus	$ 2,129,333.57

Constructive Company at the end of the calendar year. It does not, however, give any information concerning the profit and loss from the company's operations during the year. The net earnings appear in the *income statement*, which shows what income was received, what the company's expenses were, and the resulting net profits to the shareholders, including dividends paid or payable and earnings retained in the business.

(27) *SALES.* This is the total of goods and services sold during the year. It includes the cash sales and those made on credit that are now shown as an asset under Accounts Receivable in the balance sheet. A sale is usually considered as made on delivery—not upon collection.

(28) *Cost of goods sold.* Wages, salaries, overhead, supplies, raw materials, and all other expenses that are an actual part of the cost of producing the goods to be sold are a part of this item.

(29) *Selling and administrative expense.* Salesmen's commissions, advertising, salaries and wages of those not in production, and all other items of expense that are not actually a part of the production end of the business are included here. Different companies use different methods of determining how expenses should be charged to different departments.

(30) *Depreciation.* Wear and tear on equipment and buildings. This is not a cash expenditure, but it must be included as a cost to give a realistic profit figure. The amount of depreciation is reflected on the balance sheet as a reduction in value of fixed assets. When replacements are made, their costs are pro-rated over their years of useful life in the same manner.

(31) *Operating Profit.* This is the difference between income from sales of goods produced and the costs of doing business.

(32) *Interest Charges.* Interest on borrowed capital is not usually considered as one of the regular costs of doing business. Therefore, it is shown separately.

(33) *Provision for Federal and State Income Taxes.* Note that over half of the earnings before taxes goes to support the Federal and State governments. It is this high tax on corporate earnings plus the regular income tax paid by the company's owners (shareholders) on dividends received that is referred to as the "double taxation" on dividend income.

(34) The dividend on common stock shown here is unusually high in relationship to the after-tax net income. This could occur in a relatively stable business that had no intention of expanding, or it might occur when a company wished to maintain its dividend rate even during a comparatively poor year.

Other Income may appear on the statement with an explanatory footnote. It includes such items as dividends and interest received on investments in other corporations.

As with the Balance Sheet, the Income Statement provides many ratios and other figures valuable to analysts . . . these are discussed under "Income Statement Analysis."

UNDERSTANDING ANALYSIS

It is easy for the untutored investor to misinterpret financial statements. Accounting principles, difficulty of understanding the implications, the many explanatory footnotes in the statements, and the fact that different accounting methods are often used by different companies in the same industry, may cause a hasty investor to misjudge basically similar statements.

In addition, the net profit of a company can be judged only in relation to many factors. Its relationship to previous net profits is important. The year of the income statement may not be typical of the firm's usual earnings. Subsidiaries, tax considerations and adjustments, sales of capital assets, and abnormal development or promotional costs are very often not shown or explained on balance sheets or income statements. Here the services of the many financial advisory services may be helpful.

Balance Sheet Analysis

Several ratios have been developed to help interpret balance sheets. The most important are:

Book Value Per Share. This is found by adding up all the assets (generally excluding intangibles such as "good will"), subtracting all liabilities (including bonds) and stock issues ahead of the common, and then dividing by the number of shares of common stock. Book value has little significance as related either to earning power or market value of the stock. However, when book value is high relative to market value and the company is prospering, the stock may represent a favorable investment opportunity.

Working Capital Per Share. Working capital per share is computed by subtracting current liabilities from current assets and dividing the resulting figure by the number of shares outstanding. This ratio is important in determining whether a company is in a sound position for carrying on its business. The ratio can be excessive, however. Shortly after World War II, a number of companies had working capital per share substantially equal to its market value. In some cases, this led to "raids" in which speculators bought control by buying shares on the open market. They then "milked" the raided companies by declaring huge dividends out of surplus. With their working capital gone and their capitalization severely damaged, the companies were then either sold or allowed to die.

Ratio Analysis

After clarifying the figures on a balance sheet or income statement, it becomes possible to analyze various aspects of the business through the use of financial ratios.

Profitability. Profitability of a firm may be measured by these Profitability Ratios:

- The sales ratio, or sales per dollar of capital funds.
- The profit margin, or net profit per dollar of sales.
- The earnings ratio, or earnings per dollar of capital funds.
- The working capital ratio . . . see current ratio below.
- The common stock ratio, which is computed by dividing the total capital funds at book value into the common stock components. If there is only common stock the ratio is 100 per cent. The lower the ratio, the greater the leverage.
- Coverage of senior charges, which is found by dividing the balance available for senior charges by (1) the fixed charges; (2) the fixed and contingent charges; or, (3) total prior charges, if any, plus preferred dividends. Separate ratios can be computed for each type of coverage. These are important ratios for determining the quality of a bond or preferred stock.

Liquidity. Liquidity is a factor of particular importance to creditors and to stockholders as well. Various ratios, known as credit ratios have been devised as a measure of liquidity.

Capital Structure. Of particular importance especially in railroad and utility analysis are various ratios concerning capital structure. These include the common stock ratio and the debt equity ratio.

Risk. The element of risk with regard to interest payments on senior securities may be measured by the coverage of senior charges (see discussion below).

Managerial Performance. Several measures of managerial performance are discussed below. These include the various profitability and growth ratios as well as the inventory turnover ratio.

Growth Ratios. These ratios or rates of growth may apply to one year or a series of years:

- Growth in dollar sales.
- Growth of net profits in dollars.
- Growth in earnings per share.

A *growth stock* is one whose rate of growth of profit over a period of time is considerably greater than that of business generally. Some experts say a stock that grows at average rate of 10 per cent annually is a growth stock.

Stability Ratios. There are two important measures of stability over a period of years:

- The minimum coverage of senior charges. *Coverage* means the operating profits available for payment of interest on bonds and dividends on preferred stock.
- The maximum earnings decline (from the high point to the low point in a series of years).

Dividend Payout Ratio. This is the percentage of available earnings paid out in common dividends. If earnings are being retained for expansion and/or research, this ratio will be low. A company in a stable industry with little expansion planned and with little or no research may have a comparatively high ratio. It is because of this varying payout policy that the price-earnings ratio is of more importance than the price-dividend ratio in projecting changes in market value of individual stocks.

Price Ratio. Price per share may be related to the following figures in ratio form:

- Sales per dollar of common stock at market.
- Earnings per dollar of common at market (earnings yield).
- Dividends per dollar of common, at market (dividend yield).
- Net assets (equity) per dollar of common at market (asset ratio).

Other Ratios

Debt-Equity Ratio. This is often used in the analysis of public utilities. It relates the long term debt to the equity of the firm. The formula is:

$$\frac{\text{Funded Debt}}{\text{Common Stock} + \text{Preferred Stock} + \text{Surplus}}$$

The ratio is often expressed as, for example, $2 of debt to $1 of equity. The common and preferred stock will usually be valued at par or stated value. Sometimes, market value is used.

Current Ratio. The formula for this ratio is:

$$\frac{\text{Current Assets}}{\text{Current Liabilities}}$$

It is a measure of liquidity. As a rule of thumb the ratio should be at least 2:1. In some industries the ratio is normally higher. If it is lower, the company may face a shortage of working capital.

Inventory Turnover Ratio. This ratio is computed in two steps. First, an average is taken of inventory at the beginning of a period and inventory at the end of a period.

EXAMPLE:

Inventory at beginning of year	$ 650,000
Inventory at end of year	350,000
TOTAL	$ 1,000,000

Divide by two to obtain the
Average Inventory $ 500,000

The next step is to divide sales by average inventory

$$\frac{\text{Sales}}{\text{Average Inventory}} = \text{Inventory Turnover Ratio}$$

This ratio is a measure of management efficiency. The more rapid the turnover, the less working capital need be tied up in the inventory. Also, the firm can charge lower prices for its products since it can earn a better total profit on a smaller margin through higher turnover. This is a distinct competitive advantage. The inventory turnover ratio is particularly useful in analyzing a merchandising company.

Fixed Assets to Net Worth Ratio. This ratio is:

$$\frac{\text{Tangible Fixed Assets}}{\text{Tangible Net Worth}}$$

This ratio measures the proportion of capital that has been invested in fixed property. The greater the investment in property, plant and equipment, the larger the charge against earnings for depreciation. Also, the higher the ratio, the less the protection for creditors.

Sales to Net Working Capital. The formula is:

$$\frac{\text{Net Sales}}{\text{Net Working Capital}}$$

It measures the efficiency of the employment of working capital in the business. It may also indicate the need for additional working capital. It may also be useful in comparing capital expenditures with sales growth to determine the effectiveness of the expenditures. The percentages earned on sales and capitalization are sometimes helpful.

The Acid Test. The acid test is the ratio of net quick assets (i.e. current assets excluding inventories) to current liabilities. The formula is:

$$\frac{\text{Current Assets minus Inventories}}{\text{Current Liabilities}}$$

It is a measure of liquidity. A ratio of 1:1 is usually considered favorable since it means that for every dollar of current debt there is available a dollar of quick assets which can be turned into cash on short notice for payment of current obligations.

Cash Holdings. The amount of cash held is also a measure of liquidity, although an overly large holding of cash may be indicative of poor working capital management.

Physical Data

Physical data may also be used for analytical purposes.

Physical Reserves. This is a particularly important figure for companies having wasting assets. These include oil, gas and mining companies.

Capacity. This figure is important in various types of manufacturing industries such as steel, oil refining, cement production, etc. It is a useful measure in comparing one company with another in the same industry.

Production in Units. This figure is useful in analysis, particularly in comparison with the capacity figures described above.

Production by Divisions. Analysis of production by divisions can be quite useful in estimating dollar sales and earnings.

Geographical Sales. This will indicate whether sales are concentrated in one area or are diversified. If sales are concentrated in a single foreign country, an additional element of risk may be present.

Concentration of Sales. Companies whose sales are concentrated on one or two major customers are considered to be more vulnerable than those having many customers.

Income Statement Analysis

Analysis. Analysis of the income statement is particularly important in the evaluation of common stocks. The income statement helps to answer such questions as: "What are the true earnings of the period studied?" ... "What does this indicate about the future earnings of company?" . . . "How much are the present and future earnings worth to the investor?"

In studying the earnings results of a company, it is sometimes necessary to make certain adjustments in the reported figures.

1. Non-recurring items should be eliminated from year-to-year analysis.

2. Suitable adjustments should be made for arbitrary reserves as well as for depreciation and amortization.

3. Inventory changes should be taken into account.

Non-recurring Items. These are profits and losses which arise for reasons outside the regular course of business. These may include such items as:

- Profit or loss on sale of fixed assets.
- Write-downs of non-marketable investments.
- Write-downs on recoveries of foreign assets.

These items should be stated separately from normal earnings and should be eliminated from year-to-year comparisons of earnings results.

Reserves. Reserves may be set up for a wide variety of purposes. Some of these are:

- To reduce assets from original book value to some more appropriate figure.
- To reflect liabilities of a somewhat indefinite character, or of uncertain payment date, arising from past events.
- To provide for expected or possible losses arising from future events.

Insofar as reserves appear as charges to the income account, they should be treated as follows:

- Small items should be accepted as they appear.
- Reserve appropriations for income tax purposes should be considered ordinary reductions from current income, unless they clearly relate to a non-recurrent item.
- Reserve appropriations not allowed for income tax purposes should ordinarily be added back to the income account.

Inventories. Inventory accounting methods have an important influence on the reported earnings. In periods of rising prices there may be gains in the value of inventories which do not reflect true earnings.

Reserves for Contingencies. A reserve for contingencies is intended to absorb future losses or liabilities of a rather indefinite character. Such reserves may be created by a charge either to earnings or to surplus. Practice by both accountants and analysts favors the adjustment of reported earnings to take account of "true earnings" in that contingency reserve allowances deducted from income on the income statement, should be added back to income for comparison purposes.

Depreciation and Amortization. Depreciation and amortization charges are not like ordinary operating expenses which involve a current outlay of cash. Rather, they represent the estimated shrinkage in value of the fixed or capital assets, due to wearing out, or using up or their approaching extinction for whatever cause. These charges may be classified as follows:

* Depreciation (and obsolescence), replacements, renewals or retirements.
* Depletion or exhaustion.
* Amortization of leaseholds, leasehold improvements, licenses, etc.
* Amortization of patents.

In theory if a capital asset has a limited life, provision must be made to write off the asset over its period of life by charges against earnings. If it were wholly charged against earnings in the year acquired, it would give a distorted picture of that and subsequent years' earnings and would be disallowed for tax purposes.

Several methods may be used to compute depreciation charges. The straight line method is among the most common. It involves charging off a fixed annual percentage of the cost of each type of facility. *Accelerated* depreciation results in a greater depreciation deduction in the early years in an asset's life than in the case under the straight line method. In later years, the deduction declines. This method results in lower taxes for the company in the earlier years of an asset's life. This money may be put to work for the benefit of the company.

In addition to the usual depreciation charges, companies with wasting assets (e.g. oil, gas, metals) make an allowance for the using up of underground capital assets. This is known as *depletion*.

In analyzing reported earnings, it is also important to ascertain whether the corporation has paid the usual corporate income tax. Any discrepancy should be analyzed to determine the reason for it.

REVIEW QUESTIONS

1. Describe the fundamental (valuation) approach to securities analysis.
2. Of what importance is the earning record of a security to the prospective bond purchaser? To the stock purchaser?
3. What is meant by *discounting* the earnings of a stock? What theory has this led to?
4. What is the "market position" of a corporation?
5. What is the "price-earnings ratio" of a stock?
6. **What might a low price-earnings ratio indicate? A high ratio?**
7. Explain what a stock dividend is. How is its yield figured?

8. A stock purchased at $40 a share with a market value of $80 a share paid dividends of $4 during the past 12 months. What is its current *return*? What is its *yield* on its *cost*?

9. A manufacturing concern pays a dividend of 50¢ a share on its common stock. From what sources might this dividend have come?

10. Explain the basic difference between the dividend paid on preferred stock and the dividend paid on common stock.

11. What relationship does par value have to book value? Explain each.

12. What is meant by the statement that a bond is selling at a discount?

13. Which shows a greater yield to maturity, a bond selling at a discount or one selling at a premium? Why?

14. Explain the functions of the balance sheet and the income statement.

15. What is the *fiscal year*?

16. Distinguish among current assets, fixed assets, and "other" assets.

17. What is the difference between notes receivable and accounts receivable?

18. Etate the various inventory valuation methods in general use. Describe each.

19. What is the effect of valuing inventory "at market" instead of "at cost" in an industrial corporation?

20. How is stockholders' equity determined?

21. What is a liability? A current liability?

22. What term is used to describe the amount of bonds that become due and payable within the next 13 months?

23. What is the difference between a note payable and a debenture? The difference between a note payable and an account payable?

24. Are dividends payable to stockholders considered an asset or a liability? Why?

25. What are contingent liabilities?

26. What is the difference between capital surplus and earned surplus?

27. How is book value per share computed and what is its significance?

28. What are profitability ratios? Give examples.

29. Describe the computation of the common stock ratio.

30. How do you compute the coverage of senior charges?

31. What is the "dividend payout ratio"?

32. What is the formula for current ratio?

33. As a rule of thumb, what should the current ratio of an industrial concern be?

34. How is inventory turnover ratio computed? What does it measure?

35. What does the sales to net working capital ratio measure? What may it indicate?

36. What is the "acid test" and what does it measure?

37. What questions does analysis of the income account help to answer?

38. What adjustments should be made in the reported figures of earnings?

39. Describe the purposes of "reserves."

40. What is meant by "write-off" of an asset?

Chapter 9

Securities
Analysis

... the Industry Approach

GENERAL CONSIDERATIONS

Economic factors may influence market trends in particular industries or in industry as a whole. For example, interest rates tend to affect the overall market. In theory, there should be less speculation and lower prices for securities when interest rates are high. However, there have been various periods, such as 1928-29, 1954-55 and 1960-61, when interest rates were high yet the market was very bullish.

Commodity prices are often watched for influence upon stock prices. Generally, however, commodity prices seem to react after stock prices, rather than before, and are therefore unreliable as indicators. Likwise, Gross National Product and building construction, which are sometimes thought to influence stock prices, seem to reflect changes in stock prices rather than to influence them.

New orders and changes in inventories are watched closely. An increase in new orders clearly indicates a period of good business ahead, but do not always precede a move in stock prices. Changes in inventories are usually the result of business changes that have already taken effect and seldom forecast market trends.

Industrial production is a basic indicator of the state of the economy. Earnings depend upon production, and stock prices should reflect earnings. As with the other factors mentioned, stock prices seem to lead rather than follow changes in production. It is because stock prices seem to rise or fall a few to several months *before* the changes that should cause the rise or fall that is frequently stated that the stock market "discounts the future."

Political factors have become an increasingly important factor in the economic life of the country and have direct influence on market trends. War, or the lack of it, has a dramatic effect on stock prices. Presidential messages, Congressional Acts, and Federal agency releases all affect the market or a portion of it. Frequently, decisions of the Supreme Court are directly reflected in stock quotations. Most political factors are difficult to evaluate, but their importance is great.

EACH INDUSTRY IS DIFFERENT

Each major industry has its own set of problems and peculiarities. Many retail companies suffer from severe competitive conditions; business machine companies demonstrate growth; public utilities, permanence; food companies, sales stability. Public utilities operate under government regulations and restrictive conditions. The maritime industry periodically undergoes strikes and always seems to be in the throes of poor labor relations.

The economic circumstances of war or a threat of war tend to stimulate interest in almost all securities in the mineral and mining industry. Under the same conditions the securities of industries in the transportation field, which is already bound by heavy Federal regulation, might decline because investors fear even more government restrictions or perhaps an actual takeover.

Manufacturing companies are especially sensitive to sources of supply and location of markets. Impending trade laws, foreign competition, the threat of new techniques and technologies replacing or revitalizing separate branches of manufacturing, all can affect stock prices.

A particular firm must be judged on its performance within its own industry. Among similar companies it can be ranked according to its present and prospective position of size and dominance. The investor must examine a company's management, sales and earnings outlook, assets, working capital, capital structure and the reputation and intangible asset of good will which surround a solid company.

Railroads

At the turn of the century railroads were considered the financial backbone of the country. They were by far the largest group in industry. They controlled and owned vast areas of land, much of it in the then undeveloped West. Stockbrokers could think of no better investment for income and stability than railroads. They were virtual monopolies, and practically their only competition came from the waterways.

The face of America changed and the picture is vastly different today. Automobiles, buses, trucks, airlines, pipelines, as well as water carriers, compete and have left the railroads with successively smaller percentages of the transportation dollar. Railroads are not only faced with crushing competition, but with extensive regulation and control by state commissions and the Interstate Commerce Commission. The ICC has the power to fix freight and passenger rates, to pass upon the issuance of new railroad securities, to regulate accounting practices, to pass upon proposed mergers, and to supervise other aspects of railway operations. These regulations have a twofold purpose: to insure reasonable rates and service for industry and the public and to allow a fair profit.

Besides competition and regulation, railroads have an onerous basic problem. They require a high fixed investment with resulting high fixed operating costs. Maintenance and depreciation of the heavy and expensive capital equipment needed to run a railroad is exceedingly oppressive. So are labor costs, which can account for half the operating costs. Taxes, which may account for 20 per cent of the rest of the operating expenses, are also a burden. A large percentage of these costs occur whether traffic is heavy or light. An increase in volume will not usually significantly add to the costs, but it will greatly improve the profit margin.

Extensive financial and operating data is made available in the reports to the ICC and in publications from the Association of American Railroads. These figures are publicly available as are the extensive reports which the railroads put out for stockholders and other interested parties.

Financial Ratios. Key ratios in railroad analysis are:

● *The Operating Ratio* . . . the ratio of expenses (down to, but not including taxes) to operating revenue. It is useful for comparing different railroads or for comparisons of railroad performance in one year as compared with another.

● *Coverage of Fixed Charges* . . . the amount available (total income) divided by the fixed charges. A comparison over the years will help determine the growth trend of the railroad.

● *Coverage of Contingent Interest* . . . net income after payment of fixed charges divided by interest on income bonds.

● *Coverage of Preferred Dividends* . . . total income divided by the sum of fixed charges and *two times* the preferred dividends.

● *Earnings per share of common* . . . computed in the usual manner.

● *Maintenance Ratio* . . . the ratio of maintenance expenditures, including depreciation, to railway operating revenues. A comparison of this ratio among different railways may indicate a condition of under maintenance, a sign of poor management, or financial stringency.

● *Transportation Ratio* . . . relates transportation expenses to operating revenues. A low or declining ratio is a measure of operating efficiency.

Some of the more important physical or performance ratios are:

- Net ton miles per train hour.
- Average tons per loaded freight car.
- Freight cars per freight train.
- Train miles per train hour.

The results of these physical ratios show up in the financial performance ratios. They may serve to pinpoint reasons for profit or loss.

Within this profit-and-loss situation, the separate rail lines face varying problems. Some are primarily coal carriers and have little or no competition from other transportation sources, but are dependent on the amount of coal used by the economy. Others, such as the east-west railroads, are on such heavily traveled routes that they necessarily receive a share of the transportation business. But others, such as the New England railroads, are in a territory where much of their business is short-run, and heavy competition from trucks or private automobiles shows a depressing profit picture.

Recently, however, railroads have been the subject of important legal decisions on featherbedding or "make-work" labor contracts. It is possible that a combination of more efficient use of manpower plus an easing of the tax and regulation situation—which would put railroads in a better competitive position—could again make railroads more attractive to investors.

Many railroads are handicapped with heavy bonded indebtedness. During periods of business adversity, financial strains have resulted. In the depression many were forced into bankruptcy. Even today, many railroads must meet heavy bond charges before dividends can be paid on common stock.

Financial Positions. The rail industry as a whole is heavily indebted. One railroad may have many outstanding bond issues with refinancing or additional financing always a problem. It always seems difficult to increase the already large net working capital required by all railroads. A major factor in most railroads is leverage. Because of heavy fixed obligations, rail stocks often have a speculative quality.

On the other hand, many railroads receive income from investment. Coal mines, lumber, and holdings in other railroads are quite usual.

Even in the 1950s, a time of prosperity for most industries, railroad securities sold at low price-earnings ratios. Their lack of growth and financial problems of most rail lines were uncertain risks for investors.

Nevertheless, a good deal of the well-secured bonds and railroad equipment obligations are favorites of institutions and conservative investors. Lower-grade bonds, which yield more interest, and income bonds and stocks are widely held by the public.

Public Utilities

Railroads are public utilities in the legal sense but because of their economic and regulatory features are always classified separately for investment analysis purposes. Public utility securities include electric, natural and manufactured gas, telephone, telegraph, transit, and water companies. Like railroads, utilities also offer many types of bonds and preferred and common stocks.

The different utility industries show varying degrees of health and economic characteristics. In general, the growing national economy demands their increasing use, particularly of electricity, gas, and telephone.

To the investor, electric utilities are of particular importance. Even during depressions they show remarkable stability—between 1929 and 1933 total earnings declined only 20 per cent and sales volume about 15 per cent. Like all utilities, electric utilities must supply their service to all who demand it and they must be prepared to meet peak needs for service. Because electric power cannot be stored like gas or water, it must be used as it is produced. Heavy investments are necessary in production, transmission, and distribution equipment.

In the natural gas business are the pipe line operators, who buy or produce natural gas from oil fields and pump it great distances to local gas companies or retail suppliers. Manufactured gas is often sold along with natural gas to gas utilities. In areas of high electric rates, gas competes favorably with electricity.

Telephone companies have been stable investments, although less stable than gas or electricity. There is little competition and the phone companies have not been involved in struggles over franchises or in regulatory battles to the same extent as many other utilities. The giant of this utility is the American Telephone and Telegraph Company which controls over four-fifths of the telephone industry.

Western Union dominates the telegraph utilities. High labor costs and competition, particularly from the telephones and air mail, have bitten deeply into the value of this utility.

Transit lines with their high overhead costs often show unstable revenues. Many transit lines operate with low profit margins and can only be considered as speculative. Since the advent of automobiles they have faced stiff competition and are now greatly reduced in importance.

There are still some water service companies that are not municipally owned. They grow in direct proportion to the population increase in their locality and generally show stable earnings.

Regulation and Rates. The economic characteristics of public utilities are the reason for their extensive regulation. Utilities must be monopolies in their area of operation in order to be efficient. Regulatory government agencies include state public utility or public service commissions and municipal franchises whose powers cover most phases of utility operation and the Federal Power Commission and the Securities and Exchange Commission which regulate other areas of utility operation. The SEC in particular has powers in the area of public utility corporate financial matters.

Federal regulatory power has extended beyond pure interstate commerce because of the public interest it protects. While municipal regulations usually depend on whatever powers are delegated by the state, it is the state commission which determines rates, uniform accounting practices for all utilities, their capital structure ,and even the extent and quality of service and building plans.

In general, the theory of public utility regulation is to permit a company to earn a fair and reasonable return on its investment in return for which it must provide adequate service to the public. Because earnings should be sufficient to attract capital for debt issues, and to maintain a good credit rating, they have been generally set high enough to permit fairly high dividends.

The earnings represent net operating income after all expenses, including taxes and depreciation, but before capital charges such as interest and dividends. The investment in facilities is known as the rate base. It covers the company's fixed capital, or plant account, to the extent that it represents facilities used in the public service, minus the reserve for depreciation, plus an allowance for cash working capital and for materials and supplies used in operations. The general trend seems to be for regulatory commissions to allow utilities to base their rates on about a 6 per cent return on the rate base.

Balance Sheet Analysis. The principle item in a utility's balance sheet is its property and plant account which may amount to 80 per cent to 90 per cent of total assets. A ratio commonly used in utility analysis is that of *plant per dollar of operating revenue.*

Since fixed assets are of great significance in utility balance sheets, the depreciation account and methods of determining depreciation assume great importance.

Income Statement Analysis. Reserves of utility companies are broken down by types of customer, e.g. commercial, residential, industrial. These groups have different characteristics. The residential group is characterized by stability and growth. The *commercial* group may be vulnerable in the event of a severe depression, while the *industrial* load may fluctuate sharply with the general economic conditions in the region served by the utility.

Income Statement ratios. These include:

- Operating Profit Ratio . . . The formula is:

$$\frac{\text{Net Operating Income (before depreciation and income taxes)}}{\text{Operating Revenue}}$$

This ratio is very useful in following trends in a company's operations.

- Maintenance and depreciation as a percentage of operating revenue.
- Depreciation as a percentage of plant valuation.
- Gross income as a percentage of capitalization and surplus.

Other useful standards include:

- Average residential rate, use and bill.
- Average monthly residential bill.
- System peak and load factor. System peak is the highest combined demand which occurs in the system during the year. The load factor is the ratio of the average load to the peak load over a period of time, usually a year.

Financial Position. Because of their inherent stability, utilities finance largely through senior capital. Dividends on common stock are regular and higher than most industrials; in many cases dividends are three-quarters of the average earnings. The stable utility stocks do not tend to fluctuate as severely as most industrials.

Utilities are favored by institutional buyers and by investors wishing to conserve capital although there are quite a few utilities which have shown as excellent rate of growth and some utilities which verge upon speculation.

The larger utility companies are traded on the exchanges. Many small issues are actively traded over-the-counter. They have a wide market among most investors.

Industrial Securities

The group known as *industrials* include several classes of companies:

1. Mining, petroleum, and other extractive industries.

2. Manufacturing industries, which are subdivided into manufacturers of consumer nondurables, such as food and textiles, manufacturers of industrial raw materials such as chemicals and metals, and manufacturers of durable goods such as electrical and industrial equipment and automobiles. Further subdivisions are also made.

3. Wholesale and retail distributors.

The two main characteristics of this group are the freedom from the all-pervading influence of utility and rail governmental regulations and the presence of competition, often extremely severe, among industrial componies.

The supposed advantage of investment in industrial securities is that, more than rails or utilities, they tend to follow the average trend of commodity prices. Thus they appear to offer a hedge against inflation in times of expansion and/or rising prices although, of course, different industries will be affected to different degrees by the changes. As a company prospers, stock dividends and the value of the stock itself increases; senior securities, however, will be at a disadvantage because the purchasing power of their fixed dividends is lessened during a period of rising prices.

The most important factor in judging the investment quality of an industrial firm is its sales prospects. Other factors are: how essential is the industry? Can it be challenged successfully by new products or techniques? Is the company adequately diversified in case one of its divisions has a bad year? What are its long term prospects and competitive position among similar companies? How about labor costs and labor relations? Is it recession-proof or recession-prone?

The analyst has these financial elements to consider: prospective earnings, working capital position, capital structure, and dividend prospects. There may also be special features, such as accounting peculiarities, which will affect the future value of the security.

Much more than any other category, industrials present complex and varying problems which differ greatly from company to company.

Bank Stocks

Securities of most banks are truly gilt-edged. Federal Reserve requirements which specify the proportion of a bank's resources that must be held in cash reserves or government securities make this so. Other Federal rulings regulate banks as a public service in order to eliminate over-competition and duplication and to promote solvency.

Banks show two types of net earnings: net operating earnings and net profits. Net operating earnings are operating earnings minus current operating expenses and taxes. Net profits are the net operating earnings plus profits from sales on securities and on recoveries from assets and minus the necessary provisions for present and possible losses.

For many banks it is the profits on securities—the sale of Government and municipal bonds—which determines any profit if at all.

Bank capital is almost always provided by common stock. Its stock is a favored holding among many conservative institutions because of stable and regular dividends. Because of the stability of banks, their stocks probably offer smaller risks than that of most industrials.

Successful competition from outside sources is a cause of concern to some banks. Savings and loan associations, insurance companies, and finance companies all compete for loans.

Insurance Companies

There are several kinds of insurance companies: fire, casualty, and life. All are regulated for the public benefit and all show excellent records of growth.

Insurance firms act both as insurance companies and as investment companies. Their money, which is not immediately specified for payment of claims, is in reserve. This money, which is constantly being augmented by a stream of premium payments that usually outweighs claims, is invested to such a degree that normally three-fifths or more of net earnings come from such investment income. Investment policy and regulations ordinarily limit investments to high grade securities or mortgages, though a small percentage of a company's portfolio may be common stocks.

Some financial ratios are:

Loss Ratio . . . Ratio of losses to premiums paid in.

Expense Ratio . . . Selling and operating costs to new premiums.

Loss and Expense Ratio . . . Loss ratio plus expense ratio.

Underwriting Profit . . . Loss and expense ratio subtracted from 100 per cent.

Insurance companies are noted for their steady dividend rate in good times as well as bad. However, they ordinarily sell at slightly lower price-earnings ratios and yield less than most stable industrial stocks.

Note: We are discussing *stock* companies. The *mutuals*, which are in theory owned by the policyholders, do not sell stock. Mutual companies account for most of the insurance in force.

Investment Companies

Now one of the most popular types of investments among small investors, investment companies have the attractive combination of diversification of securities plus professional management. Investment companies are sold to the public in two ways: (1) by the fund undewriter which is always ready to sell to or to redeem shares from the public, and (2) through an exchange or over the counter.

There are two types of investment companies. The first is an *open-end*, known as a mutual fund. The second is *closed-end*. Closed-end companies may sell at more or less than the value of the securities they hold. Open-end funds sell at their net asset value plus any sales charges, and are redeemed at net asset value less, in a few cases, a redemption fee.

Investment companies differ from other forms of investment in that their business is primarily the business of investing in other securities. Investment companies are discussed at length in Volume 2, Chapter 2.

FACTORS IN INDIVIDUAL STOCK ANALYSIS

Valuing Individual Stocks

Over an extended period of time, a stock may sell at a wide range of prices. It may sell above what is considered its real or intrinsic value and would be termed over-priced. At other times it may sell below its "real" value and be classified as under-priced. The problem is always to determine the true value of an enterprise.

The standard method of determining future worth is called the valuation approach which projects earnings for the next five to ten years at an appropriate capitalization factor or multiplier. The factor varies with the nature of the enterprise.

Utilities, which ordinarily grow at a steady even rate and have a stable earning power, are suited to such an approach. Stocks with unstable earnings or in fields that are heavily competitive do not lend themselves easily to valuation analysis. As a rule, the more speculative a stock is, the less likely one can project its future rate of growth.

Earning power is usually estimated in one of two ways. First, to project future returns by using an earnings *base* that may go back five, ten, or 15 years. Second, to estimate future sales and profit margins from general economic forecasts.

Because earning power combines a statement of actual earnings over a period of years with the expectation that they will be approximated in the future, account must be taken of these possibilities.

(1) Basic changes in the line of products made.

(2) Basic changes in manufacturing or sales policy.

(3) Loss of some special advantages of great importance,

e.g. patents, sales contracts.

(4) A change in management.

The basic factors in common stock valuation are:

(1) Expected future earnings.

(2) Expected future dividends.

(3) Capitalization rates.

(4) Asset value.

Growth Stocks

Some industries are developed and grow because of inventions and new technologies. Others have products which meet wide public acceptance and which enjoy expanding sales year after year.

Growth stocks develop in fields where there is such a heavy demand for product that competition is not an over-riding influence, earnings are growing at a rate faster than in the average business, and it seems obvious that future growth will also be rapid. In the past few years such growth stocks have included not only the spectacular electronics, aerospace, and computer fields. Chemicals, food processing companies, and vending machine companies have been in this category.

Railroad stocks were once considered growth stocks. In the 1900s many of today's industrial, mining, and merchandise giants were showing year-to-year increases in earnings, which laid a firm foundation for future growth and resources. Many of these corporations, which include Sears Roebuck, General Electric, Eastman Kodak, and Otis Elevator are still looked on as growth stocks.

It goes without saying that it is difficult to pick and choose from among the many companies in a single industry. The mortality rate of new companies is high. Very often an investor finds he must pay a high price-earnings ratio (perhaps 40 to one) and receive a low dividend because public enthusiasm has inflated the stock price.

Many securities analysts use the following as a guide in defining growth stocks: At each peak of the business cycle earnings should show a larger gain than at the previous peak; or a growth stock is one in which the *average* rate of growth has been ten per cent or better. (The economy as a whole grows at about four per cent each year.)

Income Stocks

High and stable yields are the characteristic of this group, although the actual valuation of a particular company may not show much change. Utilities are an example of this group. Companies in the tobacco, cosmetic, and clothing industries are often income stocks.

Defensive Issues

In any declining market there are certain classes of stocks which resist the downward trend. Often they might not decline at all—they could perhaps gain as investors shift from weaker securities into these stronger issues. Industries with a stable consumer demand are often desirable defensive stocks. Food, retailing and electric utilities are examples.

Special Situations

This term is used in two senses, both speculative. A special situation is a form of speculation because the stock appears to be demonstrably undervalued and is expected to attain its true value in the marketplace when certain corporate action occurs. More loosely, almost *any* stock which is thought of as having particularly favorable near-term prospects has been labeled a special situation. An example of this special situation is a company which hopes to increase sales—or make sales—through marketing a spectacularly new product.

More strictly speaking, companies on the verge of internal changes which promise efficiencies in manufacturing and marketing are called special situations. Such changes are drastic and include:

Mergers. In a merger, all assets, liabilities, and interests of one firm are absorbed by another. On paper, at least one of the two companies gives up its independent existence. Mergers are often the method by which a company acquires an interest in a field which, because of effort, expense, and inexperience, would not ordinarily be feasible. Through mergers, companies are often able to obtain experienced management. Sometimes a company with a large tax loss is taken over in this way by another company on a sound financial basis; the tax write-off can offset some of the tax liability of the sound company.

Depending on the purchase or stock exchange terms, mergers can create worthwhile investment opportunities to increase a stockholder's capital in the merged company, particularly if the price offered in cash or stock for the equity is higher than the current sale price of the stock.

Consolidations. A consolidation occurs when two or more companies combine into one new corporation which takes over all property, rights, privileges, and contracts, and which assures their liabilities and their obligations. Generally, stockholders of the consolidating companies exchange their shares for stock in the new company. They may, however, be paid off in cash or receive in exchange for part of their holdings bonds or other obligations of the new company.

Reorganizations. These are severe shakeups in the capital structure of an insolvent corporation. The purpose of the new structure, which has been ordered by a Federal court decision, is to revitalize the company and prevent liquidation. After the reorganization the company continues in business with a new, stronger capital structure—although the bond and stockholders may not receive a full payment on their claims. Bondholders may have to take a reduction in the face value of their bonds. Stockholders usually will receive new securities which approximate a realistic equity in the reorganized company. Creditors may be asked to reduce their claims although, as a rule, much of the equity of the corporation is transferred from the stockholders to the creditors.

Most reorganizations in recent years years are under Chapter X of the Bankruptcy Act of 1938 and are known as Chapter X reorganizations. In certain cases, Chapter XI of the Act, the Mahaffie Act, or Section 77 of the Bankruptcy Act of 1898 are used.

Refinancing. A company may find it desirable to substitute one security for another in its capital structure. For example, a company with callable bonds issued at a high rate of interest may call them and replace them with a new issue paying lower interest. Issues of preferred stock may be similarly replaced. Refinancing of senior securities may affect the value of the common stock because the company has reduced a fixed debt and, perhaps, will be able to show increased earnings.

Recapitalization. The purpose of recapitalization is usually to change a company's capital stock because of adverse economic or financial conditions within the company itself. Reasons given are usually present or expected losses which force a "financial readjustment." Sometimes the purpose is to eliminate certain classes of securities by exchanging common for preferred stock (or preferred for common stock).

Other rearrangements occur when shares are retired. Changes in the par value of a stock are recapitalizations whether or not resulting from a stock split. Stock splits and reverse stock splits are themselves recapitalizations.

Stock Splits. The main result of a stock split is to increase the number of shares of outstanding stock. By reducing the price of each share, it broadens the market because many small investors feel they can better afford to buy a lower-priced stock rather than a higher-priced issue. During roaring bull markets, the average investor overvalues the importance of a stock split.

A common reaction to a stock split is an immediate increase in the stock price and the volume of trading. Although the stockholder still holds the same proportion of equity as before the split, the market becomes bullish. Stock splits often bring an increase of dividends with them, and the new stock is then worth more than the old. However, there is sometimes an adverse reaction to a stock split with a resulting drop in market price.

A *reverse stock split* reduces the number of outstanding shares, proportionately increasing the value of the remainder. The psychological impact is often to spur stock sales, because the stock purchaser may have the illusion that the stock is worth more.

Valuation of Rights and Warrants

Stock rights as options were discussed briefly in Chapter 4. Rights as stock purchase warrants (which are issued apart from the sale of securities and are not subscription warrants) may run for several years or perpetually. The value of such rights or warrants depend on:

- The option price and duration.

- Current price of the common stock.

- Number of rights or warrants outstanding relative to the common stock.

- The speculative possibilities of the common stock.

The value of a perpetual warrant, or a right before the end of its expiration period, is calculated as follows:

$$\text{Value of right} = \frac{M \text{ minus } S}{N \text{ plus } 1}$$

M is market price of common

S is subscription price of common

N is number of rights needed to buy one share

If the stock is selling above the option price, a warrant has an intrinsic value, which may be calculated.

EXAMPLE: A warrant entitles the holder to buy one share of XYZ common at $5 a share. If XYZ common is selling at $10 a share, then the warrant has an intrinsic value of $5.

In addition, since the warrant represents a call on the common and since it may move up faster than the stock, it may have an additional value or premium in excess of the intrinsic value.

Warrants offer interesting speculative opportunities, particularly in depressed markets.

Exercising rights or warrants means the issuance of additional shares with a consequent dilution of the value of the originally issued shares. The effect of the dilution ranges from negligible to very great according to the number of warrants issued and exercised.

Leverage

Leverage exists when a corporation is so capitalized that there is a large proportion of senior capital and a relatively smaller amount of common stock. As capital earnings increase, the amount remaining after interest on bonds or dividends on preferred stock shows a significant increase. Small changes in overall earnings can often produce large changes in earnings per share of common.

> EXAMPLE: ABC Railroad is capitalized as follows:
>   Long term debt $1,000,000 @ 6 per cent interest
>   Common stock 1000 shares

With gross earnings of $70,000, the common shares earn $10,000 (after payment of $60,000 interest) or $10 per share. If earnings go to $80,000, a rise of 14 per cent, the earnings on the common stock go to $20,000 or $20 per share, a rise of 100 per cent. (This example omits income taxes in order to simplify the figures.)

Leverage is a two-way street. In a period of falling earnings, the common stock will be adversely affected to a greater degree than if the leverage factor were not present. Because the chance of gain and loss are inherently greater than in stock without leverage, such stocks are considered speculative.

Taxes and Security Values

Taxes affect security values in two ways:
(1) Through their impact on corporate earnings.
(2) Through their impact on the stockholder's pocketbook.

In analyzing securities it is important to determine whether there is a tax loss carry forward, what its size is and how long it will last. Such information is usually found in the company's annual report.

Certain types of companies have special tax advantages. Companies with wasting assets, such as mining or oil companies, are allowed to deduct certain sums for depletion. Industrial companies may be allowed to accelerate their depreciation deductions.

Corporations as well as individuals pay no taxes on interest from state and municipal bonds. Insurance companies and banks, who normally invest a sizable proportion of their cash in tax-free bonds, profit greatly from this advantage.

Only 15 per cent of the dividends a corporation receives from another domestic corporation are taxable. Capital gains are also taxed at special rates. Insurance companies and holding companies are among the chief recipients of this benefit.

CORPORATE SENIOR SECURITIES

Bonds

Corporate bonds are often thought of in terms of safety. A much more realistic approach these days views them as securities with a limited return.

However, the ability of a company to pay interest on its outstanding bonds depends upon its overall financial strength. For this reason, the primary emphasis in bond *selection* should be on safety.

Some general guides in analyzing corporate bonds are:

(1) Safety is measured not by specific liens or other contractual rights but by the ability of the issuer to meet *all* its obligations. More specifically, the absence of a lien is of little consequence. This means that debentures of a sound company are as good as mortgage bonds. It is best to buy the *highest yielding* obligations of a *sound* company.

(2) Financial strength should be measured under conditions of depression rather than prosperity.

(3) Inadequate safety cannot be compensated for by an abnormally high coupon rate.

(4) Investment in senior securities should be very selective and should be subject to definite qualitative tests.

Minimum standards of safety should be set and bonds falling below this standard should not be considered *regardless of their yield*.

The nature and location of the business should be considered. Certain businesses are less stable than others. Bonds of foreign companies are subject to risks not found in those of domestic companies.

The size of the company should be considered since bonds of very small enterprises will often be less than conservative.

The provisions of the issue, including conditions affecting interest payments, the date of maturity, call provisions, limitations on creation of prior liens, requirements as to working capital and sinking funds should be considered.

Corporations issuing bonds should have a long record of successful operation and financial stability. The dividend performance is far less important than is the overall income record.

The most important specific test of safety is the ratio of earnings to fixed charges. The best method for doing this is to take the ratio of earnings to the total of all fixed charges. The ratio then applies to all issues of corporate debt both senior and junior.

The period tested should run from seven to ten years. The rule of thumb ratios to be applied using average earnings before taxes should be at least:

- For public utilities   4X
- For railroads   5X
- For industrials   7X

The earnings for the poorest year should equal at least the following ratios of fixed charges:

- For public utilities   3X
- For railroads   4X
- For industrials   5X

Also to be considered in the earnings future are:

- The trend.
- The minimum figure.
- The current figure.

Especially favorable factors are:

- A rising trend of profits.
- An especially good current showing.
- A satisfactory margin over interest charges in every year studied.

Bond Rating. The statistical services which compile bond ratings prepare various ratings, signified by symbols, which are indicators of the investment quality of the securities rated. Ratings are convenient devices for obtaining an independent evaluation of a bond and are used both by individual investors and by institutions. Ratings run from AAA (highest grade) down to D (little or no apparent value). In keeping with the old adage that "the greater the return, the greater the risk," bonds with the higher ratings generally provide lower yields than bonds with lower ratings.

Interest Rate. It is not enough to look solely to the stated interest rate of a bond. Not only should it be studied with respect to the safety of the bond itself, but also with respect to the price at which the bond is selling. In a period when interest rates are low, the bond will sell at a higher price than when interest rates are high. Thus, a bond purchased when general rates are low will probably fall in market value when interest rates rise, and vice versa.

Marketability. If the potential investor does not intend to hold a bond to maturity, he should make sure that the issue has an active market.

Conversion Privileges. The conversion privilege allows bondholders to exchange the senior issue into common stock at stipulated terms. This adds a speculative feature to the bond which would otherwise offer the holder little opportunity for capital appreciation. If the stock moves higher, the bond moves with it. If the stock falls in price, the bond will continue to sell on a yield basis.

The conversion privilege is definitely advantageous, particularly if no premium is paid for it. The conversion privilege, however, will not compensate for an inherently poor quality company. Both the bond and the stock must be appraised.

Callable Provisions. Call provisions are of particular importance with respect to convertible bonds. Through the use of the call provisions, the company can force conversion of the bonds. The investor should determine whether exercise of the call provision would be adverse to the interests of the bondholder. To do this, determine the price of the bond, the price of the stock, and the call price. If the bond is selling at a premium to its conversion value and the company has the right to call the bond in the near future, then an extra element of risk is attached to the bond.

Trust Indenture Act. The Trust Indenture Act of 1939 prescribes various rules for the protection of bondholders.

Under the Act, the corporate trustee must not possess conflicting interests; must not default; must not improve his position as a creditor to the detriment of the indenture securities within a certain period of time; must make annual and periodic reports to the bondholders; must maintain bondholders lists to provide a method of communication between bondholders as to their rights under the indenture and the bonds; and must be authorized to file suits and proofs of claims on behalf of the bondholders.

The Act outlaws exculpatory clauses which had been used in the past to eliminate the liability of the indenture trustee to his indenture security holders. It imposes on the trustee, after default, the duty to exercise the rights and powers vested in it, and to use the same degree of care and skill in their exercise as a prudent man would use in the conduct of his own affairs.

Preferred Stocks

The typical preferred stock is not an attractive type of investment. Its principal and income return are limited and the owner has no fixed claim to payment of either principal or income.

The main difference between preferred stocks and bonds is that payment of preferred stock dividends is entirely discretionary with the directors, while the payment of interest on the bonds is obligatory. To be sure, if a company is operating profitably, it will pay its preferred dividends. If it is not doing so well, it may omit the preferred dividends. It will hesitate to omit the bond interest because to do so would force it into bankruptcy or permit the bondholders to take over the management of the company.

A high grade preferred stock must meet all the minimum requirements for a high grade bond. In addition, it must exceed these limits by an added margin in order to offset the discretionary feature of the payment of dividends. Also, the business must be extremely stable since dividend payments could be suspended during a period of poor earnings. A preferred stock that meets these requirements must yield more than a high grade bond to be attractive from an investment point of view.

Income Bonds

Income or adjustment bonds are midway in position between straight bonds and preferred stock. Income bonds have a maturity date (usually at sometime in the distant future) so that, at least in theory, payment of principal is assured. Directors have almost complete discretion in the payment of interest on these bonds. Income bonds are usually issued in reorganizations and so often imply secondary credit standing of the issuer. Unless interest charges are substantially covered by earnings, income bonds should be regarded as speculative investment vehicles.

Guaranteed Securities

Guaranteed securities are of minor importance today. They are prevalent only in the railroad field. If the guarantor fails to pay the interest on the guaranteed bonds, it is forced into bankruptcy. The earnings coverage on the guaranteed bonds include the earnings of the issuing company as well as those of the guarantor. The terms of the guarantee, particularly the duration of the guarantee and whether it covers principal as well as interest, are important.

GOVERNMENT SECURITIES

Treasury Obligations

Treasury obligations are guaranteed by the United States Government as to the payment of principal and interest. It is not necessary to calculate such factors as interest coverage, since these obligations are backed by the taxing power of the world's richest country.

The first factor to analyze is whether to purchase a marketable or non-marketable issue. If liquidity is important, then a marketable issue should be chosen. If stability is required over a long period of time, then a non-marketable (saving bond) issue should be chosen.

Maturity should then be considered. For maturities up to 90 days there are Treasury Bills. For maturities up to a year there are Certificates of Indebtedness. Treasury Notes have maturities of one to five years, and Treasury Bonds have maturities of more than five years.

Virtually all Treasury obligations outstanding today are fully taxable as to interest and capital gains (if any).

Treasury notes and certificates are particularly attractive to corporations and other businesses having sums of cash on hand for which there is no immediate use. By placing these funds in these investments, the corporations are assured of both safety and liquidity as well as a reasonable return. The alternative is to leave the money in a commercial bank which pays no interest on the deposit.

Denominations range from $50 to $1,000,000 for Treasury Bonds and from $100 to $1,000 for the bills and certificates.

Municipal Bonds

State Obligations. For most states, credit standing is a function of industrialization and wealth. Only when the overall figures show a higher than average debt burden is credit standing affected. Some states have small amounts of debt outstanding so that there is a scarcity factor which raises prices and lowers yields for their obligations. In the past, property taxes were the principle sources of state revenue, but today sources of state tax revenue have widened.

Municipalities. Municipalities are corporations created by the state and are subject to the control of the state legislature. Municipal debt is often limited by state law.

In computing the debt burden of a municipality, it is customary to relate the debt to the assessed value of a real property within the city and to its population. This results in figures of net debt as a percent of assessed valuation and net debt per capita.

In addition to cities, the state may create special *districts* for purposes such as education, irrigation, and sanitation. These often have special tax powers.

A type of district is the *authority* which differs from a tax district in that it derives revenues, fees, or tolls from its operations. These include utility operation, bridges, tunnels, and toll roads. Bonds issued by authorities must usually rely on revenues for payment of interest. They are known as *revenue bonds*.

In analyzing bonds of a municipality the following factors should be considered:

- The presence or absence of diversified and growing industries within the territorial limits of the municipality.
- Transportation facilities of the municipality.
- Ratio of net debt to assessed valuations. Self-supporting debt should not be included in the net debt figure.
- Per capita debt ratio.
- Municipal tax rate.
- Past record of municipal finance.

Tax Status. Municipal bonds are presently exempt from Federal income taxation. For this reason, these issues are especially suitable for individuals in the upper top brackets. An individual in the 50 per cent tax bracket would have to receive a 6 per cent return before tax on another investment in order to equal the yield on a municipal bond paying 3 per cent. In higher tax brackets the differences are even greater.

Municipal Bond Ratios

Debt to Property Ratio. This is the total net debt divided by the actual value of all assessed property in the municipality. About nine to ten per cent is considered an average upper limit for a conservative ratio. Note that the actual (or fair market) value is the important value. Actual assessed value varies widely in different communites, running from as low as 20 per cent to as high as 100 per cent. Although the ratio of debt to total property value could be considered conservative at 20 per cent in one community, it might be considered very high in others, depending on industrialization, density of population, and local economic conditions.

Per Capita Debt. This is total net debt divided by population. It is useful to analysts as a comparative figure.

Fixed Charges. The fixed charges to budget receipts ratio is an important one. If this ratio begins to exceed about 25 percent it may be considered high. Service on the debt (fixed charges) *must* be paid; if actual receipts fall much behind expected receipts the operating budget is affected. The higher the ratio of debt service to expected receipts, the more effect delinquency will have on the municipality's ability to provide normal services to the community.

A Note on Government Federal Debt

The United States government owes roughly almost three times the total assets of all life insurance companies in the United States. While all of this debt bears interest, it is important to note that about one-third of it is working usefully for the public. Something like $25 billion is held by Federal Reserve banks. The social security reserve, pension funds for government employees, bank deposit insurance, and the assets of veterans' life insurance reserves make up about $75 billion.

CONCLUSION

Security analysis is designed to evaluate securities so that the investor may take action on an informed basis. Effective security analysis should be carried on by professionals with extensive training and experience in the field.

It is definitely not a task which can be safely undertaken by amateur investors.

REVIEW QUESTIONS

1. What is meant by industry analysis?
2. Describe the following ratios used in railroad analysis: Operating ratio; coverage of fixed charges; coverage of contingent interest; coverage of preferred dividends; maintenance ratio; transportation ratio.
3. What are public utilities? What types of companies are included? Discuss public utilities as monopolies.
5. Describe what is known as the rate base.
6. What is the principal item in an electric utility's balance sheet?
7. Name several useful standards for analysis of public utilities securities.
8. What type of investors tend to favor utilities?
9. What classes of companies are known as "industrial"?
10. Give some of the factors considered in analyzing securities of industrials.
11. What is the outstanding feature of bank stocks?
12. How is bank capital usually provided? What types of investors favor banks?
13. How do the overall price-earnings ratio and yield of insurance stocks compare with industrial stocks?
14. What are two types of investment companies? What is the major difference between them.
15. What type of stock is unsuited to the "valuation approach."
16. What is a guide used in defining a "growth" stock?
17. Distinguish between a merger and a consolidation.
18. Describe the effects of stock splits. Do they change the actual value of a shareholders' equity?
19. What determines the value of stock purchase warrants?
20. What is "leverage"? Give an example of its effect with profits. With decreased profits.
21. Discuss the effect of taxes on securities values.
22. Give the investment characteristics of corporate bonds.
23. Of a sound company, which are the best bonds to buy?
24. What are especially favorable factors in bond analysis?
25. Describe the conversion privilege.
26. Discuss preferred stocks as an investment.
27. What factors are considered in analysis of U.S. Government obligations?
28. Distinguish between obligations of a state and municipal securities issued under an authority.
29. What factors are considered in the analysis of municipal securities?

Chapter 10

Registered Representatives

Customer Accounts

NATIONAL ASSOCIATION OF SECURITIES DEALERS (NASD)

Requirements for Registered Representatives

Since its inception the NASD has used various methods to supervise sales of securities for the protection of investors. Today all partners, officers, non-exempt employees, and other representatives of a firm must become registered with the NASD and abide by its Rules of Fair Practice and Uniform Practice Code. Among the disciplinary measures for violation of those rules, members may be suspended from the Association for failure to register representatives of their firm.

Individuals associated with an NASD member firm may become registered representatives only if they:

(1) Possess all the qualifications for registration in the Association, and

(2) Have passed the NASD Qualification Examination for Registered Representatives.

The member firm itself must certify to the Board of Governors of the NASD the good character of the applicant and that he has had sufficient training or experience to handle those duties to which he is assigned. The burden is on the member to exercise reasonable care in its determination that the individual hired has the above qualifications. Improper or unwarranted certification may result in disciplinary action against the member.

For further protection of the investor, Art. 1 Sec. 2 of the NASD By-Laws state that no broker or dealer may be a member of the Association if such broker or dealer:

1. Is subject to an order of the Association suspending or revoking his registration as a registered representative;

2. Is subject to an order of the SEC denying or revoking his registration as a broker/dealer;

3. Was named as a cause of a suspension currently in effect, or of an expulsion or revocation by the Association or the SEC;

4. Is subject to an order of a national exchange revoking or suspending his registration with the exchange for conduct inconsistent with just and equitable principles of trade;

5. Has been convicted within the preceding 10 years of a felony or misdemeanor involving the purchase or sale of a security;

6. Has been convicted within the preceding 10 years of a felony or misdemeanor which the Association finds involved embezzlement, fraudulent conversion, misappropriation of funds or misuse of a fiduciary relationship.

All new personnel entering the securities business must be thoroughly trained by the member hiring them. This training must cover at least basic securities fundamentals, basic securities laws, and the NASD by-laws, rules, regulations and codes as well as the sales methods of the member. It is absolutely essential that the new employee be able to determine what may and may not be properly done in the securities business.

To terminate his registration, an individual or his employer must apply in writing to the Board of Governors. If he terminates his employment with a member, the member must promptly notify the Board of Governors. In either case the termination becomes effective 30 days after receipt by the Board unless the Board has cause not to terminate, i.e. there is an action pending against the individual. The registration of a representative is not transferable. If an individual wishes to transfer from one member to another, he must re-register with his new employer, but need not take the qualification examination again if re-registration is within 2 years of his prior termination.

The By-Laws of the NASD provide severe penalties for infractions by registered representatives. They include censure, suspension and revocation of registration, and levying of fines and costs of proceedings. Until 1964, the By-Laws of the NASD required action against a firm when a Registered Representative was involved in an infraction, but now action may be taken directly against the individual without joining the firm. Of course, the individual and the firm are always subject to both criminal and civil liability for their actions.

Registration of Principals

All persons designated as principals must be registered with the NASD which requires that they pass a Qualification Exam for Principals. Schedule C of the NASD Manual defines "principal" as follows:

> Persons associated with a member, enumerated in (a)-(e) hereafter, who are actively engaged in the management of the member's investment banking or securities business, including supervision, solicitation, conduct of business or the training of persons associated with a member for any of these functions, are designated as Principals. Such persons include: (a) Sole Proprietors; (b) Officers; (c) Partners; (d) Managers of Offices of Supervisory Jurisdiction, and (e) Directors of Corporations.

The exam for principals is more comprehensive in the securities field than that for registered representatives and, in addition, covers the supervisory functions of the principal and all applicable laws and regulations with respect to those functions.

Supervision of Registered Representatives

The NASD requires that every transaction and all correspondence of a registered representative must be approved in writing by a responsible officer of the member firm. The firm must also establish, maintain and enforce written procedures sufficient to properly supervise the representative in accordance with all applicable laws and regulations. Final responsibility always rests with the member, but the member must designate an officer or partner in each office of supervisory jurisdiction to carry out its written procedures. An office of supervisory jurisdiction is one which is designated by the member as directly responsible for review of the activities of registered representatives in that office and/or other offices of the member. A branch office may itself be an office of supervisory jurisdiction, but if it is not, its personnel must be supervised either by the main office or by the manager of another branch office that is an office of supervisory jurisdiction. The term "branch office" alone simply means an office which must be registered as one other than the main office.

NEW YORK STOCK EXCHANGE (NYSE)

Requirements for Registered Representatives

For the protection of investors, the national stock exchanges have stringent rules concerning the qualifications of registered representatives. The Report of Special Study of Securities Markets published by the SEC stated: "The qualifications of salesmen, who more than any other group represent the securities industry to the investing public, require particular attention.

The ultimate responsibility for the quality of salesmen must be in the firms which employ them and which share with the public an interest in having salesmen of good character and thorough training."

A registered representative as defined by NYSE Rule 10 means "an employee engaged in the solicitation or handling of listed or unlisted business in securities, or other similar instruments; or in the trading of listed or unlisted securities, or other similar instruments, for the account of or as a representative of his employer; or in the sale of listed or unlisted securities on a dealer or principal basis for his employer; or in handling international securities arbitrage operations of his employer; or in the solicitation of subscriptions to investment advisory or to investment management service furnished on a fee basis by his employer; or one to whom has been delegated general supervision over the foreign business of his employer. The term "registered representative" does not apply to individuals who are engaged solely in the solicitation or handling of business in, or the sale of, cotton, grain or other commodities, provided their duties in such respect require their registration with a recognized national cotton or commodities exchange."

For additional investor protection the NYSE has placed the responsibility upon members for registering certain persons:

NYSE Rule 345. (a) No member organization shall

(1) permit any person to perform regularly the duties customarily performed by a registered representative, unless such person shall have been registered and is acceptable to the Exchange, or

(2) employ any registered representative or other person in a nominal position because of the business obtained by such person.

(b) The Exchange may disapprove the employment of any person.

(c) If the Exchange determines that any employee or prospective employee of a member or member organization (1) has violated any provision of the Constitution or of any rule adopted by the Board of Governors, (2) has violated any of his agreements with the Exchange, (3) has made any misstatements to the Exchange, or (4) has been guilty of (i) conduct inconsistent with just and equitable principles of trade, (ii) acts detrimental to the interest or welfare of the Exchange, or (iii) conduct contrary to an established practice of the Exchange, the Exchange may withhold, suspend or withdraw its approval of his employment by a member or member organization; may fine such employee or prospective employee $250 for each such violation, or misstatement and may direct that he be censured. The total of the fines imposed pursuant to this Rule upon any such person at any one time shall not exceed $2,000.

(d) Any person or prospective employee of a member or member organization may require a review by the Board of Governors of any determination made under this Rule by filing with the Secretary of the Exchange a written demand therefor within 20 days after such determination has been rendered.

There are two types of NYSE registration:

(1) Full registration. This allows the representative to handle any and every type of securities business on behalf of its member firm.

(2) Limited registration. This allows the representative to handle only the sale of mutual funds and/or the Monthly Investment Plan. This registration is used for on-the-job training and may be continued only for seven months during which the representative must spend at least one half of his time preparing for full registration.

The NYSE requires those applicants without previous experience to be given actual on-the-job training for six months for full registration and for three months for limited registration. This training includes working in the various departments of the firm and is supplemented by an organized study of the securities field. The program is always under the final supervision of the member firm, but it may assign an applicant to an approved university or institute for the formal study portion. After completion of the training program, an extensive examination is administered by the NYSE to insure that the representative has sufficient knowledge of the securities field and the numerous laws and regulations relating to it to serve both his firm and the public ethically and efficiently.

Supervision of Registered Representatives

Three broad principles are followed by firms to provide good supervision and management of registered representatives:

1. Top management of the firm must always bear ultimate responsibility for proper supervision and control.

2. The person in charge of the sales force at each office must have the authority to execute supervisory procedures; and

3. The main office must have a back-up and review system of branch office procedures.

A designated principal in the main office and a branch office manager hold positions which include full supervisory responsibilities. The main task of each is to see that customers are receiving the best advice and service consistent with their investment objectives. In addition he must insure that all regulations of the exchange, the NASD, the Federal Government and the several states are followed while he operates his branch at a profit to the firm.

A branch manager must be thoroughly trained by his firm in his duties and responsibilities prior to taking the position. In addition he must have a creditable performance record as a registered representative or equivalent, must pass the appropriate Exchange examination for managers, and be otherwise acceptable to the Exchange.

The examination for managers is considerably broader than that for registered representatives. Generally, a manager is expected to know more about the securities business itself than his representatives. In addition, he is extensively tested on the NYSE rules and regulations governing conduct of offices, supervision of registered representatives, and responsibility for control of offices.

Supervision of Accounts

A program of careful supervision of all customers' accounts is required by every firm. In a branch office, supervision is by the local manager with a system of back-up and review at the main office by a partner or officer. In a one-office firm, the first check may be accomplished by the sales manager. There are usually at least two checks on each account transaction in addition to the representative's check. This supervision provides the two-fold service of protecting clients from mishandling of their accounts by inexperienced representatives and protecting the firm against fraudulent actions by customers.

Supervision procedures include a daily review of executed orders by both the branch manager and the main office. A thorough daily review acts to prevent almost any problem from becoming serious. There is also a monthly review of all accounts to give a broader picture of overall activity, payments, and concentration of accounts in particular securities.

CUSTOMER ACCOUNTS

Types of Accounts

Any responsible individual may open an account with a brokerage firm, whether it is solely an over-the-counter firm or a member of an exchange. The exact procedure varies from firm to firm, but generally the first step is to fill out a signature card. This usually records the customer's name, address, telephone number, employer, age, citizenship, and references. The purpose of such a card is to insure compliance of certain groups with regulations concerning accounts, and to determine the credit standing of the customer. For instance, brokers themselves may not have an account with another firm without special permission of their own firm, and bank employees may not have a margin account without written permission of their employer.

Accounts with over-the-counter firms must be cash accounts, as described below.

There are three types of accounts generally used by customers of the NYSE:

1) General accounts. The margin account normally utilized by customers intending to use credit for the purchase or sale of securities. This is discussed in detail later in this chapter.

2) Cash accounts. In the cash account all transactions are for cash and hence it is the simplest form of account. No purchases are made for credit, no short sales are permitted, and the customer's securities may not be hypothecated. This, however, does not mean that the customer must have the cash in his account before he is able to make a purchase. He is usually allowed to make transactions and then deposit the necessary cash within four business days. If payment is not made within seven business days, the account becomes "frozen." This is the only account which may be utilized when purchasing over-the-counter securities.

When an account is "frozen" it means that for a period of 90 calendar days all transactions in the account must be made on a pure ready-cash basis, i. e. the cash must be in the account *before* the broker may act. Extensions may be granted to modify a frozen account only if exceptional circumstances require it. Any national securities exchange or the NASD may grant the extension, but note that this applies to future transactions and not the one that initially "froze" the account.

3) Subscription accounts. The purchase of securities through the exercise of rights during a subscription period gives rise to different margin rules and hence an account dealing in such rights may be segregated from a general account.

There are also five additional types of accounts which are utilized under special circumstances:

1) Arbitrage accounts. This account is usually segregated from a general account since different margin rules apply.

2) Commodity accounts. Since trading in commodities takes place in different markets and falls under different regulations, it utilizes a separate account.

3) Specialist's accounts. These accounts must be handled separately due to the unique aspects of specialist's trading.

4) Omnibus accounts. For some purposes, accounts will be established for execution of orders of a number of persons all of whom are customers of a securities house that, in turn, is placing orders through a correspondent house.

5) Miscellaneous "memorandum" accounts. When one securities house performs special activities for another they are handled in miscellaneous accounts. This type of account may also be used for transactions in foreign exchange or collection and exchange of securities.

The most commonly used accounts, such as the cash account and the general account may be held jointly by two or more individuals. There are two types of joint accounts; joint tenancy with right of survivorship, and tenancy in common. Under the first, the survivor automatically becomes full owner upon the death of the other. Under tenancy in common there are no survivors' rights.

Some firms will also accept discretionary accounts, i. e. an account in which the broker has the authority to make purchases and sales at his discretion. Many firms do not use this type of account because of the numerous difficulties which can arise.

Accounts may also be held in the names of minors or people unable to act for themselves by registering them in the name of a custodian. This is a commonly used device and is regulated by the laws of the several states.

Handling The Account

The broker has a dual function in handling the customer's account. First, he must give the best service he can in the execution of orders, and second, he must give accurate and intelligent investment advice when solicited. Some customers will rely only upon the former, but for those who desire investment advice, the broker must know the customer's investment objective. He must be aware of the pertinent facts concerning the clients' situation before he can give any sound investment advice. Such advice must be based on sound knowledge of facts and never on rumor. It is also improper for a broker to allow his own personal purchases or sales to influence his recommendations to clients, or for him to trade a security in a manner which will adversely affect his customer's orders.

After an account has been opened and the needs of the client determined, an order may be placed by any means convenient to the client. This is usually by telephone. Immediately upon receiving the order, the broker fills out an order form and transmits it to the floor of the exchange for execution. The "back office" of the firm records all the necessary facts in the customer's and firm's records, checks the conformance to regulations and the accuracy of the execution, and prepares the confirmation and monthly statement for the customer and broker. A confirmation is mailed on the day the transaction is processed; the monthly statement, which is simply an itemization of all transactions during the month, is mailed at or near the end of the month.

Securities—Registered, Exempt and Unregistered.

Registered securities are securities that are either listed and registered on a national securities exchange or have been given unlisted trading privileges on an exchange. All registered securities are subject to the provisions of Regulation T of the Federal Reserve Board.

Exempt securities are not subject to Regulation T and hence receive very favorable margin treatment. United States bonds and municipal bonds are examples of exempt securities and may generally be purchased with five to ten per cent margin. Other exempt securities may require up to 25% margin depending on the particular issue.

Unregistered securities are those not registered on any national exchange, i.e., they are traded over-the-counter. Regulation T gives no collateral value to these securities and thus no credit may be extended on them in a margin account. Since mutual fund shares are traded over-the-counter, they may not be used as collateral for margin accounts.

Margin Accounts

The term "margin account" refers to an account in which credit is utilized by the customer on a purchase or short sale. By far the greater portion of margin trading is done with purchases as opposed to short sales. "Margin" itself refers to the amount of money which must be deposited by the customer to cover his purchase or sale. Whenever a customer has a margin account, he borrows from the broker the difference between the purchase price and the margin required. The loan carries an interest charge which is paid to the broker. The interest rate depends upon several factors such as the size of the account, its activity, and the type of securities carried. The purpose of the margin is twofold: It protects the customer from overtrading and/or buying in excess of resources, and it protects the creditor against unsound loans on securities.

The margin in an account represents the customer's equity and is therefore a constantly changing figure. The equity margin is a proportion that represents the relation between the customer's equity in the account and the value of the collateral (the securities and cash held in the account). Thus if the customer's equity is $7,000 and the collateral is $10,000, his equity margin is 70%. Or to put it another way, he is receiving credit worth 30% of the value of the collateral.

History

Prior to 1933, there was no system of uniform margin requirements. Each brokerage firm made its own requirements and, with the resulting open competition for customers, the requirements were quite low. In the early 1900's margins averaged around 10%. In the 1920's they had risen to 20%, but there still was no uniform requirement and many firms required less. As was pointed out above, trading on a 10-20% margin is exceedingly dangerous and the crash of 1929 is the prime example of what can happen when margin is this low and speculation runs rampant. Buyers on minimum margin could not meet their margin calls when stock prices dipped slightly and their resultant sales forced prices lower. This meant more margin calls, more forced sales, and still lower prices. One can easily see how the cycle feeds upon itself.

In 1933, the NYSE established uniform requirements for all of its member firms. In terms of today's computations the initial margin requirements were 33% for accounts with a debit balance of less than $5,000 and 23% for those over $5,000.

In 1934 the Securities Exchange Act of 1934 gave the power to control margins to the Federal Reserve Board. Under the Act, the Board issued Regulation T which, as discussed previously, regulates the amount of credit which can be extended on securities by brokers. It also issued Regulation U which applies similar rules to banks. Since 1934, the Board has changed the margin requirement sixteen times; from as low as 30% in 1937 to 100% in 1946 and 1947. In 1967 the existing margin requirement was 70%.

Computing Margin

In order to compute margins it is necessary to have a thorough understanding of debits and credits to a customer's account. Note that this applies to purchases only and that short sales will be discussed later. A debit to an account is made when:

1. A security is purchased.
2. Interest is charged on the debit balance.
3. Cash is withdrawn.

A credit arises from the opposite transactions:

1. Securities owned are sold.
2. Interest or dividends on securities are received.
3. Cash is deposited.

The debit balance is the basic factor in computing margins. This is the amount which the customer owes to the broker. It is a constant figure and can be changed only by one of the above six transactions. The changing value of the securities held in an account will not affect the debit balance.

The equity in the account is the value of the collateral minus the debit balance, and may be expressed by the following formula:

Equity = value of collateral—debit balance.

Since the debit balance does not change with the rise and fall of the value of the securities, i. e. the collateral, it is obvious that the equity must. Therefore a stock purchased at 100 with a 70% margin shows an equity of $7,000 at that price, but at 120 the equity will be $9,000, and at 80 the equity will have dropped to $5,000.

Margin today is determined by the formula:

$$\text{Margin} = \frac{\text{equity}}{\text{value of collateral}} \text{ or } \frac{\text{value of collateral—debit balance}}{\text{value of collateral}}$$

Using this formula one can arrive at the figures shown above:

$$\text{Margin} = \frac{10,000—3,000}{10,000} = 70\%$$

$$\text{Margin}_2 = \frac{12,000 - 3,000}{12,000} = 75\%$$

$$\text{Margin}_3 = \frac{8,000 - 3,000}{8,000} = 62.5\%$$

Margin computation on short sales is somewhat more difficult to grasp since it is in many ways the very opposite of the margin purchase. Basically, the margin will decline as the stock rises in value and will increase as the stock drops in value. For computing margin on a short sale, it is necessary to know the net proceeds of the short sale, the present market value of the stock sold short, and the initial margin. With these values known, margin can be computed with the following formula:

$$\text{Margin} = \frac{\text{Net proceeds of sale plus initial margin}}{\text{Market value of stock}} - 1$$

For example, using the same figures as above but in a short sale instead of a purchase, i. e. stock sold short at 100 with initial margin of 70%, one will have a present margin of:

$$\text{Margin}_1 = \frac{10,000 + 7,000}{10,000} - 1 = 70\%$$

If the stock rises to 120, the margin will be:

$$\text{Margin}_2 = \frac{10,000 + 7,000}{12,000} - 1 = 41.5\%$$

and if the stock falls to 80 the margin will be:

$$\text{Margin}_3 = \frac{10,000 + 7,000}{8,000} - 1 = 112\%$$

In all computations of margin, whether for purchases or sales, the present value of the securities must be known. For this purpose, the current market value is used. This value is determined by Federal Reserve Board Regulation T, Sec. 3 (C) (4):

"For the current market value of a security throughout the day of its purchase or sale, the creditor (broker) shall use its total cost or net proceeds of its sale, as the case may be, and at any other time shall use the closing sale price of the security on the preceding business day as shown by an regularly published reporting or quotation service. In the absence of any such closing sale price, the creditor may use any reasonable estimate of the market value of such security as of the close of business on such preceding business day."

Thus the broker uses the actual cost of proceeds net of commissions and taxes on the day of the trade, and the closing prices on all other days. It should be noted however, that in a period of a sharp market change, a broker may use the actual current market value as shown on the ticker tape.

Margin Requirements.

There are presently two distinct margin requirements: the initial margin and the maintenance margin. The first applies only to the margin required on the day of the transaction. The second applies to the margin required on every day after the transaction.

The Federal Reserve Board and the NYSE both have initial margin requirements. Presently, the Federal Reserve Board requires an initial margin of 70%. The NYSE requires a minimum equity of $2,000. Thus if the 70% required by the Federal Reserve Board is less than $2,000, any member firm must require additional cash to bring the initial margin up to the $2,000 requirement.

The NYSE also requires a maintenance margin of 25% of the market value of all securities purchased. Individual firms may set a higher maintenance margin. The requirement on short sales is $2.50 per share or 100% of the market value on stocks under $5,000, and $5.00 per share or 30% of the market value on higher priced stocks, whichever is greater in each case. Thus, on a purchase at 70% initial margin, the stock may decline 60% before the maintenance margin requirement is reached. Assuming the stock was purchased at 100 and drops to 40 the margin would be:

$$\text{Margin} = \frac{4,000 - 3,000}{4,000} = 25\%$$

If the stock drops further, the broker will issue a "margin call" to the customer requesting additional collateral.

When an account falls below the maintenance requirement it is considered "undermargined." Securities may be purchased when an account is undermargined, but the broker must issue a margin call at the time of the transaction. There is no rule as to how much additional margin will be required, but the usual practice is to require enough to bring the margin up to 35%. Of course, the new purchase itself will have to be fully margined at the initial rate. If the customer "switches," i. e. makes a combination of a purchase and sale, he need not deposit additional margin. A switch must be made on the same day to be effective. This is an extremely important point since it allows unlimited activity in a restricted account without the deposit of additional margin.

The Federal Reserve Board has no maintenance requirements, but they restrict accounts that have less than the initial margin requirement. In a "restricted account" there are several rules on withdrawals of cash, securities, and dividends. If stock is sold from a restricted account, the customer may withdraw the difference between the market price and the retention rquirement. This requirement, as defined by the Federal Reserve Board in Regulation T, is 50% for registered non-exempt securities and the maximum loan value for exempt securities. In addition the NYSE requires that the account shall not become undermargined by such a withdrawal. In other words, generally only one-half of the proceeds of a sale from a restricted account may be withdrawn.

Securities which are unregistered may be withdrawn from a restricted account only if the maintenance requirements are met after the withdrawal. Registered or exempt securities however, may be withdrawn only when the customer:

1. Pays his entire debit balance leaving no loan outstanding against the account; or

2. Substitutes on the same day registered or exempt securities with at least the same retention requirement value as those withdrawn; or

3. Deposits cash on the same day equal in amount to the current retention requirement on the securities withdrawn; or

4. Deposits cash to bring the account to the full initial margin requirement.

Dividends, whether cash or stock, receive special treatment in the restricted account. Cash dividends may be withdrawn for up to 35 days after their deposit provided they have not been used for a margin purchase. Stock dividends may be withdrawn if they do not exceed 10% of the market value of the stock itself. In all cases, the maintenance margin of the exchange must still be met after the withdrawal.

Again as mentioned previously, a customer can buy and sell or vice versa on the same day i. e., "switch," without having to deposit additional margin.

Using Margin.

There are strong advantages and disadvantages to using margin. When investing a particular sum of money, the investor can buy more shares if he buys on margin than he can if he buys for cash. For instance if the initial margin requirement is 50%, the investor can purchase twice as many shares (ignoring extra commissions and taxes), and if the requirement is 20%, as it was during the 1920's, he can purchase five times as many shares as he could with the same amount of cash. Thus, if a share of purchased stock rises from 50 to 75, the investor on a cash basis receives a 50% gain on his investment while one who purchased on margin of 50% receives a 100% gain. The one on 20% margin would have a 250% gain on his investment!

While this may appear very attractive at first, it is important to realize that the identical situation occuring in the reverse will cause disastrous results. If the share purchased falls from 50 to 25, the investors on a cash basis suffers a 50% loss while the one on 50% margin has lost 100% or his entire investment. One on the 20% margin would be wiped out entirely by a fall of only 20%!

Certainly, there are advantages to margin trading, but one must be careful to insure that the other side of the coin is also recognized. If the inherent risks of margin trading are recognized and provided for, the investor may utilize margin to advantage.

CONCLUSION

It is clearly evident from the foregoing that one of the main objectives of both the NASD and the national exchanges is to require numerous safeguards for the protection of the investing public. To this end, they have devised regulations strictly governing the qualifications of registered representatives and principals, the handling of customer's accounts, and the supervision of the representatives and customer accounts. Through this extensive system of checks and controls, the abuses which sometimes occurred in the past have been eliminated to a large extent and the investing public is receiving the protection it rightfully deserves.

REVIEW QUESTIONS

1. What qualifications must an individual possess in order to become registered with the NASD?
2. Who must be registered with the NASD?
3. What does the training of a registered representative consist of?
4. How is the registration of an individual terminated under the NASD?
5. What are some of the penalties imposed by the NASD for infractions of their rules?
6. Can a registered representative of the NASD write sales letters without approval of an officer of his firm?
7. Distinguish between an office of supervisory jurisdiction and a branch office.
8. Must an individual who handles only international arbitrage operations be a registered representative under the NYSE?
9. What penalties may the NYSE impose upon an individual for violation of its constitution?
10. Distinguish between full and limited registration under the NYSE.
11. Under the NYSE Rules, may an individual become a manager if he passes the appropriate examination?
12. Generally, what supervision is maintained over customer accounts?
13. What are the three general types of customer accounts?
14. What kind of account must be used for the purchase of mutual funds?
15. What is a "frozen" account?
16. What is the dual function of a broker in handling customer accounts?
17. Distinguish between registered and unregistered securities.
18. Define "margin."

19. Who establishes the initial margin requirements? What is the rate today?
20. Does an increase or decrease in the value of collateral affect the debit balance?
21. Given the following facts, what is the margin?
    a. Stock is purchased at $70 and rises to $84. The initial margin rate is 70%.
    b. Stock is sold short at $70 and falls to $63. The initial margin rate is 70%.
22. How is the collateral value of a security determined?
23. Distinguish between initial and maintenance margin.
24. What is the advantage of using margin?

INDEX
Please see back of Volume 2.